KIERKEGAARD AS PSYCHOLOGIST

KIERKEGAARD AS PSYCHOLOGIST

Vincent A. McCarthy

Northwestern University Press
Evanston, Illinois

Northwestern University Press
www.nupress.northwestern.edu

Printed in the United States of America

10 9 8 7 6 5 4 3 2 1

Library of Congress Cataloging-in-Publication Data

McCarthy, Vincent A., 1947– author.
Kierkegaard as psychologist / Vincent A. McCarthy.
pages cm
Includes bibliographical references and index.
ISBN 978-0-8101-3131-6 (cloth : alk. paper) — ISBN 978-0-8101-3181-1 (pbk. : alk. paper) — ISBN 978-0-8101-3132-3 (ebook)
1. Kierkegaard, Søren, 1813–1855. 2. Kierkegaard, Søren, 1813–1855—Influence. 3. Heidegger, Martin, 1889–1976. 4. Psychology—Philosophy. I. Title.
B4378.P79M33 2015
198.9—dc23

2015011506

In gratitude to
Robert McAfee Brown
and
William J. Richardson, S.J.
inspired teachers, inspiring persons

Contents

Acknowledgments

This work is the product not only of many years, but of many hands and of many minds. In particular I would like to thank Steven N. Dunning, emeritus professor at the University of Pennsylvania, for his suggestions and encouragement for this project, as well as David Law, professor of Theology at the University of Manchester, UK, for his steadfast assistance and keen editorial eye. The staff of Northwestern University Press has been a pleasure to work with.

Early versions of some chapters appeared in the International Kierkegaard Commentary series, edited by Robert L. Perkins, and I am grateful to Mercer University Press for their ready agreement to my using them.

Chronology of Kierkegaard's Writings

1843

Either/Or: A Fragment of Life, edited by Victor Eremita (*Enten-Eller. Et Livs-Fragment*, udgivet af Victor Eremita)
Two Edifying Discourses, by S. Kierkegaard (*To opbyggelige Taler*, af S. Kierkegaard)
Fear and Trembling: A Dialectical Lyric, by Johannes de Silentio (*Frygt og Bœven. Dialektisk Lyrik*, af Johannes de Silentio)
Repetition: A Venture in Experimenting Psychology, by Constantin Constantius (*Gjentagelsen. Et Forsøg i den experimenterende Psychologi*, af Constantin Constantius)
Three Edifying Discourses, by S. Kierkegaard (*Tre opbyggelige Taler*, af S. Kierkegaard)
Four Edifying Discourses, by S. Kierkegaard (*Fire opbyggelige Taler*, af S. Kierkegaard)

1844

Two Edifying Discourses, by S. Kierkegaard (*To opbyggelige Taler*, af S. Kierkegaard)
Three Edifying Discourses, by S. Kierkegaard (Tre opbyggelige Taler, af S. Kierkegaard)
Philosophical Fragments, or a Fragment of Philosophy, by Johannes Climacus, published by S. Kierkegaard (*Philosophiske Smuler eller En Smule Philosophie*, af Johannes Climacus, udgivet af S. Kierkegaard)
The Concept of Anxiety: A Simple Psychologically Oriented Reflection on the Dogmatic Problem of Original Sin, by Vigilius Haufniensis (*Begrebet Angest. En simpel psychologisk-paapegende Overveielse i Retning of det dogmatiske Problem om Arvesynden*, af Vigilius Haufniensis)
Prefaces: Light Reading for Certain Classes as the Occasion May Require, by Nicolaus Notabene (*Forord. Morskabslæsning for enkelte Stænder efter Tid og Lejlighed*, af Nicolaus Notabene) (published on the same day as *The Concept of Anxiety*)
Four Edifying Discourses, by S. Kierkegaard (*Fire opbyggelige Taler*, af S. Kierkegaard)

1845

Three Addresses on Imagined Occasions, by S. Kierkegaard (*Tre Taler ved tænkte Leiligheder*, af S. Kierkegaard)

Stages on Life's Way: Studies by Various Persons, compiled, forwarded to the press, and published by Hilarious Bookbinder (*Stadier paa Livets Vej. Studier af Forskjellige,* sammenbragte, befordrede til Trykken og udgivne af Hilarius Bogbinder)

Eighteen Edifying Discourses, by S. Kierkegaard (a collection of the remaindered Edifying Discourses from 1843 and 1844)

Article in *Fædrelandet* under the pseudonym Frater Taciturnus asking to be criticized in *The Corsair*

1846

Concluding Unscientific Postscript to Philosophical Fragments: A Mimetic-Pathetic-Dialectic Compilation, an Existential Plea, by Johannes Climacus, published by S. Kierkegaard (*Afsluttende uvidenskabelig Efterskrift til de philosophiske Smuler.—Mimisk-pathetisk-dialektisk Sammenskrift, Existentielt Indlæg,* af Johannes Climacus, udgiven af S. Kierkegaard)

A Literary Review: "Two Ages"—novella by the author of "An Everyday Story"—reviewed by S. Kierkegaard (*En literair Anmeldelse,* af S. Kierkegaard)

1847

Edifying Discourses in Different Spirits, by S. Kierkegaard (*Opbyggelige Taler i forskjellig Aand,* af S. Kierkegaard)

Works of Love: Some Christian Reflections in the Form of Discourses, by S. Kierkegaard (*Kjerlighedens Gjerninger. Nogle christelige Overveielser i Talers Form,* af S. Kierkegaard)

1848

Christian Discourses, by S. Kierkegaard (*Christelige Taler,* af S. Kierkegaard)

The Crisis and a Crisis in the Life of an Actress, by Inter et Inter (*Krisen og en Krise i en Skuespillerindes Liv,* af Inter et Inter)

The Point of View for My Work as an Author: A Direct Communication, a Report to History (*Synspunktet for min Forfatter-Virksomhed. En ligefrem Meddelelse, Rapport til Historien,* af S. Kierkegaard) (published posthumously)

1849

Second edition of *Either/Or*

The Lilies of the Field and the Birds of the Air: Three Devotional Discourses, by S. Kierkegaard (*Lilien paa Marken og Fuglen under Himlen. Tre gudelige Taler,* af S. Kierkegaard)

Two Ethico-Religious Treatises, by H. H. (*Tvende ethisk-religieuse Smaa-Afhandlinger*. Af H. H.)
The Sickness unto Death: A Christian Psychological Exposition for Edification and Awakening, by Anti-Climacus, edited by S. Kierkegaard (*Sygdommen til Døden. En christelig psychologisk Udvikling til Opvækkelse*, af Anticlimacus, udgivet af S. Kierkegaard)
"The High Priest"—"The Publican"—and "The Woman Taken in Sin": Three Addresses at Holy Communion on Fridays, by S. Kierkegaard (*"Ypperstepræsten"—"Tolderen"—"Synderinden": Tre Taler ved Altergangen om Fredagen*, af S. Kierkegaard)

1850

Training in Christianity, by Anti-Climacus, nos. I, II, III, edited by S. Kierkegaard (*Indøvelse i Christendom*, af Anti-Climacus, udgivet af S. Kierkegaard)
An Edifying Discourse, by S. Kierkegaard (*En opbyggelig Tale*, af S. Kierkegaard)

1851

On My Activity as a Writer, by S. Kierkegaard (*Om min Forfatter-Virksomhed*, af S. Kierkegaard)
Two Discourses at Holy Communion on Fridays, by S. Kierkegaard (*To Taler ved Altergangen om Fredagen*, af S. Kierkegaard)
For Self-Examination: Recommended to the Contemporary Age, by S. Kierkegaard (*Til Selvprøvelse. Samtiden anbefalet*, af S. Kierkegaard)
Judge for Yourselves! Recommended to the Present Time for Self-Examination. Second series, by S. Kierkegaard (*Dømmer Selv! Til Selvprøvelse Samtiden anbefalet.* Anden Rœkke, af S. Kierkegaard) (published posthumously in 1876)

1854

"Was Bishop Mynster 'a Witness to the Truth,' one of 'the True Witnesses to the Truth'—Is This the Truth?" by S. Kierkegaard, in *Fædrelandet* ("Var Biskop Mynster et 'Sandhedsvidne,' et af 'de rette Sandhedsvidner,' er dette Sandhed?" af S. Kierkegaard)
The Instant, by S. Kierkegaard (*Øjeblikket*, af S. Kierkegaard)
Christ's Judgment on Official Christianity, by S. Kierkegaard (*Hvad Christus dømmer om officiel Christendom*, af S. Kierkegaard)
God's Unchangeability: A Discourse, by S. Kierkegaard (*Guds Uforanderlighed. En Tale*, af S. Kierkegaard)

Abbreviations

Complete citations can be found in the bibliography.

Kierkegaard

Danish

SKS	*Søren Kierkegaards Skrifter*

English (translations by Howard V. and Edna H. Hong, except where noted)

CA	*The Concept of Anxiety, translated by Reidar Thomte*
CI	*The Concept of Irony*
CUP	*Concluding Unscientific Postscript*
E/O 1	*Either/Or, part 1*
E/O 2	*Either/Or, part 2*
FT	*Fear and Trembling*
JP	*Journals and Papers*
LD	*Letters and Documents, translated by Hendrik Rosenmeier*
R	*Repetition*
SLW	*Stages on Life's Way*
SUD	*The Sickness unto Death*
TA	*A Literary Review: Two Ages*

Freud

SE	*Standard Edition of Freud*

Heidegger

GWH	*Gesammelte Werke*
SZ	*Sein und Zeit*
BT	*Being and Time*
QCT	*Question concerning Technology*

KIERKEGAARD AS PSYCHOLOGIST

Introduction

Kierkegaard has become a classic author not only in his native Denmark, where he remains a major literary stylist, but also in much of the world, especially the western European and English-speaking worlds. But, like so many such authors, after the passage of time he runs the danger of being more cited than understood, of being more referred to than read. The reasons are complex but several are understandable. He is not, after all, our contemporary and he wrote in the increasingly distant literary and philosophical style of another century. In the case of psychology, he was using the word before there was a formally recognized academic field bearing that name. And so he pursues philosophical psychology without any knowledge of an alternative way. His use of pseudonyms seems odd and psychologically tempting for Freudian and post-Freudian interpreters, even though their use was not uncommon in his time. In indulging in pseudonymity he does not seek to circumvent a censor but rather to enhance literary effect and to have readers focus on the text rather than on the author.[1] But in Kierkegaard's usage pseudonymity also became a tease for the reading public to figure out who the real author was and then took on a life of its own, as one puzzling Latinate name succeeded another. The many learned references in Kierkegaard's writings presume a European classical education that occasionally succumbs to a display of learning for its own sake. They also assume an exposure to the folk literature that was awakening interest in the early nineteenth century (e.g., the works of the Brothers Grimm and Hans Christian Andersen, the latter Kierkegaard's contemporary).

While still cherished as a master of the Danish language and as a religious reformer who has had significant influence on the theologies of the twentieth century, Kierkegaard was above all a daring and an original philosophical thinker who not only saw the dangers of Hegelianism when it was at its apex in Denmark but was also a prescient voice whose insights on a wide range of intellectual and cultural problems to come, so much so that he can with good reason be seen as a forerunner of existentialism, a proto-phenomenologist and psychologist, and he can even sometimes be plausibly construed as a proto-postmodernist. While his psychological thought has always been acknowledged as rich (Reinhold Niebuhr hailed him as the greatest psychologist of the soul since Augustine), and while he has had a major influence on the psychological thought of Heidegger, Sartre, and the school of existential psychoanalysis, his accomplishment has not always been fully appreciated, in part because it is cast so widely across his works.

Indeed an alternative title for this work (imitating the title of his famous *Philosophical Fragments*) might well have been "Psychological Fragments," but that might have confused uninitiated readers of Kierkegaard. Instead, in this work I try not to presume deep initiation into the works of Kierkegaard, even as I hope to pass muster among other Kierkegaard specialists. This book is intended to highlight the incredibly rich and deep psychological dimension of Kierkegaard's thought, to offer an appreciation and assessment of it, and to serve somewhat as an introduction and commentary on Kierkegaard's psychology for general readers with an interest in, but not necessarily in possession of detailed knowledge of, Kierkegaard's corpus and Kierkegaard scholarship as such. The work is limited to the so-called pseudonymous works, where his psychological thought is essentially contained. There are elaborations and fine insights of course in his religious discourses, but that is perhaps the task of another day.

It is hoped that this work will be of value to a general readership at least somewhat familiar with the main currents in philosophical and theological thought since the Enlightenment. Kierkegaard was of course a man of his times, as one should expect—and despite his strong critique of his times. He was steeped in the writings of Enlightenment and post-Enlightenment authors, not to mention his contemporary writers in the Golden Age of Danish arts and literature and not to overlook the ancients, with whom he was also intimately familiar. His works are in many senses a conversation with the times and with the tradition, often in the form of a very heated argument. He takes on the Hegelians with zest, but equally Socrates.

His notion of psychology was existential and experimental (even if still in the sense of intellectual experimentation) and oriented toward the individual, but it was also inductive, unlike the highly speculative and deductive psychology that would derive from Hegel and speculative idealism. His method is surely not Freud's, nor is his perspective. Kierkegaard, despite his struggles and final battle with the church establishment in Denmark, remained a believing Christian and at several points (such as in *Either/Or*) seems to be updating Augustine's self-psychologizing in the *Confessions.* At the same time he can seem like a proto-Bultmannian[2] (among his other "proto-" epithets) for his attempt to understand important Christian teachings with an emphasis on the existential rather than on the literal. For example, his *Fear and Trembling*—a kind of pre-Sartrean meditation on Danish Christian "bad faith" deluded into thinking that it is the real thing—is an existential attempt to think about faith as an actual ongoing experience rather than a passive creed or mere baptismal certification. He holds up Abraham, whom people of faith have hailed as "the father of faith," and, in an in-your-face inquiry, asks his reader in effect, "If this is who Abraham was and if this is what faith was for Abraham, what does this say about your own very different stance that you are calling 'faith'?" In *The Concept of Anxiety* he sets out to make existential and rational sense of what became known as the doctrine of original sin in Christian theology. As a rationalist, he believed, along with Kant, that original sin could not mean guilt inherited from another, no less from the first human ancestor. It made sense only if a notion of original sin spoke of one's own original deed and its effect upon one's own current existential condition, which he then proceeded to analyze in sometimes opaque language and categories but in which he achieved important breakthroughs, as recognized, for example, by the central role that *Angst* has played in existential philosophy and psychology.

Augustine of Hippo, author of the *Confessions*, would recognize in Kierkegaard's young aesthetes elements of the young Augustine himself. But one can look forward as well as backward, and Kierkegaard's nineteenth-century poets and spiritual patients (often modeled on himself) have their counterparts today in the fashionable culture of sensitivity and self-actualization that constitute the new romanticism of California and, by extension, contemporary American culture. Kierkegaard knew nothing, of course, of sensitivity groups, self-fulfillment groups, and the like. But nineteenth-century Denmark and Germany had their cultural equivalents. Kierkegaard fully granted the alienation that such groups pointed to and agreed about the self-alienating quality of modern society. But, having himself experimented with the alternative life views celebrated by such groups, he came up against their limits and came to regard proposed novel cures as worse than the disease—worse, since they did not cure the disease but had the effect of either distracting one from it or driving one further away from one's self in a kind of spiritual attempted suicide that Kierkegaard would come to analyze as "despair."

Kierkegaard is thus an analyst of the individual psyche as well as the psyche of the time and he emerges as an undisguised critic of modernity. At the same time, he is very much a man of his century who accepts certain psychological insights of his age but considers them not sufficiently profound, and so takes the seemingly reactionary stance of holding that, at bottom, the analysis of the psyche in earlier Christianity was much closer to the mark. This was as hard to hear then as now for religion's cultured despisers, as Schleiermacher would subsequently term them,[3] mostly because they never grasped the central existential and experiential message of Christianity. For, in this view, Christian faith did not consist of creedal statements to subscribe to so much as experiences to be open to.

Kierkegaard was not fixated on the externals of early Christianity and allows the insights of early Christianity to be "translated" into the discourse of his age. Thus, for example, in his thoroughgoing reconsideration of the meaning of original sin he joined up with rationalist demythologizers and in its place offered a deep deliberation on the meaning of our own incontestable sense of fallenness. For Kierkegaard, sin is a real and unhappy fact that reflects missed opportunities and lost possibilities. But it need not be spoken of in terms of a medieval balance sheet of debts and credits on some divine accounting sheet. "Sin" and "forgiveness" are terms that can even be discarded if necessary, but the process they point to takes place, he would hold, in the living, struggling spirit of every person, whether in the fourth century, the nineteenth, or the twenty-first.

What Kierkegaard criticizes in modernity is, on the one hand, the overconfidence of the scientific worldview that was still on the ascent in the nineteenth century and, on the other hand, the fanciful notion that moderns, by virtue of their increased knowledge and mastery of the planet, are somehow essentially different from the human species in ages past. The consequence of a fanciful notion of a new humanity was that moderns began to believe that by experimenting with themselves and with society they could radically and essentially change things and themselves. Kierkegaard held this to be dangerous nonsense. And a prime example of this sort of thinking was Jean-Jacques Rousseau then (or Karl Marx later), who emphatically denied anything like original sin and blamed the evils of the world on wicked societies. While Kierkegaard tended to be politically conservative, his philosophical thought is by no means incompatible with economic, social, and political progress. He was a harsh critic of bourgeois Danish society and equally of self-designated reformers, whom he viewed as dangerously superficial. He also stands against the self-proclaimed individualists in the excessive new climate of individualism—the poets, literati, intellectuals, and aesthetes of every stripe who set themselves up as models of modern self-fulfillment.

Kierkegaard recognized that the malaise of his age was, at root, a very old malady indeed, that modern dis-ease revealed a spiritual disease that he would analyze in *The Sickness unto Death.* He also increasingly came to believe that the truest modern medicine for the human spirit was really a very old one and recognized that this would be very hard swallowing for an age that considered the past as surpassed. He set himself the unenviable task of persuading the heirs of the Enlightenment and the partisans of Hegelianism, who were convinced that they had advanced from darkness to light not only in natural knowledge (the sciences) but in supernatural knowledge as well, that the "old truths" were truer than ever, even if they needed modern reformulation. Kierkegaard would call for a break with the lingering naive optimism of the Enlightenment and subsequent Romanticism in order to point to the humbling truth of a humanity circumscribed not only by its nature but also by its own deeds of self-impairment. He knew too that he was breaking with the modern notion of history, and of historical social progress, for the sake of the higher history of the individual soul. Indeed, Kierkegaard saw that the essence of the fall from a transcendent calling was not so much a matter of distant ancient history as it was forever new and recurring. Distracting contemporaries from this were the poets and would-be geniuses of his age with their seductive image of sensitivity and creative suffering frequently disguising a diabolical willfulness and concealing an inner hell.

In Kierkegaard's view, the poets (and intellectuals too)—the cultural heroes and models of nineteenth-century self-fulfillment—were seducing the age by celebrating feeling and imagination, by holding up various attractive versions of an imaginary self. The young Kierkegaard had made his own personal experiment and then reverted to unglamorous older ways described in such "outdated" terms as "sin" and "forgiveness." But having caught himself in time, as he thought, he could not rest content to let the age go the path it seemed to have sketched for itself. For he saw clearly that the imaginary "new" self so celebrated by his age could never be actualized and that those who pursued such fancies of the imagination never moved a step closer to overcoming the self-alienation that had been their starting point. In the process, Kierkegaard disputed and sometimes mocked the analyses and cures offered by the informal psychologists of his time: the poets and novelists, the philosophers and the Christian clergy. In his view the root problem was that of a human being coming to peace with itself and with its Ground, and this was not a matter of poetry or sheer feeling or lofty concepts. The nineteenth-century therapies of art and literature had no lasting effect beyond the moment, any more than currently popular fads of massaging and various forms of soaking do today. What was needed in his view was a timeless cure based on a correct understanding of the eternal template of the self in relation to its Eternal Ground and yet pointing in a surprising way to the inevitably unique individual quality to every such God relationship.

Kierkegaard's authorship stresses what he holds to be a timeless prescription as it engages in a profound analysis of forms of alienation and dis-ease with oneself. The "patients" he selects are modeled on nineteenth-century types, but he quickly penetrates beneath the nineteenth-century surface to reveal souls whose restlessness and discontent Augustine in the fourth century and we in the twenty-first have little trouble recognizing. And it is because of his penetration to a problem that transcends but is not unconnected with any particular age and society that Kierkegaard can seem very modern indeed, that he can sometimes seem a contemporary of Freud and Maslow and not just of Brahms and Liszt.

Kierkegaard's psychological insights into the nature of the self are not presented as if they were the last word on the subject. For while Kierkegaard's work does have an influence that is much broader and deeper than frequently recognized, Heidegger, for example, does go further than Kierkegaard and succeeds in secularizing an analysis that Kierkegaard could express only in the older language of Christian metaphysics.

Kierkegaard is indeed a psychologist but one whose principal patient, as with William James and Sigmund Freud after him, was none other than himself. But from his analysis of that self he discovered and described the depths of a universal human condition that he set out not just to analyze but also, most centrally, to induce his readers to attend to and resolve.

1

Kierkegaard, Psychology, and Freud

Kierkegaard's *Either/Or* and *Repetition* rival the best psychological novels of the eighteenth and nineteenth centuries, while his treatises *The Concept of Anxiety* and *The Sickness unto Death* anticipate the great psychological breakthroughs of the end of the nineteenth century. He was an astute observer of Copenhagen society, of himself, of the human condition, and of "the self" as he understood it. Paralleling Augustine, he understood himself in effect as a microcosm of a universal human condition, and he believed that self-examination under the microscope of rational reflection would be revealing not only about the universal human condition but also, and even more important, about the cure.

Kierkegaard also did the things that many of us associate with psychology in the twentieth and twenty-first centuries but that were not at all uncommon in the nineteenth century and before. For example, according to a contemporary, Kierkegaard often consulted his Copenhagen professor Sibbern as a psychological and spiritual advisor.[1] The same Hans Brøchner also valued Kierkegaard as a listener who knew how to provide comfort and understood the wisdom of not covering up the causes of sorrow but rather of bringing them to clarity.[2] Brøchner reports in particular Kierkegaard's service to a Mrs. Spang as a spiritual counselor in 1846 in precisely this respect.[3] Kierkegaard also provided psychological help to his crippled cousin, Hans Peter Kierkegaard,[4] and no doubt to others as well. In his *Journals* in 1846 he wrote, "I have considered my task to be like that of one who himself became unhappy in loving men but wishes to help others who are capable of happiness."[5] In other words, he recognized himself as someone who had derived insight from personal suffering and understood that he could thereby help others.

All this could equally be called pastoral, and for many centuries pastors and wise friends conducted much of what we nowadays call psychology and even psychotherapy. This may seem a trivial observation, but it bears remembering that modern psychotherapy is less radical and novel than some might think. In many ways it is a refinement and systematization as well as an important attempt to transform a very traditional service to others into an effective science.

But it is equally important to remember that the emergence of psychology and psychoanalysis as formal disciplines occurred only subsequent to the life and death of Kierkegaard, that "psychology" in our contemporary understanding of the word did not exist at his time. The word certainly did, and we know that Kierkegaard himself used it in subtitles of pseudonymous publications. He employed the phrase "experimenting psychology" in the subtitle of *Repetition.*[6] But we would be naive if we were to look to it as if it might be an early example of "experimental psychology," for *Repetition* is a very different creature indeed. It is a masterly literary rebus worthy of at least a Freud, if not already beyond him. But it is no experimental psychology (nor for that matter is much of the Freudian corpus).

Thus, it would be well to review the meaning(s) of the term "psychology" at the time of Kierkegaard and in Kierkegaard's own usage as a cautious preamble to an appraisal of Kierkegaard's psychology and a consideration of some of its parallels with subsequent Freudian psychology and psychoanalysis and its influence on existential psychological thought.

While Kierkegaard certainly does not engage in "psychoanalysis" in Freud's usage, he certainly would have understood himself as engaging in analysis of the psyche in a very long tradition that goes back to the pre-Socratics, that then was given definitive shape by Aristotle, a Christian-Plotinian content by Augustine, an updating by Descartes, and important philosophical impetus in the eighteenth century by Christian Wolff. It was elaborated in Hegelian categories by Karl Rosenkranz, who used the structure provided by Hegel's *Encyclopedia* (Anthropology, Phenomenology, Pneumatology) in his *Psychologie* of 1837, a text that Kierkegaard owned and cited.[7] But Rosenkranz serves only as Kierkegaard's point of departure. We do not know how well Kierkegaard studied Rosenkranz's influential work. However, if one takes Rosenkranz's entry on melancholy as an example, one recognizes immediately that Kierkegaard was no disciple but a very independent psychologist. For Rosenkranz, viewing melancholy classically as one of the humors, regards the melancholy temperament as oriented only toward the past and the memory of past events (in contrast to the choleric temperament, which is oriented toward change and the future). Rosenkranz cites Chateaubriand as the example of the person who seeks to study the past and almost to live in the past, with melancholy results. Kierkegaard begins with the Romantics' notion of melancholy as unfulfilled longing for an object never possessed, and he develops it further in observations of a deeply brooding and crisis state of melancholy that he terms *Tungsind*[8] and that begins to reveal the need for a new and higher Object of desire. Thus one could say that for Kierkegaard, melancholy is, yes, about the past and the present but, most important, about the future. In addition, and as Nordentoft notes in his attempted systematization of Kierkegaard's psychological thought, Kierkegaard was on new ground when he dealt with what he viewed as "mixed emotions"—as, for example, in his important treatment of anxiety as "sympathetic antipathy" and "antipathetic sympathy."[9] He is on even newer ground with his careful attention to and emphasis upon emotions with no clear object, that are, in a sense, about "nothing."

Kierkegaard's is ultimately and emphatically *philosophical* psychology, indeed part of a long tradition of philosophical anthropology. As observed above, the academic discipline of psychology, as we currently know it, did not emerge until the latter part of the nineteenth century.[10] For its part, the philosophical use of the term "psychology" can be traced back to at least 1575.[11] Equivalent words were "pneumatics" and "pneumatology," which were part of the vocabulary of the metaphysical and theological traditions and still current in Kierkegaard's time. "Psychology" was essentially a *metaphysical* term until the second half of the eighteenth century, with 1750 considered the date of its emancipation from metaphysics. Thus Kierkegaard employs the term during what we now view as a transitional phase: the term was no longer just a traditional metaphysical term, but it was still very far from being a social science term in the modern sense.

Other intellectual figures who wrote on psychological themes from a philosophical perspective clearly influenced Kierkegaard, and the influence in psychology of such figures as Descartes and Leibniz is still seen today. Indeed, Cartesian dualism is still the presupposition for most psychological language today, even if the terms "mind" and "soul" are used loosely. But Christian Wolff's eighteenth-century psychological thought, for example, was concerned to articulate a *Seelenlehre*, or doctrine of the soul, that incorporated a Leibnizian harmony of soul and body.[12] The independent existence of an immaterial soul substance remained a "given" through the succeeding centuries, and thus psychological reflection at the time of Kierkegaard was still directed toward an understanding of the soul through self-reflection.

Literature as Psychology before the Twentieth Century

While Kierkegaard is naturally influenced by the philosophical psychologies of his time, he is far more influenced by the psychological insights of literature. Indeed, in psychological matters, Shakespeare and Goethe are far stronger influences upon Kierkegaard's psychological thinking than any eighteenth or nineteenth century book that included "psychology" in its title.[13]

We know of course that literature has played this role for centuries, indeed millennia. Kierkegaard is heir to this tradition both as reader and also of course as writer, for some of his most astute psychological material is found in the quasi novels *Either/Or*, *Repetition*, and *Stages on Life's Way*. These works do more than illustrate theoretical problems later schematized in *The Concept of Anxiety* and *The Sickness unto Death*, the two works in Kierkegaard's corpus generally held to be of greatest psychological interest. Indeed, when a commentator such as Kresten Nordentoft writes that Kierkegaard's entire psychology is contained in these works, he is correct in the sense that all Kierkegaard's literary characters are illustrations of the existential problem of non-self-actualization that Kierkegaard is concerned to analyze. But they are more than this. For these literary works of Kierkegaard at the same time constitute an "anatomy of melancholy," much in the style of William James's 1902 classic *Varieties of Religious Experience*, with its exploration of sick souls, but equally in its disguised inclusion of much autobiographical material.

Kierkegaard's most extensive commentary on psychology is contained in an excursus within *The Concept of Anxiety*, when Haufniensis observes,

> It is not my intention to write a learned work or to waste time in search of literary proof texts. Often the examples mentioned in psychologies lack true psychological-poetic-authority. They stand as isolated *notarialiter* [notarized facts], and as a result one does not know whether to laugh or to weep at the attempts of such lonely and obstinate persons to form some sort of a rule. One who has properly occupied himself with psychology and psychological observation acquires a general human flexibility that enables him at once to construct his example which even though it lacks factual authority nevertheless has an authority of a different kind. The psychological observer ought to be more nimble than a tight-rope dancer in order to incline and bend himself to other people and imitate their attitudes, and his silence in the moment of confidence should be seductive and voluptuous, so that what is hidden may find satisfaction in slipping out to chat with itself in the artificially constructed nonobservance and silence. Hence he ought also to have a poetic originality in his soul so as to be able at once to create both the totality and the invariable from what in the individual is always partially and variably present. Then, when he has perfected himself, he will have no need to take his examples from literary repertoires and serve up half-dead reminiscences, but will bring his observations entirely fresh

> from the water, wriggling and sparkling in the play of their colors. Nor will he have to run himself to death to become aware of something. On the contrary, he should sit entirely composed in his room, like a police agent who nevertheless knows everything that takes place. . . . His observation will be more reliable than that of others, even though he does not support it by references to names and learned quotations. . . . His observation will have the quality of freshness and the interest of actuality if he is prudent enough to control his observations. To that end he imitates in himself every mood, every psychic state that he discovers in another. (*SKS*, 4:359–60; *CA*, 54–55)

He later adds,

> The observer must especially exercise the caution of physicians who when they take the pulse make sure that it is not their own that they feel but that of the patient. In the same manner, the observer must take care that the movement he discovers is not his own restlessness in carrying out his observation. (*SKS*, 4:375; *CA*, 71)

Obviously, this kind of psychology is far from what we today term "experimental psychology," but for Kierkegaard it is quite clearly experimental insofar as the mind of the careful, cautious psychological observer takes an observed condition further by appropriating it and internalizing it, and then imaginatively taking it to its conclusion. In the process he dissects every new detail and contemplates the logical possibilities that emerge and the "decision tree" that they present. This is systematic observation. It is more literary than scientific by our standards yet careful not to be dependent on the literary observations of the past but instead to require fresh personal observations by the "psychologist," first of the other (the observed) and then of oneself as one imaginatively re-creates and develops the psychological condition in oneself. It is still close to the spirit of the best psychological literature and even to the spirit of later literary detectives such as Sherlock Holmes at the end of the nineteenth century or Miss Marple in the twentieth.

For various reasons, then, one should hardly expect a formal psychology from Kierkegaard, even less a systematic one. Kresten Nordentoft did an admirable job of tracing Kierkegaard's positions on a broad and fairly standard range of topics in psychology as currently understood. But this still does not mean that Kierkegaard had a psychology in any contemporary sense of the word. Nor did Kierkegaard himself pull together his psychological observations into anything even resembling a formal treatise (which would have run counter to his maieutic interest in stimulating the reader's own reflections). There are large fragments of a psychology, and they are very interesting pieces indeed. But they never amount to aiming to be a full or systematic psychology. Moreover, Kierkegaard had no such formal interest or goal. His interest was in the direction of psychology of conversion. (Strictly speaking, his pseudonymous fragments do not extend to the moment of conversion itself, or beyond, but only to the moment of the recognition of the need for decisive action.) Kierkegaard presents a rich psychology and analysis of religious crisis, and he leaves us with acute psychological insights into many personality types. But his fullest contribution is toward the psychology of conversion and inner healing, with a pastoral interest always in the background. He traces the movements and momentum pressing an individual to turn away from a dead-end way of life and to embark in an alternative direction that could satisfy deeply felt needs, the direction having been discerned from the exploration of deeply felt dissatisfactions as failed experiments in alternative directions. His observations constitute a phenomenology of the existential effects of what he sees as an individual's having turned away from God and a taking stock of the high cost of continuing on such a lost path, as revealed in the disquietude of an aesthetic existence that never rises above the categories of pleasure and the interesting.

Nordentoft's schematization of psychological material in Kierkegaard's writing can have the unintended effect of obscuring Kierkegaard's main point: namely, that his interest in presenting a psychology of religious crisis is to alert the reader to the rumblings of spirit in the reader him- or herself and to stimulate the reader to respond. At the same time, in presenting the existential manifestations of what his theological pseudonymous speakers call sinfulness, Kierkegaard, in advance of twentieth-century phenomenologists, is clear about detecting and pointing out the direction that the emotional data point to (what phenomenologists will term their intentionality).

Kierkegaard never issued anything like a modern psychological treatise, even when in *The Concept of Anxiety* we have the *form* of a treatise (albeit a *theological* treatise) and the expressed psychological interest in plumbing the meaning of the mood anxiety. Instead, his writings are a Socratic-existential nudge/provocation/plea to the reader to listen, to feel, and to recognize the pulse of spirit, to hearken to its message and direction, and always and above all, to make the process and natural further movements one's own. In Kierkegaard's views, this constitutes the true seriousness of his work, and he for his part would scoff at any idle formulation of a concept for intellectual reasons only.

For a variety of reasons, therefore, it would be a mistake to call Kierkegaard a psychologist in the contemporary usage of the word. He is neither a trained therapist in one of the established schools nor a social scientist. The laboratory for his experiments is himself, in inward self-examination. He is from the old school of pastoral and literary psychology and brings a definite Christian metaphysics to his analysis. The reality of such things as soul, sin, grace, forgiveness, and the encounter of the human spirit with divine Spirit are his starting point.

Kierkegaard and Freudianism

Freud shares none of the views just mentioned, but he too ultimately moved into the realm of metaphysics, albeit of a secular kind, and his so-called metaphysical turn is the objection on the part of some critics to Freud's late works such as *Beyond the Pleasure Principle.*[14] Moreover, as recent Freudian criticism has shown, Freud is far more a literary author than was thought, not just for the prose and detective-story quality of the case histories but also because of his manipulation of the case histories that he recounts for storytelling effect. As such, he has long since been revealed as less the disinterested scientist than he at first portrayed himself.

Narcissism and Melancholia

Both Freud and Kierkegaard discuss the narcissistic and the melancholic personality. Their analyses are significant, but equally significant is their linking narcissism with melancholy. Freud's 1915 "Mourning and Melancholia" can in fact be viewed as a continuation of his 1914 essay "On Narcissism." In Kierkegaard's *Either/Or,* part 1, narcissism and melancholy are found together in one and the same character, Aesthete A. Although Kierkegaard never uses the term "narcissism," both Freud and Kierkegaard cited the Roman poet Ovid, who gave us Narcissus and who would have no trouble in recognizing the dangerous self-infatuation of Aesthete A. (See chapter 5 for a more complete treatment of this theme.)

Melancholy and Depression

When Kierkegaard presents the lost young aesthete in emotional crisis, he generally terms the problem "melancholy." There is no question but that the self-presentation of his young aesthete in *Either/Or,* part 1 (but other aesthetic characters in his authorship too), constitutes a partial checklist for what we nowadays would recognize as clinical depression: low self-esteem, self-loathing, lack of energy, awakening in the morning still tired and with the immediate wish to return to bed.

But Kierkegaard would not have had the category clinical depression and did not have a clinical interest. His first inclination, after all, would not have been to prescribe Prozac for his lost young aesthete, even if it had been available, but instead Plato and Augustine and wisdom philosophy, as well as the Bible.

There may not be an adequate English translation for the Danish term *Tungsind.* "Brooding melancholy" is one suggestion.[15] In the end, the term to use may be Freud's own, namely "melancholia," for in "Mourning and Melancholia" Freud is covering much of the same ground as Kierkegaard (but with a different agenda, of course).

Freud's linking narcissism with melancholy would not at all have surprised Victor Emerita, Kierkegaard's pseudonymous editor of the melancholy and narcissistic papers of Aesthete A in *Either/Or.* Freud's essay, for its part, attempted a careful comparison of regular mourning with the phenomenon of melancholia and sees distinctive features of melancholia emerge. To his credit, Freud stresses the tentative nature of his work and warns against over-overvaluation of his tentative conclusions (*SE,* XIV:243). Moreover, Freud subsequently made important revisions to his theory in *The Ego and the Id* (1923) that viewed the differences between mourning and melancholia as far more nuanced than in 1915.[16]

In "Mourning and Melancholia," Freud characterized mourning as reaction to the loss of a loved one or to the loss of some abstraction that has the same power as a loved one—for example, one's country or liberty or some other ideal (*SE,* XIV:243). Mourning was viewed as the working through of the loss. Freud stressed that it is not normally regarded as pathological, and it is overcome after a certain period, when, as he described it, the ego has detached itself from the lost object and libido is free to attach itself to a new object. In contrast, melancholy knows no such "mourning period" after which it readjusts to the living world and to another love.[17] This line of thinking might lead to the consideration of whether Kierkegaard's presentation of melancholy in two formulations might be restated along Freudian lines as loss or absence of a love object (*Melancholi*) and the brooding refusal to move on to a new and higher love object (*Tungsind*). But *Tungsind* contains the consciousness that a new human love object will not deliver the fulfillment sought, that only a higher and spiritual love Object (namely, God) will solve the root problem. (Freud can imagine no such thing as *Tungsind* in Kierkegaard's sense and would no doubt reduce it to prolonged mourning.)

Freud wrote,

> The distinguishing mental features of melancholia are a profoundly painful dejection, cessation of interest in the outside world, loss of the capacity to love, inhibition of all activity, and a lowering of the self-regarding feelings to a degree that finds utterance in self-reproaches and self-revilings, and culminates in a delusional expectation of punishment. (*SE*, XIV:244)[18]

Most of these qualities are well known to Kierkegaard readers from the "Diapsalmata" of *Either/Or*, part 1, and Kierkegaard's early journals from which they are drawn.

Freud noted that the key difference between mourning and melancholia turns on self-regard, which is undisturbed in mourning. There is a period of suffering, but "when the work of mourning is completed the ego becomes free and uninhibited again" (*SE*, XIV:245). In melancholia, on the other hand, one's self-regard is undermined and one turns one's energies ultimately against oneself.

For Freud, both mourning and melancholia are reactions to the loss of a loved object. The loss in mourning is associated with death, whereas the loss in melancholia is of a more ideal kind. Freud regarded melancholia as "in some way related to an object-loss which is withdrawn from consciousness," versus mourning, which has nothing unconscious about it (*SE*, XIV:245). In short, in melancholia one does not entirely understand what it is that has been "lost." Its object is ideal, indefinite, unconscious.

The melancholic person does not know what is absorbing him. And so melancholia is an inward matter. "In mourning it is the *world* which has become poor and empty; in melancholia it is the *ego* itself" (*SE*, XIV:246; emphasis added). The melancholic turns his considerable energies against himself, and, in an observation that Kierkegaard would surely have agreed with, Freud notes that the melancholic "has a keener eye for the truth than other people who are not melancholic" (*SE*, XIV:246). "When in his heightened self-criticism he describes himself as petty, egoistic, dishonest, lacking in independence, one whose sole aim has been to hide the weaknesses of his own nature, it may be, so far as we know, that he has come pretty near to understanding himself; we only wonder why a man has to be ill before he can be accessible to a truth of this kind." In the final clause, Freud almost seemed to be investing the insights of the melancholic with objectivity and universality. The melancholic understands *himself* more keenly. Freud was not claiming that the melancholic has insight into the human condition generally, just heightened personal sensitivity, whereas Kierkegaard regards melancholy as a window upon the human condition and falsely directed desire.

For Freud, the outstanding feature of the self-dissatisfaction of melancholia is the ego's dissatisfaction with itself on moral grounds. Note that for Freud this is a psychological observation, not an ethical judgment. For Kierkegaard, it is precisely the problem.

Finally, Freud observed the extreme and violent self-accusations that the melancholic utters against himself and interprets them as reproaches against the failed love object that have now been shifted onto the person's own ego (*SE*, XIV:248) (hence the connection with narcissism). An object relationship was shattered and the ego identifies with the object and loves itself in its identification with the love object, in what constitutes a regression from object love to an original narcissism (*SE*, XIV:249). Freud thus sees the disposition to melancholia as lying in the power and predisposition to narcissism (*SE*, XIV:250). The melancholic loathes and hates himself for having failed to possess the idealized object of love. One mourns the other not for him- or herself but for what the other means to oneself. In this sense it is narcissistic.

Kierkegaard's view of melancholia is similar in its externals but quite different in its underlying meta-psychology. Kierkegaard's analysis is characterized by its religious metaphysics; the self, in Kierkegaard's view, is spiritually grounded, and it is that spiritual grounding that has been seriously severed and subsequently obscured by modern life.

Kierkegaard's standpoint has just as strong a claim as Freud's own eventual meta-psychology. In Freud's mind, Kierkegaard would simply be applying unscientific religious ideas to psychology. From Kierkegaard's position, Freud's view is a kind of reductionism to the finite, to the ego understood as nonspiritual.

Freud wrote, "We see that the ego debases itself and rages against itself and we understand as little as the patient what this can lead to and how it can change" (*SE*, XIV:257). In contrast, Kierkegaard is sure that melancholy, properly reflected on, does see where it is leading and how the personality can change.

Indeed, how it changes is precisely what Kierkegaard set out to show in *The Concept of Anxiety* and *The Sickness unto Death*, but it is already intimated in the ending of *Repetition*, where the nineteenth-century amateur psychologist Constantin Constantius suggests that it is a religious crisis that underlies the melancholy of the young man he is scrutinizing.

Repetition and Repetition Compulsion (*Beyond the Pleasure Principle*)

Kierkegaard's "The Banquet" ("In Vino Veritas") in *Stages on Life's Way* (1845) has frequently been compared to Plato's *Symposium*, but his earlier work *Repetition* actually shares the same existential interest of the well-known speeches of both Aristophanes and Socrates (Diotima). For, while *Repetition* begins playfully as a work in search of the meaning of its own title, it eventually reverts to the literal Danish meaning of "getting back again" (thus *Gjen-tagelse*). The Latin phrase *redintegratio in statum pristinum* (reintegration into the pristine original state) is a further clue and recalls the words in Aristophanes' speech, "We used to be complete wholes in our original nature, and now "Love" [Eros] is the name for our pursuit of wholeness, for our desire to be complete" (*Symposium* 192E–193A). Kierkegaard's work passes beyond Aristophanes's remedy of seeking one's other half and allies itself with Diotima's ladder of ascent to the divine. This is of course a meaning of "repetition" that Kierkegaard does not share with Freud. (He does share, uncannily, with Freud the themes of constancy, compulsion, and the talking cure.)

Anxiety/*Angest*/*Angst*

Kierkegaard's concept of anxiety is perhaps his greatest contribution to psychological thought of the twentieth century. It is the first major modern consideration of this mood from a philosophical perspective, but it is not a complete consideration of what contemporary psychiatry and psychology would mean by the term, which would be much broader. For that reason, it would be tempting to leave the term in Kierkegaard's original Danish *Angest,* or the more familiar German *Angst,* for his concern is with *existential anxiety,* the disturbing encounter in emotion and then in consciousness with one's own unfulfilled possibilities. However, there would be problems using those terms as well that would require constant footnoting. It is best to bear in mind that Kierkegaard is quite specific in what he means by the term and informs the reader of what he is speaking. The careful reader must then keep this in mind. The analysis is begun in *The Concept of Anxiety* and continued in *The Sickness unto Death.*

Both are manifestly "meta-psychological" works, which is to say that they take psychological states as their starting point but go far beyond the data in their analyses. But the important point to remember is that they are each empirical and profoundly existential, not just in the sense that each of them has also had enormous influence on existential philosophy and existential psychologies of the twentieth century but also in that they recall the reader to individual existential reflection and personal decision. The pseudonymous Haufniensis's formal treatise stresses the correct mood for his "simple psychologically orienting deliberation on the dogmatic issue of hereditary sin" (subtitle). That mood, he tells us, is *not* the mood of (philosophical) psychology, which is mere curiosity, nor is it the metaphysical mood of indifference. It is, instead, the mood of seriousness, of serious engagement with the problem of personal anxiety.

Kierkegaard-Haufniensis's work begins in the form of a medieval theology treatise, centered on the theological problem of sinfulness and its origin in the first sin of Adam. But while Kierkegaard personally accepted the historicity of a biblical Fall, his discussion parallels Kant's *Religion within the Limits of Reason Alone, Book One,* where Kant rejects the historical fall as an irrational idea and concentrates on its symbolism. Both ultimately give a personal, existential meaning to the theological notion of "inherited sin" " or "original sin." Kierkegaard means *subjective* anxiety as real, experienced, and revelatory of a crisis in the personality in which the personality becomes attuned to a self-inflicted wound that can be healed. The meta-psychology (or theology) of the work, like Kant's, is its tracing empirical psychological data back to a necessarily inferred personal deed. But its psychological importance is its existential emphasis on the anxiety experience as an index of where one stands with regard to the issue of reintegration of the personality. (See chapter 9 for a fuller discussion of anxiety and Heidegger's debt to Kierkegaard.)

Freud initially viewed anxiety as a product of sexual repression. He had revised this theory by 1926 and in 1932 wrote, "It was not the repression that created the anxiety; the anxiety was there earlier; it was the anxiety that made the repression!"[19] But Freud never, of course, pursues anxiety into the theological realm of sinfulness.

Kierkegaard's analysis of sin continued far beyond giving existential content to original sin as his pseudonymous Anti-Climacus developed the problem in the large meta-psychological essay *Sickness unto Death,* which schematized various ways of continuing in sin. But it too is concerned with overcoming the problem, not just understanding and schematizing it. Whereas Kierkegaard maintained the theological term "sin" and gave it existential content, Freud termed similar phenomena "neurosis" and "repression."

Freud is concerned too with the phenomenon of anxiety not only as an indication of a problem in the personality (neurosis) but also a problem that stands unresolved (repression). Freud did attend to the phenomenon of guilt, but merely as an observation. Even in his meta-psychology he stays far away from theology. For Kierkegaard as for Kant, there is a *feeling* of guilt precisely because *one has become guilty*, and one needs somehow to get back and undo the original deed. This is an important difference with Freud, of course. One not only feels guilty but also *is* morally guilty and responsible. Furthermore, the only cure is in becoming conscious of the responsibility and acknowledging it. Freud, from a Kierkegaard point of view, remains on the level of the feeling of guilt, and this is not enough.

It can be tempting to lump Kierkegaard together with traditional theological metaphysics and to have his work share its current fate of being mostly dismissed by our culture, and this for the simple reason that he has not abandoned the language of theological metaphysics. It *can* be freed, as Heidegger's secularization of Kierkegaard demonstrates. Kierkegaard's phenomenology and meta-psychology of human non-reintegration is no more meta-psychological and no more metaphysical than Freud's explanation of birth trauma, Oedipus complex, and so on. Kierkegaard uses the un-novel and un-pagan categories of Christian theology, not merely because they are part of an established tradition that he is part of but also because he sees in them a valid expression of deep truth about the human condition. Freud shares neither his perspective nor his language. Heidegger will show that the perspective can be freed of the language.

The Kierkegaardian's Debt to Freud

Repressed sexuality, anxiety, melancholia, narcissism: these are some of the themes shared by both Kierkegaard and Freud, for all of which readers and scholars of Kierkegaard should be grateful for Freud's highlighting them and an appreciation in hindsight of Kierkegaard's equal, perhaps even superior, accomplishment a half century earlier. That they have entered into our everyday thinking is of course the contribution of Freud and Freudianism. The cultural success of Freudian terms and a Freudian perspective (even if increasingly challenged) can also lead us to appreciate the depth and acuity of Kierkegaard's own, earlier insights, the equal plausibility of his own meta-psychology, but above all the difference in perspective, its significance and its implications for understanding a troubled self. Here the key difference between them is that, for Kierkegaard, spirit is not an empty name but something that is real, and, as he has the character Judge William write, when spirit is mocked and not allowed to have its evolving, dynamic life in oneself, melancholia is the result.

Kierkegaard's psychological thought is ultimately maieutic in intent, which is to say Kierkegaard, true to his Socratic method, is not concerned with laying out a definitive or full-blown psychology so much as getting the individual to think about his or her own condition and to do something about it. This is also to say that Kierkegaard is not a whit less interested in cure than Freud would be.

But Kierkegaard would surely think that consulting Constantin Constantius, of *Repetition*, and engaging in talk therapy would not be enough. The therapy that Kierkegaard points to, beyond the coming to self-consciousness, choice, and the will to overcome the fragmentation of the self, is set out in the therapy of *Works of Love*: the therapy of spiritual love that embraces love of neighbor in manifold senses. Indeed, Kierkegaard is nowhere more eloquent and nowhere more profound than when he writes very simply and in his own name in *Works of Love*, "For *to love God, that is in truth to love oneself; to help another person to love God is to love another person; to be helped by another person to love God is to be loved.*"[20]

Restated in more secular terms, to love oneself truly is to love oneself in all one's depth, that is, in a deeper and common ground of our common being. To love another person truly is to help another to know and experience this same deeper common ground. And truly to be loved means to be assisted by the lover to know and experience the deeper common grounding.

This grounding is of course what Christians term God. Cicero, in his famous essay on friendship's meaning for Stoicism (*De Amicitia*), speaks very similarly when he says that two persons can call their relationship friendship only when it is grounded in the Good, understood not as something intellectual but as a Socratic existential commitment and experience. Friends thus help each other to be grounded in the Good and to be better, moral persons and thereby fulfilled human beings.

A (re)reading of Freud after Kierkegaard helps us to appreciate that Kierkegaard may not only have uncannily anticipated many of Freud's famous themes but may also have gone further. The Kierkegaardian's debt to Freud is the Freudian perspective's leading one to appreciate the greater profundity of Kierkegaard in his own much earlier work. It remains an important alternative to Freud. For a therapy that understands the human person as participating in the transcendent reality called spirit is significantly different not just in its details but also in the end point toward which it conducts a troubled self. If that end point is real and not just imaginary—in other words if it can be *experienced* in the here and now—then it is significantly richer than Freud's.

2

Sex and Sexuality

Sex and the erotic are not identical, despite contemporary confusion on the subject. Writing about eros and what the human heart is after is a subject that goes back at least as far as Plato. Kierkegaard's inclusion of the erotic is therefore not, on the surface, surprising. What is different, however, in such an otherwise conservative figure are his discussions of sensuality and sexuality, surely in the abstract, but nonetheless telling. This is best reflected in his extended essay on eros and desire in Mozart's operas, most particularly in *Don Giovanni* with its musical expression of the myth of the self-destructive sexual rake. But he was and remains a pre-Freudian writer. Given his conservative stance on so many subjects,[1] we may be surprised that he took up the subject of sexuality at all. His contribution to the subject is not extensive, but it is real, provocative, and an advance challenge to the Freudian views that would dominate much of twentieth-century thought.

His views on sexuality are sometimes surprisingly modern, sometimes courageous, as when he critiques religion's mistaken stance toward sexuality and the disastrous equation of sexuality with sinfulness. Kierkegaard tried to show that what is regarded as sexuality in the modern world is a distortion of the natural. And so he seeks a return to "natural" sexuality (as if there is or was any easy agreement on its meaning), freed of both cultural and religious distortions, recognized as a means of individual pleasure and fulfillment, as well as the continuation of the species, but not as a final end. Ultimately, he thinks, the dynamism present in human sexuality is part of a higher eros and leads to an even higher realm.

While sex and sexuality are openly discussed by the twenty-first-century public, such candor is relatively recent and dates back only to the 1960s. The nineteenth-century public, for its part, was not a bit less interested in the topic of sex but was restricted to mostly indirect references to it. Repression often finds creative outlets, and sometimes memorably creative portrayals of eroticism arose as a result, to which Kierkegaard also contributed.

Yet while Kierkegaard was part of a culture of sexual indirectness, a few direct theoretical mentions of individual sexuality do emerge in his writings, if executed with broad theoretical brushstrokes. In his private journals we find only cryptic and indirect mentions. Still, Kierkegaard would term his main interest the *erotic*, rather than sexuality, and he has a great deal more to say about the former than about the latter. This is not due simply to the fact that discussion of the erotic was more permissible in the nineteenth century. Kierkegaard is interested in the dynamism of the erotic, which, in his view, certainly includes the human sexual chase that leads to reproduction of the species. But he suggests a higher eros that involves participation in the creation of a higher self.

It is no accident that his literary banquet in *Stages on Life's Way* harks back to Plato's *Symposium*, where the sexual and the erotic are the principal themes. While his own speakers restrict themselves to a discussion of woman, and even how women of the nineteenth century are to be criticized for having become too willingly what men reduced them to, his own standpoint is akin to that of Socrates, who, in Plato's dialogue, told the story of a ladder of erotic ascent to the spiritual.[2]

Anyone expecting to learn something about Kierkegaard's own sexuality will be disappointed by the silence and impenetrable ambiguities in Kierkegaard's published writings and private papers. In his Danish equivalent of the Victorian age, proper persons did not speak openly or directly about animal passions and embarrassing drives. There is very little that he tells directly, but a bit may reasonably be inferred from his indirect remarks (as Joakim Garff does on the subject of masturbation on the part of the Kierkegaard brothers).[3] To the frustration of some, Kierkegaard's sex life cannot be constructed from his writings and journals. Yet Kierkegaard's published works draw so heavily on his biography and make so many half-veiled references to events in his life that it is virtually impossible to consider this and other topics without inquiring into his own life.

There are only a few relevant episodes in Kierkegaard's largely literary existence that touch upon the sexual, most especially his famous brief engagement to be married. In 1840 Kierkegaard surprised everyone, perhaps himself included, by suddenly proposing to the eighteen-year-old Regine Olsen (1822–1904), who had been close to being engaged to another when Kierkegaard asked for her hand. No sooner was he engaged than he was seized with private doubts. Despite them, he did not return his own formal engagement ring until nearly a year later. A marriage engagement in nineteenth-century Denmark was a very serious commitment, ushering in a period of ritualized family integration. Breaking an engagement in nineteenth-century Denmark was scandalous, a source of gossip, shameful for the families and engaged couple, but mostly for the young woman. Regine Olsen's plea to Kierkegaard not to break with her, her father's equal desperation, and the unbridgeable chasm that resulted from such a rupture must be viewed in this context. By the standards of the twenty-first century, this is exaggerated, hysterical conduct over a mere marriage engagement, but not by the standards of the nineteenth century.

For her part, Regine Olsen was by all accounts a charmingly innocent girl and there is no reason to think that relations between Regine and Kierkegaard were anything but proper by the standards of the day. In short, it is unimaginable that they would have had anything approaching sexual relations. Indeed, Kierkegaard worried about appearances and was shocked when the distraught Regine came alone to his apartment after the rupture. To the gossipy Copenhagen public, Kierkegaard tried to appear a cad so as to protect Regine and draw all criticism to himself.[4]

What most people would have regarded as a minor event in the grand scheme of things was evidently a trauma in Kierkegaard's life, and he spent much of his literary life trying to write his way out of it. The point is not the engagement itself (although an engagement, as noted, in the nineteenth century was a very serious undertaking) but what the engagement meant *for* him and what breaking it did *to* him. It became the literary inspiration for several works: *Either/Or*, part 1, including "The Seducer's Diary"; "The Aesthetic Validity of Marriage" (*E/O* 2), in which Judge William argues that eros, marriage, and Christianity are compatible; "'Guilty?'/'Not Guilty?'" (in *Stages on Life's Way*) and *Repetition*, both of which deal with broken engagements; as well as *Fear and Trembling*, which dwells on the miraculous restoration of an innocent sacrificial victim (Abraham's Isaac). After the trauma is worked out in literature, tinges of regret and a deep sense of loss continued to permeate Kierkegaard's writings, as well as ambivalence about breaking the engagement. Kierkegaard's multiple broken-engagement stories may well represent the manifestation of a classic Freudian repetition compulsion, nowhere more clearly than in the work *Repetition* (see chapter 6).

Perhaps adding to the trauma was his shock when he learned that Regine had become engaged to Fritz Schlegel, her original intended, at a time when Kierkegaard had been privately indulging thoughts of a re-engagement (even if it is hard to imagine that he ever would have acted on them). She married in 1847, and he mourned her loss but evidently never really gave her up. He dedicated his authorship to her, had copies of his work specially bound for her, and hoped for some sort of reconciliation, perhaps in their old age or else in eternity. More than ten years after the rupture he was writing about her as his heavenly bride and made her his heir before his early death (to the consternation of Regine Schlegel's husband).

Why Kierkegaard broke with Regine makes for rich speculation but is ultimately an unanswered and unanswerable question. That does not and will not stop speculation. Since the dawn of the age of Freud, some have conjectured that Kierkegaard was impotent or homosexual. Was the rupture due to a Freudian, masochistic self-castration resulting from a sense of guilt? Or—to consider an extreme view—was it the Sadeian culmination of toying with and emotionally torturing an innocent girl, as Johannes does to Cordelia in "The Seducer's Diary"?[5] Did he intuit that his marriage as the precocious, intellectual, twenty-seven-year-old son of a wealthy merchant to an innocent girl of eighteen from a good family would have been a mismatch? There is no solid evidence for any theory, but that does not stop the theories from recurring.

Kierkegaard does comment that he did not want to introduce Regine to his melancholy and to family secrets.[6] Among the dark secrets: Kierkegaard's father, Michael Pedersen Kierkegaard (1756–1838), had impregnated a family servant, Ane Lund (1768–1834), while his first wife was ill and married her soon after his wife's death. Not much of a scandal at all for us, and not much more unusual in the nineteenth century than in the twenty-first. But such things were hushed up and repressed in his time. Ane Lund Kierkegaard became the mother of all seven Kierkegaard children. Before his father's death in 1838, five of the seven children and their mother had already died, and Kierkegaard expressed a strong sense that the family was cursed. A journal entry after his father's death expressed his hopelessness about leading a happy family life and the continuity of the family line.[7] This was two years prior to his engagement.

It is not so much the embarrassing fact of his mother's pregnancy before marriage and the sad facts of so many deaths in the family that are central here but rather their effect on Kierkegaard. There are reasons to think that he thought of himself as a sacrificial victim for his father's sins (playing Isaac to his father's Abraham, in a sense). But he was also possibly haunted by youthful dissipation, to which he makes obscure references but that may be purely literary or only partially personal.[8] Kierkegaard has one of his pseudonymous figures examine street urchins' faces on Copenhagen boulevards, searching for signs of having fathered one with a prostitute.[9] His journals contain a version of this parable that is (only) possibly applicable to Kierkegaard's life:

> Once in his early youth a man allowed himself to be so far carried away in an overwrought irresponsible state as to visit a prostitute. It is all forgotten. Now he wants to get married. Then anxiety stirs. He is tortured day and night with the thought that he might possibly be a father. . . . He cannot share his secret with anyone; he does not have any reliable knowledge of the fact. . . . This very ignorance is the basis of his agitated torment. . . . His misgivings do not really start until he actually falls in love.[10]

In another journal entry, Kierkegaard writes that if he had gone through with the engagement, Regine would have been more like a concubine than a wife, since he could not have been totally open with her.[11] And he has his character Judge William write, "If in some way or another you have swallowed a secret that cannot be dragged out of you without costing your life—then marry."[12] As a result, "the curse that hangs over me is that I never dare let any person become deeply and intimately attached to me."[13] The literature that he subsequently produced is full of attempts to spin out the meaning, and perhaps the residual emotional trauma, of his overpowering reaction to his engagement.

Kierkegaard lamented,

> I would have had to initiate her into terrible things, my relationship to my father, his melancholy, the eternal brooding night within me, my going astray, my lusts and debauchery, which, however, in the eyes of God are perhaps not so glaring; for it was, after all, anxiety which brought me to go astray, and where was I to seek a safe stronghold when I knew or suspected that the only man [his father] I had admired for his strength was tottering.[14]

One can cautiously conclude that, because of family and personal secrets, Kierkegaard felt he could not fulfill what he understood as the ethical requirement of openness in marriage and therefore recognized that he should not marry.

Despite his sense of sinfulness, sharpened by the Pietism of his time and his family experience among the Moravian Brethren in his childhood, Kierkegaard apparently knew he was being hard on himself, as the tradition of reformed sinners from Augustine onward encouraged one to be. Yet we know that the deeds of self-described great sinners in Christianity are often rather minor. It is the guilt and suffering produced in and by the sinner that makes them great. In short, what we have here is a classic case of a tortured soul that a William James would have readily identified and perhaps included in his *Varieties of Religious Experience* had he known about Kierkegaard.

But if Kierkegaard comes to a discussion of sexuality and the erotic with unresolved personal issues, that should neither disqualify him nor distract us from what he wishes to say directly on the subject. Kierkegaard is not a major theoretician on sexuality. But let us not underestimate him either: Kierkegaard does in fact, and well in advance of Freud, posit sexuality as central to the understanding of human psychological life. The only nineteenth-century contemporary who gives similar importance to sexuality is Schopenhauer. His 1819 *The World as Will and Idea* did not become known to Kierkegaard until 1854, well after the composition of the psychological works of the 1840s.[15] On the subject of eros and desire, he takes his place with the great thinkers of the West.

Kierkegaard's pseudonymous Haufniensis boldly asserts in *The Concept of Anxiety* that there can be no exclusion of sensuality and sexuality in an integrated personality, which is to say that an integrated personality requires the sensual and the sexual. In his thinking, they must ultimately be (re)integrated with spirit, and in fact Kierkegaard takes the Christian tradition to task for having separated them quite erroneously.[16] Here Kierkegaard is not only temporally in advance of Freud but also, if one shares his spiritual perspective (whether in Christian categories or not), possibly *beyond* Freud in seeing the need for the integration of the sexual and the spiritual. This means nothing less than affirming the sexual and grounding it in a higher eros connecting to spirit itself.

Kierkegaard's thoughts on sexuality are first set out in his lengthy portrayals of desire and eros in *Either/Or* of 1843. His term in Danish for desire is *Atraa*, the standard Danish translation of the Greek *eros*. While Kierkegaard's corpus does refer to sex and sexuality, the erotic and sensuality are the major terms in his writings of the 1840s. In his famous Mozart-related essay "The Immediate Stages of the Musical Erotic,"[17] Kierkegaard's anonymous Aesthete A writes of three stages of desire represented in three famous Mozart operas. Cherubino in *The Marriage of Figaro* symbolizes desire in its first stage, when desire is not yet conscious: the desirer desires something without knowing what she or he is looking for. Desire at this point does not have a clear object, as symbolized by young Cherubino's swooning over and chasing women—virtually any woman and every woman. In love with love, Cherubino darts wildly in all directions toward the possible gratification of his sexual needs. Any woman will do. As a result he is comical, nearly farcical, even if charmingly so. Papageno of *The Magic Flute* symbolizes awakening desire: he knows that he seeks another but is not clear who that other would be. He has no idea what she looks like, but he does know her name: Papagena, the feminine version of his own name. He is naively convinced he will recognize his "true love" when he finds her. And he merely winces when she eventually reveals herself disguised as homely, even ugly. This suggests that any girl who knew the magic word "Papagena" might have had the same success, whether beauty or beast. Desire at this secondary state is understood as recognition of a need for a specific, single other to be the possibility of one's emotional and physical satisfaction.

Genuine self-conscious desire—the third stage—emerges fully in Mozart's *Don Giovanni*. Kierkegaard's Aesthete A sees a development from Cherubino, who wants anybody, to Papageno, who wants somebody named Papagena, to Don Giovanni, who wants a succession of women, of whom Elvira and Anna are only the most recent names inscribed on a very long list. Interestingly, all three characters are comic, and we even laugh briefly at Leporello's aria about Giovanni's 1,003 (*mille tre*) in Spain. Ultimately, the large number of conquests names a compulsive womanizer who is profoundly unfree. As he moves from one exploit to another, he is depicted as having a store of seemingly inexhaustible sexual energy but with unspecified deeper desires that remain unsatisfied. When, at the opera's end, Don Giovanni accepts the challenge of the Commendatore to dinner (and to death), he very tellingly chooses the fires of hell over the inexhaustible yet exhausting fires of sexual desire.

Another section of *Either/Or*, part 1, presents an important and generally unacknowledged *fourth* stage of aesthetic desire in the figure of another variant of the name John, namely Johannes, the infamous psychological seducer of "The Seducer's Diary." In contrast to Don Giovanni, Johannes desires only one woman. More precisely, *he desires to make her desire him*, and this is more important to him than physical desire itself. Indeed, in this psychological thought experiment, physical conquest is almost an afterthought. For what Johannes truly desires is *her desire*, that she desire him. In his devilish diary of emotional manipulation, he believes that he outdoes Don Giovanni and his 1,003 bodies. In desiring her desire, he actually desires her "soul." Johannes's desire is more demonic as well as he plots and achieves the seduction of Cordelia's will. But here too Johannes is not his own master, and he knows it. His own hell can be taken to be chronicled in the chilling "Diapsalmata" that Kierkegaard places at the front of the volume: hymns and epigrams of restlessness and self-loathing.

In *Repetition*, the pseudonymous psychologist Constantin Constantius considers the unsatisfied desire of another Papageno who has found and become engaged to another Papagena. *Repetition*'s nameless young man has fallen in love with and become engaged to a nameless young woman. His enduring melancholy (*Melancholi*) is the negative index and negative definition of his desire and eventually leads him to the insight that *it is not she* that is desired. In fact, no woman can satisfy a deeper and objectless desire that he detects in himself. His mistake was to think that she might. Constantius declares the young man's melancholy to have a *religious* depth requiring a *religious* solution, and Kierkegaard thereby indicates where his analysis of desire will eventually lead. As if to prevent readers from missing the point, the story line is virtually repeated in the novella "'Guilty?'/'Not Guilty?'" in *Stages on Life's Way*. By way of emphasizing the gravity and depth of a melancholy not satisfied by an earthly beloved, the terminology changes and the term *Melancholi* is replaced with the darker term *Tungsind*, which, as noted, suggests a self-destructive melancholic longing about to implode. But the most theoretical comments about sexuality itself are to be found in *The Concept of Anxiety*, which is formally a treatise about the roots of sinfulness. Here, sexuality is considered in its relationship to anxiety, which Kierkegaard analyzes as a summons to self-actualization. Technically and formally speaking, *The Concept of Anxiety* takes the form of a theological treatise, focusing on sin as a pressing existential problem to be overcome. Comments on sexuality emerge from an exploration of the unfortunate medieval theological link between sinfulness and sexuality. But this is only a point of departure, and Kierkegaard's understanding of sexuality goes well beyond the traditional association of sex and sin. Ultimately he proposes a higher form of sexuality linked with spiritual striving, after an analysis of eros as a dynamism propelling one beyond the merely sensuous to a mostly ignored higher realm.

The Concept of Anxiety first considers sexuality in the narrow sense—as a drive to gratify sensuality combined with a drive to reproduce—and then moves on to sweeping cultural comments. Greek paganism's philosophy of beauty is represented as the positive flowering of sensualism, while Judaism is presented as the other pole of sexuality, namely perpetuation through reproduction. Both of these are contrasted with the spirituality in sexuality, which he asserts Christianity, when properly understood, really did introduce, despite the theological distortions that have emerged during Christianity's nineteen hundred years.

Kierkegaard contends that spirituality transcends both sensuality and the reproductive urge by subsuming them into the larger and higher spiritual life that Christianity introduced in the person of Christ.[18] He goes so far as to say that, within the perspective of the spiritual, no difference any longer exists between man and woman. The true victory of Christian love in a person will mean that the sexual is transcended—but not annihilated or ignored. This is the ideal that he claims can be made real, but he does so without empirical support of any kind.

While granting preeminence of the spiritual, Kierkegaard wanted to affirm a positive relationship between spirituality and sensuality/sexuality (spirit and flesh). He regrets that sexuality through traditional biblical interpretation of Adam's original sin had come to *signify* sinfulness.[19] But despite this association of sexuality and sensuality with the sinful in human history, Kierkegaard emphasizes that neither sensuality nor sexuality is per se the sinful.[20]

However, Kierkegaard's argument is not just with the mistakes of past Christianity. There were new errors in Christianity in the nineteenth century as well. In his view, the formal Christianity of his day had betrayed its spiritual core in trying to accommodate a philosophy of spiritless sexuality and sensuality. Much of Kierkegaard's early aesthetic authorship is a literary portrayal of this cultural problem. *Either/Or*, part 2, speaks of a healthy sexuality that is at least not indifferent to things spiritual, that is, not just beyond the physical but also beyond the intellectual and aesthetic. It is the task of *Either/Or*, part 2, to show how spiritually indifferent sexuality can be elevated. Judge William critiques Aesthete A of *Either/Or*, part 1, who is lost in sensuality. William argues (and demonstrates in his own life) that sexuality finds its proper place in the ethical state of marriage, which he characterizes as open, committed, and charitably loving.[21] For William, (Christian) married love leaves room for the pleasant eroticism of first love, while elevating lovers above mere erotic chase of male or female to become nothing less than spiritual equals before God.[22]

In sum, Kierkegaard, at least in his pseudonymous authorship, says yes to healthy sensual pleasure. Subsequently, writing under his own name, he will direct readers toward what he holds to be the higher stage of Christian love. In *Stages on Life's Way*, his pseudonymous author writes, "The lover's desire presumably is not selfish in relation to the beloved's, but the desire of both together is absolutely selfish insofar as they in union and in love form one self."[23] The problem here is a union that eliminates one form of selfishness only to replace it with another and does not rise to a higher spiritual form of self. The more that two I's come together in an attempt to merge as one, the more the lovers love only themselves. Kierkegaard argues that erotic love weighed down by self-interest and passionate preference is thus incompatible with Christian love.

Kierkegaard, in his later, private *Papirer*, eventually rejects as inadequate the married lifestyle that his character Judge William led and proposed to Aesthete A of *Either/Or*. Kierkegaard does so not to return to aesthetic sensuality but, with Plato and Paul, to point toward a form of eros that is both higher than the sexual chase and higher even than marriage. But this was already implied in the dialectic of *Either/Or*, where each part cancels out the other in a veritable neither-nor and where the astute reader realizes she is left on her own to find resolution.

> The hearty twaddle of family life constitutes the worst danger for Christianity, and not wild lusts, debauchery, terrible passions and the like. They are not so opposed to Christianity as this flat mediocrity, this stuffy reek, this nearness to one another. . . . There is no greater distance from obedience to the either-or than this flat, hearty family twaddle.[24]

At first reading, "the hearty twaddle of family life" takes one aback, but the emphasis is on the hearty twaddle as the danger to the Christian life. The point of this harsh-sounding dismissal of bourgeois married life is the danger that mundane everyday life can distract spouses from attending to the spiritual dimension of life, unless elevated by a higher interest. This position echoes Aristophanes's famous myth in Plato's *Symposium* and the frequently forgotten first stage in his tale when the newly split beings seek their other half and forget that they once sought nothing less than the realm of the gods themselves.

Kierkegaard's goal is first to free healthy, normal sexuality from its unhealthy association with the sinful and then to link it to the spiritual. He thus aligns himself with the best attempts of Christian theology to make married love and sexuality compatible with the spiritual. But he wants to make his readers recognize that married love is not entirely free of selfishness and that it too needs to be transcended. How this would work out in the kitchen and the bedroom is beyond his married character Judge William and never set out except in Kierkegaard's religious discourses. Nonetheless, the reader misses an examination of the fully integrated subjectivity that Kierkegaard repeatedly holds out as an ideal.

Kierkegaard's authorship is concerned largely with the transformation of individuals from beings merely in search of satisfying animal needs to beings in whom a religious dimension has subordinated all others, rather than being subordinated to them. This begins when individuals transcend mere aestheticism, including all sensuality, and emerge into the greater sphere of the ethico-religious and culminates in the Christian teaching of love properly understood (*agape*).

For Kierkegaard, human sexuality is finally to be understood as part of a deeper, more powerful, more enveloping movement toward (re)union with the One, the Absolute, the Creator God. His is therefore a far more positive view of sexuality than many might think, and this despite the fact that his own outward life did not effectively support his message. But it is significant for its attempt to reunite sensuality and spirit and for the prominent, decisive role assigned to this reunification.

This is a very different theory from Freud's. To be sure, there is no mention of such things as infantile sexuality or polymorphous perversity or an Oedipus stage. Fascination with these acute and controversial observations of Freud's have often led readers to forget how meta-psychological these theories really are. Kierkegaard's theory is surely no less meta-psychological, but ultimately also no less interesting and no less profound. His suggestion that the history of Christianity has had the unfortunate effect of separating sexuality and spirituality and that the two must be acknowledged and integrated is as much a challenge to Christianity as it is to secular psychoanalysis.

For not just in advance of Freud on sexuality but also in advance of Nietzsche's "Death of God" Kierkegaard recognized that for the modern world "spirit is dead" and that as a result sexuality is misunderstood. Indeed, in this new materialistic world, the word "spirit" no longer seemed to name anything. The danger is a vitiation and eclipse of the spiritual. To counter the unnecessary and fatal separation of the sexual and the spiritual, Kierkegaard tries to call attention to what he believed to be the forgotten wellspring of psychic integration, namely the individual human spirit in relationship to transcendent Spirit.

3

Emotions about Nothing

Kierkegaard, author of a philosophical masterpiece with the unserious title *Philosophical Fragments*, has also left us a series of *psychological* fragments that are consciously incomplete. He never intended to be systematic in his treatment of emotional life, nor does he ever engage in a fuller philosophical exploration of human nature and emotions as did David Hume. And while his avowed interest in the moods selected for sustained attention is resolution, he explores only the crisis phase.

Yet while Kierkegaard never declared a programmatic plan for exploring psychological topics, he in effect engaged in a phenomenology of moods, in a wide exploration of a set of emotions that are particularly distinctive for having no clear object and, in effect, revealing themselves to be emotions about "nothing." The phrase "emotions about nothing" does not mean here emotions of insignificance or worthy of dismissal from consideration but exactly the opposite: emotions that are powerful and real and uniquely revelatory about the human condition and where "nothing" ultimately emerges as a highly important negative ideogram of something that holds the greatest significance.

Given the role of "nothing" in his psychological explorations, it is somewhat ironic that Kierkegaard wrote in 1844 that if ever there were to be such a thing as Danish philosophy, it would not begin with nothing.[1] And yet his important contributions to psychology begin with an exploration of world and self-dissatisfaction that quickly reveal not only a non-object but point toward an exploration of the paradoxical "nothing" in play.

For in boredom, I discover that I am interested in nothing, that nothing at hand interests me. In irony I reject the unsatisfactory world but do not know what will satisfy or fulfill me, and turn on it with scorn in the false initial impression that nothing will provide fulfillment and relief. In anxiety my fear has no object and I am thrown back on myself and eventually the "nothing" that is at the center of my own being. (See chapters 8 and 9.) In despair I am on the verge of giving up hope of ever solving the riddle of myself and of my existence, a riddle that seems to defy answers and come to nothing.

It is well known from his *Journals* and from later biographies that Kierkegaard suffered serious emotional crises.[2] In the emotional depths into which he was plunged, he explored the self, *before* Existentialists and *beyond* Romantics, with an eye for detail and with reflective brilliance. His analysis of the emotional life must to some extent be understood in relation to the Romantics of his times and seen as a strong corrective. Kierkegaard set out to show that an individual's emotional life can have a meaning, depth, and ultimate clarity that go far beyond popular wisdom, poetic *Schwärmerei*, and philosophical group psychologies of a Hegelian cast. Ultimately Kierkegaard proposes the religious (or spiritual) sphere as the deepest ground of the person and as the realm to which his analysis of indeterminate emotions points. What Kierkegaard means by the religious is not a set of doctrines or documents or practices but a personal experience and a personal discovery of the grounding and equilibrium-restoring source for a series of emotional upheavals in the personality. He sought to portray and then conceptually articulate the meaning and intentionality of certain emotions.[3] Kierkegaard explores a "logic of the heart" through an examination of the truth of human growth. He does so empirically and reflectively and speculatively and then moves on to formulate a philosophical statement of the underlying elements that make sense of emotional life. He also engaged in existential experimentation—personal and imaginative.

What is particularly distinctive is the emphasis on the meaning of individual experience. Thus while there is general language about becoming a self, every self is understood as a distinctive and individual self-creation.[1] To some extent, Kierkegaard's analysis can be considered an updating and elaboration of the well-known quote from Augustine's *Confessions* (addressed as a prayer to God): "Our heart is restless until it finds rest in you,"[5] but with added emphasis on each individual's distinctively individual experience.

The Concept of Moods

Kierkegaard's authorship is to a significant degree an analysis of the stormy emotional life of the potentially religious subject, a presentation of the human spirit weathering the internal storms involved in reaching the transcendent. Kierkegaard limited his psychological explorations to emotions that eventually pointed the way toward a higher subjectivity. Further, he had a concept of these moods, even if he never wrote a formal treatise on moods as such, as Heidegger was among the first to see clearly and then to articulate in a very different philosophical project of his own. Kierkegaard's presentation of certain moods is not straightforward, and for this he had his deliberate reasons.[6] Moreover, despite the extensive descriptions he provides, he never directly defines a mood as such; and the four moods that he emphasizes, as well as their manner of presentation, make for a surprising list for the twenty-first-century reader, namely, irony, anxiety, melancholy, and despair.

Anxiety and despair are each the clear subject of a treatise by a transparent pseudonym[7] (*The Concept of Anxiety*, by Vigilius Haufniensis, and *The Sickness unto Death*, by Anti-Climacus). Irony, which is initially the most surprising "mood," was the subject of Kierkegaard's Copenhagen dissertation, for which he was awarded a degree by the university and the epithet "master of irony" by the public. But for him irony was not essentially a matter of wit or a sharp tongue but a coloration of the entire personality, a tonality (Danish *Stemning*) that characterized the way one experienced the world and oneself in the world. It is a mood of rebellion and rejection of finitude—the givens and limits in which one always finds oneself as a human being. Melancholy is longing for a beloved, not as nineteenth-century Romantics understood it but ultimately as Christian mystics did. Kierkegaard's concept of the moods of religious subjectivity also contains a discernible dialectic of moods. And his rational examination of emotional life constitutes a logic of moods, a clear and meaningful ordering of crisis and resolution in what would at first appear to be merely a chaos of emotions. Moreover, in each instance he would hold that crisis is both predictable and necessary for personal growth to occur.

Kierkegaard is interested principally in moods that trigger reflection and self-consciousness, moods that intensify the experience of subjectivity and call one's identity into question. A mood is an attunement, a coloration affecting perception. "Being in a mood" is a way of indicating its hold. For some, such as Heidegger, one is always in a mood, always colored, attuned. One does not choose one's mood in the sense of selecting it, but for Kierkegaard, as for Heidegger, once in a mood one needs to accept it and the new knowledge about the self that it brings.

The four moods of dawning subjectivity that Kierkegaard examines have no external objects and are essentially about the self, as indicated by their intensification of subjectivity. These moods have the effect of making one more conscious of oneself and of the problem of the self, in two senses: (1) the self as shattered and a burden and (2) the self as task to be accomplished.

Moods come and go, but all four that Kierkegaard considers are tied to one fundamental existential condition, namely a shattered self in need of reconstitution. These moods can, however, lie dormant, and a dialectic of moods, as Kierkegaard portrays them, occurs only in a subject awakening from the slumbering condition of alienation to a growing consciousness of its truth and the crisis of choice that it reveals. Each of the moods examined has a direction and a kind of revelation. But its message is implicitly present in the personality. The moods lead to awakening in which the consciousness and task of subjectivity emerge.

The solution to a mood, or the way out of the emotional crisis that Kierkegaard targets, is to choose oneself in light of the directionality that a mood reveals to the discerning subject. While moods come and go, the underlying problem does not. Each eventually builds to a crisis stage demanding resolution. However, resolution does not happen by itself. It is not automatic and there is no assurance that one will arrive where the moods ever more clearly direct one. This is true in two senses: first, in that each step requires an act of the will that one is not compelled to make (even if one is emotionally punished for not making it); second, in that the final re-fusion of the self results from a feeling of outside input, which he terms a "grace."

As a free being experiencing the possibilities but also the task of freedom, one is equally free to actualize oneself or to destroy oneself in inaction and resistance; and Kierkegaard's writings portray characters that rather clearly will *not* go the whole way, most notably the central character of *Either/Or*.[8]

Hegelian Terminology

Such terms as "concept," "dialectic," "crisis," "contradiction," and "necessity" are shared Hegelian vocabulary and part of the metaphysical tradition. Hegelian terminology is clearly visible in Kierkegaard's works, and the dialectic of moods in Kierkegaard has a Hegelian structure: each mood has an initial state; a crisis phase in which inner opposition is brought into open contradiction and then intensified to the point of requiring resolution; and finally a resolution akin to a Hegelian *Aufhebung*—cancellation and preservation, and nowadays frequently translated with the coinage "sublation."[9] Kierkegaard's psychology of moods is a detailed examination of the second (i.e., crisis) phase. The principal difference between Hegel and Kierkegaard is contained in the Kierkegaardian category of the "individual." For him, the existing individual seemed to have been forgotten or dissolved in the Hegelian system of philosophy, where attention focused on the progress of an abstract humanity seemed to take over. In contrast, Kierkegaard emphasized individuals and their individual freedom.

His writings therefore begin with a highly individualized subject who, while surely an intellectual and philosophically inclined, increasingly agonizes over the meaning of his subjectivity. And although Aesthete A of *Either/Or* is a creation of Kierkegaard's mind (if partly based on his own romantic youth), there is still no question of privileged access to him. Anyone can see his problem and one's own very similar problem in him.

While in the later works the analysis is of the problems of every individual self—rather than the highly individualistic and fantasizing self of *Either/Or*—the emphasis remains upon the *individual*, who must *individually* realize the universally open destiny of authentic subjectivity. In contrast, Aesthete A of *Either/Or* possesses only a false and deceptive individuality, which unmasks itself over time. And the authentic individuality promised is no less individual or genuine for being available to every subject. Human destiny here is never thought of as a collective experience or a collective destiny but as individual and distinctive.

Diagnosing a Moody Aesthete

Aesthete A of *Either/Or* is a formidable and fascinating character, an individualist and would-be individual who, because his existence is rooted largely in imagination and personal willfulness, never achieves authentic individuality. Kierkegaard's aesthete is burdened with and tormented by his self-consciousness and awareness of his perverse stance. He can neither let himself go nor quite contain himself. No sooner does a possibility occur to him than his fantasy spins out every conceivable variation, which he then compares and judges. In the process, he wears himself out without ever taking action on anything. He both loves doing this and hates it; but more significant still, he cannot stop it. (See the fuller discussion of the psychology of Aesthete A in chapter 4.)

He is above all an *intellectual* aesthete: his are the pleasures of thought, of fantasy, of the detailed plan of action. His alter ego, Johannes the seducer, author of "The Seducer's Diary" in *Either/Or*, has his greatest pleasure in the *idea* of seduction rather than in the real thing. His pleasure is in executing his idea, and, odd though it may seem, for him the idea is clearly more important than the physical deed. Moreover, it is precisely his intellectuality as seducer that makes him so diabolical. Unlike the famous Don Juan and his 1,003 conquests, Johannes boasts of only one conquest and feels he compares very well.[10]

Kierkegaard's inclusion of the intellectual into the aesthetic stage is an important point in his writing. His major point against Enlightenment philosophy, Romanticism, and idealism is that an exclusively intellectual life is existentially bankrupt. The roller-coaster moods of the aesthete are witness to the frenzied bankruptcy of a life lived exclusively for personal pleasure (the aesthetic) and nothing more.

But Kierkegaard does not merely depict an intellectual Romantic who is a prisoner of moods, who is ironic and melancholy, anxious and despairing, in our usual senses of these words and also in the special sense he will emphasize. He scrutinizes the emotional life of his intellectual aesthete as others in his time did not and thereby takes emotional life with the utmost seriousness.

The sole solution Kierkegaard holds out for every aesthete—namely, experiencing a transcendent dimension in oneself—emerges gradually from the aesthetic writings but is declared openly along the way in parallel religious discourses that Kierkegaard published under his own name. The solution for this crisis of reflection is not grandiose absolute knowledge in the manner of Hegel but, more modestly, accurate knowledge of the self unencumbered by theories of human individuality that are intellectual fancies ungrounded in individual experience.

Irony as the Mood of Rebellion against Finitude

Irony is an early crisis mood in an existence lived on the level of pleasure (sensual and intellectual) and centered exclusively in oneself.[11] As the pseudonymous Johannes Climacus remarks,

> Irony is an existence qualification, and thus nothing is more ludicrous than regarding it as a style of speaking or an author's counting himself lucky to express himself ironically once in a while. The person who has essential irony has it all day long and is not bound to any style, because it is the infinite within him. (*SKS* 7:457; *CUP* 503–4)

That is, it is something higher within the person calling out to be freed. Irony represents a heightened consciousness about the world (finitude) and about oneself in the world. It begins in the reflection in which one realizes that one feels unsatisfied, uncompleted by the world, and begins to reject and resent the world for failure to satisfy. Kierkegaard thus speaks of irony as raising one out of a nonreflective existence but leaving one in midair (*SKS* 1:109n; *CI* 48n).

One ironizes, according to Kierkegaard, because the world has lost its validity (*SKS* 1:297; *CI* 259). The implicit promise of the world to satisfy a person's full needs is experienced as broken and increasingly recognized as unfulfillable. Disappointment in the world breeds resentment, and the ironist turns increasingly bitter against the world and his fellows, and sometimes against himself.

Kierkegaard did of course recognize the more usual understanding of irony as a tool of discourse, which he views rather as a surface phenomenon. Thus the rebel against finitude sometimes employs rhetorical irony: saying the opposite of what he means but at a deeper level reflecting the difference between reality and appearance; sometimes he indulges in the private irony of showing up others in their own illusions as he watches from some pseudosuperior viewpoint. In the first instance he plays on the fact that everything is not as it appears or sounds; in the second he engages in exploding the cherished illusions of others.

Kierkegaard draws a line between the ironist and the satirist. His view is that the satirist is a reformer at heart, seeking to correct the foibles of mankind (whether in the gentler Horatian mode or in the harsher Juvenalian). But his point in the contrast is that the ironist at this stage in his development has no ethical concerns: he does not take others into account for their own sake but merely for his own purposes. In short, he has no serious concern for others. His goal in engaging in ironic discourse is a kind of one-upmanship, the self-satisfaction of an ailing and solitary self taking some brief pleasure in exposing others to their own illusions, a kind of *Schadenfreude.*

When Kierkegaard's dissertation turns to the deeper manifestations of irony in an ironist's existence, he breaks new ground. He recognizes the rebellion of irony as representing the first moments of genuine subjectivity, of the break with the masses and the emergence of an individual, even if at this point individuality is still negatively defined. Kierkegaard terms irony an incitement to subjectivity, and the ironist himself he calls an unfulfilled prophecy about a complete personality (*SKS* 1:199; *CI* 149). When he says that no genuinely authentic human life, no life worthy of being called human, is possible without irony,[12] he is to some extent reformulating the famous line of Socrates in *The Apology*, "The unexamined life is not worth living." He means that breaking with everyday illusions is a prerequisite for achieving a more authentic mode of being human.

Irony is negativity itself—"infinite absolute negativity," as he terms it. Irony as negativity means quite simply that it *only* negates. Here we return to the indeterminate. For irony does not provide content to the existence that it has severed from the world. The ironist merely feels cut off from and superior to the masses in their enduring ignorance. He no longer looks to the world for the sustenance of his inner life, yet he still requires sustenance and feels its absence. He becomes alienated from others. Even a relationship to other ironic subjects proves illusory since irony cannot provide the positive bond that establishes a relationship. The danger is that the ironist succumbs to the illusion that he can identify something positive.

Irony breaks other illusions but must catch itself before it plunges into an empty infinity of fantasy. For having realized the unworthiness of former objects of desire, it may seek to satisfy itself through the creation—and destruction—of imaginative objects of desire.

Without genuine content, without continuity, and without perspective, the ironist by degrees moves into crisis in his rebellion against the world: he has rejected the world but has nothing in its place. Kierkegaard speaks of living in a hypothetical and subjunctive way, under the sway of moods and feelings (*SKS* 1:319; *CI* 284). And the only unity in discontinuity is the superficial profundity and hungry satiety of boredom, that other central experience of the indeterminate.[13] Boredom is finally only an index of the uninteresting: it lets me know what does *not* interest me, but it tells me nothing about what will or should interest me, and so it seems to set me before an infinite task of eliminating the uninteresting in the hope of stumbling upon something truly interesting and in my interest.

One may thus schematize the life of an ironist as follows: an initial moment of seeing through a finitude that cannot satisfy the infinite longing of the human spirit; a moment of opposition between the self and the world that leads to rejection of the world but needs to master itself before it can reconcile with a world that it still needs. This would constitute a "mastered irony": an irony in which one is freed from finitude. One does not, however, come to a controlled or mastered irony before passing through other crisis moods and their ever more explicit revelation of the depths of the self.

Anxiety as the Mood of Possibility

Kierkegaard writes of anxiety in a restricted sense. He would regard anxiety about a decision or an exam or a doctor's report or even the stock market as surface manifestations of a more fundamental personal anxiety about oneself. An individual's anxiety in its grounding is always about himself, even if, on the surface, it is about another or something else.

In Kierkegaard's view, a special anxiety crisis begins to dissolve a life centered on intellectual and sensual pleasure and leads to rising above mere aesthetic categories. A human being as a living, changing organism, always has possibility according to Kierkegaard. And the freeing but challenging experience of one's own possibilities is precisely what the mood of anxiety is about. But since possibility is by definition something that has not been actualized, Kierkegaard and subsequent existentialist writers term it the "nothing" of anxiety. The continually erupting experience of possibility ultimately points to one *essential* possibility of crossing over to the plane of the ethico-religious. The resolution of anxiety in choosing to actualize one's possibilities as a centered and ethical being is also the resolution of the negativity of irony. The seriousness of the mood is reflected in the alarm and fascination that attend it.

In his exploration, Kierkegaard uses conventional theological language, but his point is not conventional at all—he demythologizes theological language and recognizes beneath it the narrative and description of the human condition never satisfied with stasis and always seeking to actualize itself on a greater scale. Experimentation is possible, failure is sometimes the outcome, and each must find his or her own way.

Kierkegaard centers on the existential meaning of the Fall story as a symbolic depiction of the state in which every human finds him- or herself at the moment when she or he is also confronting personal possibility: fallen, responsible, and guilty yet aware of the personal need and freedom to overcome this condition in a resolute act of the will. Choice of the self gives positive content to the "nothing" of anxiety. But further possibility remains and thus anxiety with it. Anxiety is most decisively—but still not completely—overcome in the mood of despair, with which Kierkegaard links anxiety in several places.[14] So long as a subject lives, he has possibilities, and hence anxiety is never annihilated.[15]

Among the intellectual debates that raged in the early centuries of Christianity, one of the most central had to do with finding the right expression for recognizing an individual's ability to affect his own psychic growth while feeling that a greater and transcending Reality (namely God) was also involved. It is heard in the faith versus works debate of the Reformation. Kierkegaard can be understood as emphasizing both, but the divine input retains the status of a sine qua non, that is, an indispensable element, even if it also seems to be able to be counted on to materialize at the right moment. (Something similar seems to be expressed in the Hindu teaching about the monkey-hold or cat-hold theory of salvation, and in the Zen teaching of sudden versus gradual enlightenment.) Kierkegaard-Haufniensis's teaching in *The Concept of Anxiety* culminates in chapter 5, "Anxiety as a Saving through Faith." The emphasis is upon both saving experience and faith experience. For only the term faith, in Luther's sense of a personal involvement with the Transcendent, properly identifies that which will restore the fallen self—that is, restored relationship to God as the ground of one's being.

The Mood of Melancholy as Longing for the Infinite

It is no small task to explain to contemporary readers what Kierkegaard could have meant by describing two types of melancholy when the contemporary person might hardly be expected to understand any longer what would be meant by even one of them.[16] For we stand at a considerable distance from the Romantic period, when most everyone would have understood what it meant to speak of a young man's melancholy. Of course it meant that he had not found the right young lady yet, that he was actively seeking and tenderly suffering in the meantime, and that we felt for him as someone who deserved success. As observers we would also have taken pleasure in the awakened memories and sympathetic tender feelings in ourselves. In short, we would have been somewhat in love with our own feelings and admired the sweet suffering of young lovers who had not yet fully culminated their search. All that is changed now. We live in a very different time, and, while a bit of this phenomenon may survive, it is far less visible in a culture where early sexual activity has frequently displaced traditional courtship and romance. Certainly there are still unhappy lovers, but they usually do not call themselves melancholic.

The task at hand is to understand what Kierkegaard meant by his use of not just one but two terms for melancholy, corresponding to two stages of the dark emotion. The term was already in decline in the late nineteenth century but went into total eclipse after Freud.[17] And one of the problems is that it has meant many things across the centuries. "Melancholy" (literally "black bile") has Greek roots and dates from a theory of a balance of four humors (yellow bile, black bile, phlegm, and blood) that had crystallized by about 400 B.C.E. in Greek medicine but seems to have even older roots in Egyptian thought. It gained its greatest popularity as a theory under Galen in the second century and dominated medieval medical thinking. Under Avicenna, the theory was extended to encompass mental and moral life. In fact it was only definitively undercut as a theory in the mid-nineteenth century with the theory of cellular pathology.

Kierkegaard's use of the language of melancholy is purely metaphorical and not allied with the vanishing medical theory of humors for the psychological explanation of mental dispositions and inclination. There is—metaphorically—both "black bile" (*Melancholi*) and "blacker bile" (not the literal meaning of his term *Tungsind*, which is "heaviness of spirit").[18] This latter form is portrayed as a more intense and critical state of mental-emotional life, presaging a personal crisis about "nothing." It is the melancholy of a subject become reflective in the wake of the failure of all finite objects to satisfy an unquenchable longing.

In Kierkegaard's description, *Melancholi*, the first moment of this condition, and its English cognate, "melancholy," is the longing of poets and young men, the sweet and seductive pain of not possessing a beloved or object of desire. *Tungsind* (German *Schwermut*)—which might better be translated with the antiquated term "melancholia"—is portrayed as an advanced case of the same psychic-emotional-spiritual malady. Ultimately, Kierkegaard sees it as pointing to a spiritual problem: the longing for the highest object of desire, the Transcendent itself (although Kierkegaard uses traditional Christian God language). In this second and reflective stage of melancholy, the impossibility of finding an all-satisfying object of desire among the realities of this world becomes increasingly clear. This occurs for his several melancholic aesthetes in a process of elimination of finite objects until they are left with "nothing," which ultimately points to the Infinite (=God) as the real possibility. But before then, *Tungsind*, which literally means "heavy spirit," comes to stand for gloom, reserve, and empty isolation.[19]

Kierkegaard depicts *Tungsind* as the natural development of *Melancholi* and would thereby imply that the lighter form thought to be curable by romantic love is not the genuine article. Kierkegaard analyzes melancholy in three works. *Either/Or*, part 1, is the presentation of an engaging melancholic. Aesthete A is well on his way to becoming reflective about his melancholy and knows that his attempt to live in aesthetic categories—sensual and intellectual—cannot succeed. But he refuses to affirm himself in a relationship to something higher than himself. The chaos and eruptions in the aesthete's inner life are interpreted by Judge William, in part 2, as spirit's revenge: "But the spirit does not allow itself to be mocked; it avenges itself on you and binds you in the chains of [*Tungsind*]" (*SKS* 3:197; *E/O* 2:204). However, the judge also tries to console the suffering aesthete with the positivity of melancholy: it indicates the movement of the human spirit toward something.

Kierkegaard's Judge William engages in a brief but insightful two-page analysis of *Tungsind*, which includes an analysis of the "nothing" of *Tungsind*. He writes,

> There is something unexplainable in [*Tungsind*]. A person with a sorrow or a worry knows why he sorrows or worries. If a [melancholiac] person is asked what the reason is, what it is that weights [*tynge*] on him, he will answer: I do not know; I cannot explain it.[20] (*SKS* 3:183; *E/O* 2:189)

Repetition, by the pseudonymous amateur psychologist Constantin Constantius, is a self-proclaimed psychological examination of a young man whose melancholy has not been cured by romantic love.

The young man of *Repetition* was melancholy, fell in love, and comes to his amateur psychologist friend Constantin more melancholy than ever. He is puzzled and troubled, for the so-called cure, falling in love, has not worked. He is in fact more melancholy than before. He also begins to feel that he cannot carry through to marriage under these conditions. Gloom and despair begin to weigh him down, and he is on his way to the heaviness of spirit that is the "blacker bile" of *Tungsind.*

"Never in my practice had I seen such melancholy [*Melancholi*] as this," remarks the surprised psychologist (*SKS*, 4:13; *R*, 136). And once he concludes that the religious is the base of the problem, he acknowledges reaching the limits of his competence. Constantin and the young man simultaneously discover the potential religious element in melancholy—the latter through reflection on his own experience, the former through observation of the young man and the young man's self-analytical letters.

Stages on Life's Way contains another version of a broken engagement and a presentation of a melancholy already at the stage of *Tungsind* in "Quidam's Diary" ("'Guilty?'/'Not Guilty?'"), where in alternating morning and evening entries the gloomily melancholy young man recounts by day the breakup of his engagement one year ago and, by night, agonizes over a lingering guilt.[21]

The diarist in question is in a gloomy state of melancholy from the very first page. By degrees he begins to think that his root problem is religious in nature, and one of the reasons for the rupture with the young fiancée is that he thinks that she has little or no understanding of the religious. His last hope of reconciliation is to stir the religious in her, if possible, but it proves not to be so.

Frater Taciturnus, the observer and editor of the larger work, sums it up: "Thus the [melancholia] of my character is the crisis prior to the religious" (*SKS*, 6:398; *SLW*, 430). If he recognizes coming to terms with the religious dimension of his life as his main problem and task, he is still a long way off, as he observes, "I am really no religious individuality; I am just a regular and perfectly constructed possibility of such a person" (*SKS*, 6:240; *SLW*, 257). The religious crisis in melancholy can be stated using some of the terminology employed to describe anxiety, with which it is intimately connected. The nothing of melancholia is ultimately connected to the nothing in anxiety that Schelling called the dark ground of God—the nothing from which God was held to have created the world and from which a person now feels challenged to create him- or herself.

This *Melancholi* is the innocent throb of longing within a sensitive nature, and it indicates both sensitivity and religious potentiality. (It remains even in the individual who exists in religious categories, for, so long as he lives, he has always greater religious potential.) *Melancholi*, to Kierkegaard's way of thinking, indicates a personality with a developing, spiritual dimension. But in its initial phases, it indicates a gestating condition. In the language so frequent in the works, spirit sleeps. However, it will awake, as the reader witnesses in *Repetition*. The beginning of the evolutionary movement is referred to as the stirring of spirit, or the stirring of the Idea.

The stirring within the personality reveals, to Kierkegaard's mind, that an encounter with the Absolute is sought, i.e., with the grounding power of our self. The painful longing expressed in the metaphysical language of Absolute, Ideal, and Eternal might thus be spoken of as a "metaphysical wound." It is a wound which festers so long as it is not healed and, as we have occasion to be reminded by Kierkegaard, a wound that is never entirely healed (thus the enduring bit of melancholy even in the religious person).

Despair as the Mood of a Conscious, Shattered Self

Kierkegaard's treatises on anxiety and despair are companion pieces. For in many senses *The Sickness unto Death* (1849) (by the pseudonymous Anti-Climacus) is in part a continuation of the 1844 treatise by Vigilius Haufniensis, *The Concept of Anxiety*. While their styles are technically different, their principal concern is sin, or human failure and brokenness, and related psychological states. *The Sickness unto Death* proceeds with the same seriousness as the work on anxiety and turns that seriousness, in part 2, to a consideration of despair as a continuation in the failed state. Like *The Concept of Anxiety*, it is profoundly and self-consciously existential and is intended to be seen as having nothing to do with scholarly works that have no practical application.

Kierkegaard describes despair in two ways. The first is despair as a structural imbalance in the personality[22] (e.g., the despair of possibility is the failure to recognize one's limits; the despair of necessity is the failure to recognize one's freedom and possibilities, etc.). The second way is as a profound experience of a split in one's being and simultaneously the crying out for healing. It is a personal earthquake with a high Richter-scale reading.

Overcoming the mood of despair involves rising to a more acute consciousness of one's personal dilemma in becoming an authentic self: not only the awareness of a higher personal possibility and one's responsibility for the present condition but also the recognition of one's limited ability to finish the job and agonizing confession of inability to finish it without outside help. (This description sounds vaguely similar to contemporary twelve-step programs, with which it has some points in common.) It is here that the "hopelessness" suggested by the term "despair" can be seen. But the paradox is that the subjectively experienced mood of hopelessness is not hopeless. It is a mood of helplessness, out of which one can be helped. The "nothing" of despair is the recognition of the nonselfhood in which one is suffering, consciousness of the nonattainment of a psychic imperative.

Despair is thus in a true sense also a mood of possibility, as is anxiety. But it is a mood of intensified anxiety that turns on one specific possibility, namely, taking on the consciousness of the need for a grace to become an enhanced whole.

The issue in despair as a state of being is either to remain in an increasingly agonizing situation of self-alienation or to respond to the promptings already detectable and detected in irony, melancholy, and anxiety.

Of course, no one is forced to become his or her true self (i.e., a self formed on the basis of a true understanding of the dynamism that a human being is), and Kierkegaard in his novelistic writings has portrayed and analyzed aesthetic characters who clearly will not do so, either out of weakness or from defiance. The despair of defiance even leads to a kind of nihilism that seeks to prove the wretchedness of all existence:

> Rebelling against all existence, [the despair of defiance] feels that it has obtained evidence against [existence], against its goodness. The person in despair believes that he himself is the evidence, and that is what he wants to be, and therefore he wants to be himself, himself in his torment, in order to protest against all existence with this torment. (*SKS*, 11:187; *SUD*, 73–74)

And this despairer is adamant that no one take his despair away from him, for he needs his own despair and unhappiness to prove to himself that he is right. To repeat: the final agonizing, but paradoxically hopeful, moments in despair are the recognition of one's ultimate helplessness to get oneself out of the existential hole that one has dug oneself into. The pseudonymous Anti-Climacus speaks of it as sin consciousness and describes the marvel of human self-becoming in the corresponding theological category of grace. But the experience of helplessness is not a passive mood of weakness but rather a crisis moment attained only after an arduous effort of self-recovery, so that, if this is grace, it is not "cheap grace"—a giveaway that one has in no way striven to merit. Kierkegaard wants to maintain the theological sense here of an experience of recovery that is felt to be beyond one's deserts.

If what Kierkegaard describes is to any extent accurate, one would need to be a very sensitive and well-trained pastoral psychologist nowadays to distinguish between someone suffering the last phases of cure and someone in need of medication. Kierkegaard is not writing about those troubled selves who might be helped by Prozac and other modern equivalents. The psychologist Anti-Climacus focuses on the total cure for an underlying problem, for those who are in a condition able to face up to it. Thus he is not interested in the temporary alleviation of symptoms, and he would be harsh in his judgment of anyone offering further distractions to one on the verge of spiritual recovery. For he thinks that so long as total cure is not attained, sickness of the spirit will break forth again.

Kierkegaard never describes or portrays the reconstituted, refocused, and cocreating human subject after the breakthrough moment. With the revelation-proclamation of the need of help from a transcendent source, Kierkegaard's exploration abruptly ends. It advances toward a definition of the modern self, with admittedly metaphysical underpinnings and an undisguised religious presupposition.

4

The Psychology of *Either/Or*

Either/Or has long been recognized for its rich psychological character portraits, its psychological insight, and its philosophical-psychological ideas. And even before its formal publication, Judge William, in part 2, weighed in with a psychological commentary on and evaluation of part 1. Some of the principal psychological characteristics of Aesthete A in *Either/Or*, part 1, are later broadened to become the subjects of thinly pseudonymous treatises, most notably in *The Concept of Anxiety* and *The Sickness unto Death*, works that schematize the full breadth of the condition and thus naturally go beyond just Aesthete A. In time, both works would have a profound influence on twentieth-century existential philosophy and on the existential psychologies that grew up from Freudian roots and Kierkegaardian (as well as other) graftings. Although melancholy figures importantly in *Either/Or*, not to mention Kierkegaard's own life, there is no formal treatise on melancholia in his works, except insofar as *The Sickness unto Death* names and analyzes the underlying root problem, just as it complements the analysis of critical possibilities for selfhood and nonselfhood first presented in *The Concept of Anxiety*. The substance of melancholia is already there in *Either/Or*, just as a range of conditions of anxiety and despair is equally present. (Anxiety and despair have survived into the twenty-first century as psychological categories, whereas melancholia is now sometimes regarded as a suspicious cultural construct.[1])

Joakim Garff, in his 2005 Kierkegaard biography, essentially reads the anxiety of *Either/Or* going forward toward *The Concept of Anxiety*, as did Kresten Nordentoft before him.[2] Theirs is both a sensible and insightful line of interpretation with which I have no real disagreement. Yet in one sense, I propose to do exactly the opposite of what Nordentoft and Garff have done, namely, to read the works, in their association, in *reverse order* and also to ask what, in retrospect, the later schematization of anxiety in *The Concept of Anxiety* (1844) tells us about the nature of anxiety as presented in *Either/Or* in 1843, and then to move on to a similar inquiry with regard to the forms of despair schematized in *The Sickness unto Death* (1847).

Either/Or

In *Either/Or*, part 1, we have the rich psychological and fragmented literary self-portrait of Aesthete A and the portrayal of a fictitious, subjunctive Johannes of "The Seducer's Diary," whose novella in diary form will, following the pseudonymous editor Victor Eremita, be attributed to Aesthete A. Not to be overlooked is the psychology of the equally subjunctive Cordelia, as represented and intimated by Johannes.[3] The character behind the "Diapsalmata" is the victim of wild, often violent, mood swings. The cause, we are to infer, is not his failure to take his medication! (which in any case would not have been available in 1843) but rather his lifestyle, and his life view. But both of these proceed from who he is.

How might we imagine him as our contemporary in the early twenty-first century rather than as Kierkegaard's in the nineteenth? Perhaps as follows:

> A voracious reader with a fast-paced intellect and a fast-paced pen. A twenty-one-year-old Harvard junior perhaps or recent graduate.[4] A young man of comfortable family background, precocious yet in many respects immature, wildly self-confident to the point of arrogance about his intellectual ability (but also essentially correct in his self-regard), and certainly pretentious in taking on major cultural figures as, at most, his intellectual peers. Someone who has kept up with the fast crowd—at least the small circle of the intellectually serious fast crowd—and maybe outdone them in some respects. Someone who knows the taverns where the elite let off steam after a hard day of reading and ruminating, and maybe who knows some of the other places where drunken young men used to go before there were co-ed universities and more convenient, dormitory liaisons. Someone always ready to debate at a tavern or in the debating club, whether he really knows what he is talking about or not. And someone quickly able to wax intense and convince himself, by virtue of his own intensity, that every spirited comment and critique that passes his lips is actually true. Sometimes he waxes passionate, but here, at least privately, he may draw back a little from some of the thoughts and utterances that are a little "over the top."
>
> Yet all this passion and sparkle have not come cheaply. The price of the imbalance is emotional immaturity, and that is why he sounds still sophomoric at times—a bit juvenile in his Juvenalian barbs. Yet emotional immaturity by no means implies the absence of emotions. While he endures emotional explosions (he calls them earthquakes) that, to his credit, he does not seek to repress, neither does he seek to surmount them. He wallows in his sorrows and knows that they give him,

> at minimum, something new to write about. And the memories of his sufferings supply him with a wellspring of resentment and world hatred that can be drawn up almost at will.
>
> In short, a great character actor before character acting. A poet, a performer, an exhibitionist. A potential suicide.

Nowadays there are not many who fill this bill. It takes some daring, after all, to let oneself develop in this direction to begin with. To our own current way of thinking, there has got to have been some emotional wound that has set someone apart from the crowd like this and individuated him or her—even if eccentrically—at the very time in life when most are only beginning to emerge from the firm grip of conformist pressures.

In addition, the individual who emerges in the pages of part 1 has not come to his sense of himself only recently. It has already been a while, and he already has a solid sense of himself as standing alone, and standing tall, if somewhat shakily when moods and emotions overwhelm him. In his thinking and in his feelings, he has been a rebel for a long time already, even if his sentiments could not be given utterance until relatively recently.

> And if it is at a college like Harvard that we might find his twenty-first-century equivalent, he knows that he still has a lot of intense competition for attention, despite his personal brilliance. It is no longer to himself and to his small circle of convinced admirers that he must prove himself but to a group of similarly talented others who are equally interested in obtaining recognition for themselves, not in granting it to others. And so he is wont to put others down, and they him, in a dialectic in which no one is affirmed. And, if in his moments of self-hatred, he also puts himself down, this requires demoting others even further in his estimation, so that the proper rank ordering can be maintained. He appears to be well on his way to being a young misanthrope, yet a social misanthrope all the same, for while he rejects the crowd, his feet are firmly planted on the soapbox at its center.
>
> It is more than incipient misanthropy that is in evidence here; it is already wide reaching. He lashes out not just at himself and others but also at "the world"—at everything around him that pretends to be important but that he knows, deep down, is not. And he dwells on this negative knowledge, not (yet or not ever) daring to explore the "deep down"—the depths in himself that are the source from which flows his negative insights and his growing disdain for the vanity of vanities surrounding him.

Judge William's Commentary on the Psychology of Aesthete A

The psychological component of *Either/Or*, part 1, was immediately recognized by its first readers, but the first (and highly astute) commentator on the psychology of Aesthete A was none other than Judge William himself in part 2 of *Either/Or*, who is portrayed as knowing Aesthete A personally but who indicates no knowledge of A's papers.[5] "You who always pride yourself on being an *observateur*," he writes, "must, in return, put up with becoming an object of observation" (*SKS*, 3:17; *E/O*, 2:7). And, after having already done so for some eighty pages, he now proposes, "Allow me to point out the dark side of your life" (*SKS*, 3:88; *E/O*, 2:84).

The first twenty pages of "The Aesthetic Validity of Marriage" are a highly critical personal attack on the existence stance of Aesthete A and a biting critique of his psychology. It is in fact so passionate and zealous as to make us wonder whether Ethicist B is not just formally frustrated with his younger friend but also possibly reliving his own rejection of very similar positions and problems before his own ethical turn (which may very well be what the more sober thirty-year-old Kierkegaard was also doing in these pages vis-à-vis his own wayward student period).

In advance of the reading public of *Either/Or*, part 1, Judge William recognizes the psychological power of Aesthete A. Ethicist B takes a dim view of Aesthete A's self-psychologizing. He chastises him for a psychological interest that lacks seriousness and that he dismisses as mere "hypochondriacal inquisitiveness": in effect—and more in the language of William James than of Judge William—a "sick soul" running wild with reflection that is nonetheless not genuine "introspection" because it fails to *see*. Going beyond but in the spirit of B, it might be added that Aesthete A's *experimenting* psychology—experimenting upon himself and others (including the subjunctive Johannes of "The Seducer's Diary")—is also not to be confused with "*experimental* psychology" of the twentieth century, since the former lacks serious interest, focus, and control, to say nothing of open-eyed analysis of the data produced. That, in fact, is ultimately left for *The Concept of Anxiety* and *The Sickness unto Death*, although Ethicist B ventures a number of observations about anxiety and despair that anticipate, by one and six years, respectively, the schematization of anxiety and despair in those subsequent works. And if Constantin Constantius subsequently raises the level in his own "venture in experimenting psychology" later that year, he too is still far from the seriousness that Vigilius Haufniensis, in *The Concept of Anxiety*, judges the only appropriate mood for considering the underlying problem.[6]

The Augustinian and "retro" soul psychology of Ethicist B comes through in many places but is nicely summed up in the comment "Instead of saving your soul by entrusting everything to God, instead of taking this shortcut, you prefer the endless roundabout way, which perhaps will never take you to your destination" (*SKS*, 3:23; *E/O*, 2:14). The only thing that results from the moods of Aesthete A, according to B, is mere better acquaintance with moods. There is no progress, no action or deed, no *Bildung*. Just idle knowledge. This position will be echoed and sharpened by Vigilius Haufniensis, who will stress that the point of thinking about sin is not to wallow in it or one's understanding of it but to get out of it. And if Aesthete A mistakenly thinks that mood is the province of aesthetes alone, Ethicist B (Judge William) instructs him in his second letter, "The person who lives ethically is also familiar with mood, but for him it is not the highest; because he has chosen himself infinitely, he sees his mood beneath him" (*SKS*, 3:220; *E/O*, 2:230).

In putting the young aesthete, whom he calls "a total incarnation of mood" (*SKS*, 3:21; *E/O*, 2:11), under his critical gaze, William even begins a schematization of melancholia (*Tungsind*) when he distinguishes between "egotistic" melancholia and "sympathetic" melancholia, the former associated with the attempt to avoid real involvements with others, the latter having the somewhat redeeming characteristic of being oriented toward others, at least in fearing itself for the sake of others (*SKS*, 3:33; *E/O*, 2:25). But both forms are evidence of "self-indulgen[ce] in enjoyment." William calls *Tungsind*, with his emphasis on *tung* (heaviness), the defect of the age, present even in the *letsindig* (light-minded) laughter of the times.[7] "Is it not [Melancholia, *Tungsind*] that has robbed us of the courage to command, the courage to obey, the power to act, the confidence to hope?" (*SKS*, 3:32; *E/O*, 2:23–24). William views the manic and melancholiac aspects of Aesthete A's personality and intellect on the one hand as a cold, sharp, and biting March wind (the manic) and, on the other hand, as the shrunken—and literally introverted—pouch form assumed by a jellyfish (the melancholiac) (*SKS*, 3:46; *E/O*, 2:38).

In his second letter ("The Balance between Aesthetic and Ethical"), he calls melancholia "hysteria of the spirit" and the refusal of spirit to evolve and act:

> There comes a moment in a person's life when immediacy is ripe, so to speak, and when the spirit requires a higher form, when it wants to lay hold of itself as spirit. . . . Now spirit wants to gather itself together out of this dispersion, so to speak, and to transfigure itself in itself; the personality wants to become conscious in its eternal validity. If this does not happen, if the movement is halted, if it is repressed, then [melancholia, *Tungsind*] sets in. (*SKS*, 3:183; *E/O*, 2:188–89)

He goes on to call it the mother of all sins, the refusal to will deeply and inwardly, and then to link it to original (hereditary) sin. It will be up to Vigilius Haufniensis to lay out the fuller, theological schematization of the states of sinfulness and the types of anxiety associated with them. William calls melancholia spirit's revenge for mocking spirit by ignoring it in inaction (*SKS*, 3:197; *E/O*, 2:205). In declaring Aesthete A's life to be despair, he also anticipates the fuller analysis of despair's multiple forms in *The Sickness unto Death.*

So it is William who first identifies the problematic psychology of Aesthete A and it is William who puts his finger on the issue of moods—far in advance of the Heidegger who perceptively saw and powerfully seized upon this aspect of Kierkegaard's work.[8]

We cannot treat the publication order of the papers in *Either/Or*, part 1, as a chart of moods, since Victor Eremita warns us in his literary fiction that the papers fell out of the desk and ended up in the random order in which he presents them to the reading public. Still, the order makes an impression, and the passionate "Diapsalmata" would have been any editor's dramatic choice to open the work. Here we meet an Aesthete A who hates the world, who hates living, and who hates himself. Moreover, his world hatred is clearly an extension of self-hatred. If he really had been Johannes of an actual "Seducer's Diary," we could understand his self-hatred after the fact, much as we can understand the quasi-suicidal choice of Don Giovanni to accept the Commendatore's invitation to supper (and to a different kind of hell). He cannot stand the life that he has defiantly chosen; he refuses any other life. He is turned in upon himself; he refuses to turn outward. He is estranged from others, a misanthrope in the making, but he is equally estranged from the shallow existence that he has chosen for himself and remains defiantly closed to exploring deeper depths that he knows are there. If he is as sharply ironic as he is darkly melancholic, his is not the *mastered* irony that Magister Kierkegaard's dissertation alluded to. He merely rages in negativity, refusing anything positive.

He speaks of his nighttime battles with pale, nocturnal shapes that are more frightening than anything in fiction (*SKS*, 2:32; *E/O*, 1:23). He writes of the emptiness and meaninglessness of his life, and in the process provides commentary in advance on his sparkling essays that follow: they are quick-passing, intellectual entertainment but provide no longer-term, deeper satisfactions. His only friend is echo—the echo of his own voice. For all his knowledge of Greek myth, he fails to recognize the self-destructiveness of his narcissism that stares him in the face. But unlike Narcissus, he does not embrace himself even figuratively. Instead, he rejects himself. In a poetic example of Roman *praeteritio*, he asks himself whether he should communicate his sorrow to the world and says that he will not, precisely while he is doing so. He speaks of movement within which presages an earthquake and refers to a chain of *inexplicable* anxieties, although he already indicates an inkling of what they are about, which he summarily resists. The "Diapsalmata" in fact documents his fascination with his own sorrows and suffering, his intention to continue in what he is doing, and his illusion that this is really a longer-term possibility. After all, the images of loss of energy, of shrunkenness (the references to the Hebrew *sheva* and *dagesh lene*: *SKS*, 2:30; *E/O*, 1:22), have their own nihilistic logic and, combined with expressions of boredom, emptiness, meaninglessness, and an inability to respond to desire (*SKS*, 2:50; *E/O*, 1:41), paint a portrait that is the nineteenth-century literary foreshadowing of Edvard Munch's *Scream*.

In "The Immediate Erotic Stages," he proves himself an insightful musical critic but, more important, a very capable analyst and theoretician of sensuous desire. We are to infer, thereby, that he has moved beyond the stages of the Page and Papageno (in Mozart's *Marriage of Figaro*, that he has lived through the emptiness and desperation of Don Giovanni with his compulsive sensuousness leaving him suicidally unfree. He will eventually try to outdo Don Giovanni in "The Seducer's Diary," but this is a fiction (as is, of course, Don Juan and his various literary incarnations across Europe).[9] Full of insight into what it means to seduce rather than merely act upon physical desire, he ultimately gives us only a glimpse into, and one example of, the rich, outer intellectual life that provides distraction from the inner emptiness witnessed in the "Diapsalmata." Others follow, and the moods of the "Diapsalmata" are rejoined in the gloomy peroration that is "The Unhappiest One" and then in the desperately ironic "The Rotation of Crops," although these are not direct personal statements.

"The Seducer's Diary" constitutes approximately one-third of *Either/Or*, part 1. According to the editor, Victor Eremita, it is a subjunctive remembrance on the part of a fictitious Johannes. "How it might have been." "The Seducer's Diary" would formally seem to be about Johannes, but in some ways it is more about Cordelia, for she is the personality that develops, that experiences anxiety (as we shall understand from Vigilius, all do and must) but who actualizes possibility, whereas Johannes undergoes no change. Her opening letters to him contain all the bitterness of an Elvira in *Don Giovanni*, but Elvira is a mature woman, we assume, before her seduction by Don Giovanni, whereas Cordelia was an innocent young girl. "She has imagination, spirit, and passion—in short, all the essentials" (*SKS*, 2:332; *E/O*, 1:343). By degrees, Johannes stimulates the stages of desire in her, so that in the end she cannot be satisfied with an Edvard/Papageno but takes notice of one whom she can desire absolutely, namely the Johannes who has been charting and guiding her development through desire.

Johannes's psychological mastery of the interesting is demonic and fascinating. If only in the nonsubjunctive world things could proceed at such a controlled pace! He woos Cordelia through misunderstanding and repulsion, so that she takes serious notice of him and becomes increasingly interesting as Edvard becomes increasingly boring. His narrative has the perfection that one finds only in fiction: "One would not believe it possible to plot so entirely accurately the history of the development of a psyche" (*SKS*, 2:348; *E/O*, 1:359), and the savvy reader takes him literally. Where does one meet such a systematic seducer, such a psychologist, he asks rhetorically (*SKS*, 2:351; *E/O*, 1:363). Only in literature.

The improbable psychological "seduction" of Cordelia, with the attendant manipulation of Edvard and Cordelia's aunt, is the drama of the work that initially catches the reader's attention, but from Johannes's viewpoint the real story begins after the engagement as he tries to bring her to his preordained goal of breaking the engagement.

"Strictly and abstinently, I keep watch on myself so that everything in her, the divinely rich nature in her may come to full development" (*SKS*, 2:373; *E/O*, 1:385). Not quite: his notion of development stops at the erotic. In his ensuing letters to her, he continues the manipulation that he started in the Baxter family parlor.

Is this really psychology? There are insights along the way about the power of the interesting, but the seduction is neither real nor realistic. And even if it were, we have learned only about the twisted psychology of a most unusual individual, in effect "abnormal psychology." This is not "Unum noris omnes," the oft-cited (and altered) dictum from Terence's play and the stated purpose of Augustine's own introspection: in knowing oneself essentially and deeply, one knows what is most universal and most important about being a human being.[10] This is *not* what the "Diary" is about.

Johannes sees Cordelia developing to the point where she will seek to take him captive by means of the erotic (*SKS*, 2:409; *E/O*, 1:421) In the process of the disengagement, Johannes concedes that she has become his preoccupation (*SKS*, 2:422; *E/O*, 1:435) (his obsession), and to that extent he has lost control.

The Concept of Anxiety

In *The Concept of Anxiety*, Haufniensis-Kierkegaard elevates anxiety to a major philosophical-psychological category and proceeds to view its data through the lens of the (Augustinian) theological doctrine of original sin ("hereditary sin" in Danish and German).[11] If the theological doctrine is false, this would of course make the consequent analysis faulty to possibly useless. But it is not false, even if neither it nor the biblical tale at its origin is literally true.

While eighteenth-century Enlightenment philosophy argued the illogic of the idea, and the divine injustice of inherited sin (based on eighteenth-century notions of individual rather than tribal or species justice), most recognized the profound but nebulous truth that the doctrine attempted to articulate: that there is something amiss about the present human condition that needs positive action to be set right. Whether one thinks of this call to "perfection" as the need for completion (from incompleteness to completeness) or for restoration (from fallenness to perfection), it powerfully identifies the mood of anxiety with our current, incomplete, in-process, intermediate stage, sees anxiety as the tension (unconscious and conscious) between the what-is and the what-can-be, and then examines a variety of stances that one can take in relationship to the current stance or stage.

As such, the doctrine is shown to possess great psychological truth about the human condition, while not an accurate historical account of its origin.

The Concept of Anxiety is as distinctive in its genre as *Either/Or* is in its own. Formally, *The Concept of Anxiety* appears to be a theological treatise, with topics logically divided. It gives extended treatment to a category never so fully treated before. Like so many treatises, it does not necessarily give equal distribution to each part, and so while "Objective Anxiety" and "Subjective Anxiety" are set up as a paired section, so-called objective anxiety seems considered mostly for formal purposes, whereas subjective anxiety is clearly where the author's interest lies. "Subjective Anxiety" explores the kind of anxiety that emerges in individual subjects.[12]

Structurally, the emphasis of the work is on the sections "Subjective Anxiety," "Anxiety about the Good," and the "pneumatic" (spiritual) aspects of the latter. This would be in keeping with its opening statement about seriousness, rather than mere academic observation, and its pastoral and therapeutic interest in overcoming anxiety—not in idealist speculation, Romantic observation, or perhaps contemporary psychoanalytic talking but in acting, in taking on the self-consciousness that brings the promise of overcoming anxiety. But, alas, it is his being stuck in thinking and feeling that is precisely the problem, the predicament and the adamant stance of Aesthete A.

Kierkegaard's citation of *King Lear* by Shakespeare—that nonpsychologist most cited by psychologists—is very apt here. King Lear is a figure that may be said to have driven himself mad by out-of-control reflection, and this is a threat lurking beneath the surface of the "Diapsalmata" as well. The blinded Gloucester, who has earlier been told by Lear that he does not need eyes to see the madness of the world, speaks to the fallen, shrunken figure of Lear in Tieck-Schlegel's German and says, "O thou ruined masterpiece of Nature" (cited by Kierkegaard as "O du zertrümmert Meisterstück der Schöpfung"[13]), and continues, "And so will the great cosmos itself one day wear itself down to nothing" ("So nutzt das große Weltall einst sich ab / Zu nichts" [*King Lear*, IV, 6]).

All the characters of *Either/Or* must of course be considered to populate a world where there is objective anxiety, but in their cases too it is their subjective anxiety that is of most interest. The author of *The Concept of Anxiety* makes reference to *Either/Or* and to the problem of melancholy that emerges there and its relation to anxiety, writing in a footnote that the first part of *Either/Or* "expresses the melancholy in its anguished [*angestfulde*] sympathy and egoism, which is explained in the second part" (*SKS*, 4:348; *CA*, 43).

Kierkegaard-Haufniensis's exposition of anxiety presupposes that human beings are a dualism of matter and spirit. It locates anxiety in the spiritual capacity of human beings, but a spiritual capacity that is as yet "nothing," and it is from this reified nothing that anxiety arises.[14]

Anxiety is held to be possible because human beings are both physical and spiritual. In an oft-quoted passage, Vigilius writes,

> "Anxiety is the dizziness of freedom, which emerges when the spirit wants to posit the synthesis and freedom looks down into its own possibility, laying hold of finiteness to support itself. Freedom succumbs in this dizziness. Further than this, psychology cannot and will not go." (*SKS*, 4:365; *CA*, 61)

Aesthete A lives in a world of objective anxiety, in which anxiety has been increasing by generation, in which sensuousness has become sinfulness because of sin. Aesthete A's anxiety is essentially Anxiety about the Good, and this is confirmed by his own declaration of enclosing reserve, which is one of its principal marks in *The Concept of Anxiety*. He is anxious in the face of the possibility of the Good, of overcoming his current deficient lifestyle and life view. At the same time, his anxiety is also Anxiety about Evil, because his problem, namely, his stance in the sensuousness that is sinfulness (because of sin), has not been negated. And in this aspect of anxiety, there is the possibility that one can sink further. It is no doubt in order to dramatically emphasize the further sinking that Kierkegaard-Haufniensis chooses the tragic figure of King Lear, who in every scene of the play sinks to yet a lower level, until he recovers himself internally after the death of Cordelia.

Vigilius Haufniensis will eventually help us to see, in retrospect, that his objectless fear is his own unactualized possibilities of becoming an authentic self, and so it is as yet still a "nothing." He has the sympathetic antipathy and antipathetic sympathy to which Vigilius will eventually refer, without having Vigilius's terminology. For he is fascinated with himself and his own sufferings, as the "Diapsalmata" amply documents. And he enjoys scrutinizing himself, without going the whole way toward serious introspection. In the "Diapsalmata" he dissects himself more thoroughly than the subjunctive Johannes ever does to Cordelia, or Edvard in the "Diary." He senses that he is out of control, that the movement within himself is not under his power, any more than an earthquake would be. His resistance and insistence on standing still, rather than making any movement, testify to the impotence of his life view. That is clear enough to the outsider, the reader, but not at all clear to Aesthete A himself.

He laments the absence of possibility in his life, but rejects possibility. He hates his present, no less the past, and he dreads a future that is mere repetition of the present. Any real and possible future he rejects out of hand,[15] He is in "anxiety for the good," according to Vigilius's schematization, insofar as he attempts to refuse the movement of possibility from its inception. But since he cannot kill possibility, he is always subject to the inner eruptions, the earthquakes to which he refers.[16] This defiant stance is the demoniacal in him, even if the diarist Johannes will ultimately strike us as more demon-like, and he gives voice to it in a defiant, sharp, sometimes bitter irony—not the softened irony of remembrance and reflection but the hard irony of pained experience.

Apart from insights that will be developed by subsequent so-called existentialist philosophers and psychologists, what does all this tell us about Aesthete A?

It makes clear that Kierkegaard regards the problem of Aesthete A as a conflict between flesh and (emerging) spirit, and that the emergence of spirit must be understood in relationship to the universal existential fact of personal fall into sinfulness (or not being the self that one is impelled, but not compelled, toward becoming).

The emergence of spirit here must in fact be understood in terms of a de facto semi-Pelagian theology of self-recovery, in which the individual has to do certain things for himself, even if it is maintained that only God's grace can ultimately conclude the process.[17] (In Kant's version, the problem is justification before God, being counted righteous in view of the fact that one has sinned and therefore can never be considered fully righteous before God as the Author of the Moral Law.)

The problem of Aesthete A, and the cause of his ongoing sufferings, is that he will not do anything to alter his situation. He rejects possibility even as he laments the absence of possibility in his life. For what he rejects is what is truly possible for him, whereas the possibilities he laments are the speculative, fanciful things that proceed from his lively imagination rather than from his actual being. This can be understood as something like my lamenting the now impossible possibility of my being a Dane—something that is genetically and culturally a nonpossibility to me—rather than fulfilling the genetic and cultural possibilities that I do have by virtue of the nationality and homeland that are actually mine.[18]

When all is said and done, what, if anything, have we learned about Aesthete A from *The Concept of Anxiety* that we might not already have known from *Either/Or*? From a Kierkegaardian perspective, we learn that the essence of his problem is *spiritual*, that the dead-end nature of his battle with sensuousness is only an appearance: he is not trapped, except insofar as he insists on being trapped. There is a way out, if only he will take it, but we have no indication that he will and every suggestion that he will not. His underlying problem, theologically, is sin. His surface problem is lack of will to do the one thing about his problem that can be done and that he himself already senses needs to be done: move beyond merely aesthetic categories to become a more fully developed human being. We also learn from *The Concept of Anxiety* that the apparent answer, offered in the insightful analysis of Judge William, is only part of the answer: moving into ethical categories is part of the solution, but he needs to enter that widest sphere of the ethico-religious.

The difference between the anxiety of Aesthete A and that of Cordelia is that the character of Cordelia, and thus her anxiety, evolve before our reading eyes in the "Diary": she begins as a naive young girl in near "spiritlessness" because she is an individual in whom spirit has not yet stirred. "In spiritlessness there is no anxiety" (*SKS*, 4:398; *CA*, 95), but anxiety lies in wait. It is Johannes's self-appointed role to stir spirit in her, until she has emerged as the very formidable personality whose passionate letters of hate open the "Diary."

The Sickness unto Death

The Sickness unto Death, like *The Concept of Anxiety*, reflects a schematization that could be presented as a checklist against which to visualize the full range of forms of anxiety and despair that Aesthete A actually has. In some sense, he has most of them catalogued, for many of them are overlapping. And he has all the most essential and critical forms of both. That is the point already being made in *Either/Or* in dramatic fashion and that is then underlined in theoretical fashion in the two practical treatises. Neither of them is interested in merely observing forms of anxiety and despair. Each is concerned about getting out of the condition, not wallowing in observation or any possible pleasures of theorizing.

The Sickness unto Death helps us to see Aesthete A more clearly, for it presents us with a chart of personality development in which we can see for ourselves where Aesthete A would be placed. Since despair is universal, of course he is to be regarded as in despair, but he is also aware of the fact, as he reveals in his "Diapsalmata." While Aesthete A is not totally transparent to himself about his condition, he does have a clear inkling about what is wrong. He shares the same theory of the movement and development of spirit as Kierkegaard has Johannes the seducer manifest in his seduction of Cordelia and as Anti-Climacus articulates in fuller philosophical-theological explicitness, and so he implicitly knows that it applies to himself as well. Yet Johannes suggests an emotional wound unlocks spiritual development, which is to say that he is not subscribing to any theology of baptism.

Anti-Climacus captures Aesthete A very well when he writes,

> [T]hose who say they are in despair are usually those who have so deep a nature that they are bound to become conscious as spirit or those whom bitter experiences and dreadful decisions have assisted in becoming conscious as spirit: it is either the one or the other; the person who is devoid of spirit is very rare indeed. (*SKS*, 11:142; *SUD*, 26)
>
> . . . Eternity asks you and every individual in these millions and millions about you only one thing: whether you have lived in despair or not, whether you have despaired in such a way that you did not realize that you were in despair, or in such a way that you covertly carried this sickness inside you as your gnawing secret, or in such a way that you, a terror to others, raged in despair. And, if so, if you have lived in despair, then regardless of whatever else you won or lost, everything is lost for you, eternity does not acknowledge you, it never knew you—or, still more terrible, it knows you as you are known and it binds you to yourself in despair. (*SKS*, 11:143–44; *SUD*, 27–28)

When we leave Aesthete A, we know he risks remaining in despair—risks spending the rest of his life spinning his wheels, as it were, in aesthetic pleasure, including the mixed pleasure of psychological self-observation. But the problem is that his psychological acuity is limited to observation and does not proceed to analysis. He describes but does not ask himself what is *wrong*. To do that, he would need some standard of measurement and judgment. And so he merely observes and catalogues his psychological states. He never asks about a cure. And so after becoming emotionally exhausted, he falls into sleep and forgetfulness before it starts up all over again. *The Sickness unto Death* provides its theory of the remedy, of the long-term cure, of what its author believes to be the sole cure for the problem of Aesthete A and every aesthete, of every "sinner" or non-self.

Reading *Either/Or*, we would already recognize that Aesthete A is conscious of the fact that he is in despair. Yet something is wrong beyond the fact that he is unwilling to do anything about it. *The Sickness unto Death* makes clear that part of his problem is that he does not have the correct conception of despair: "The true conception of despair is indispensable for conscious despair" (*SKS*, 11:162; *SUD*, 47). Aesthete A has more than dim knowledge of his condition, but he is far from having perfect clarity (he seems in fact to be engaging in a stratagem of distracting himself from his self-knowledge through various kinds of mental busyness, whether it be in aesthetic essays or self-observation).

His is not the despair of the earthly. That is left for conformists and external practitioners of Christianity. His is rather despair of the eternal, which is regarded as "a significant step forward" (*SKS*, 11:176; *SUD*, 61), and one of its principal indicators is enclosing reserve [*Indesluttethed*] (*SKS*, 11:177; *SUD*, 63), as is his longing for solitude. Carried to its extreme, in which one remains totally secretive and a secret to all, without a confidant or the ability to have a confidant, it brings with it the danger of suicide. In *Either/Or*, we do not know how far the character might eventually go toward this, but we do know that the young man of *Repetition* was, in an early draft, slated for suicide, before a repetition occurred that even the author had not contemplated.

Despair of the eternal is also characterized as the despair of a self with apparent self-mastery, but on the part of one who is in effect an absolute ruler who presides over nothing, the proverbial king without a country (*SKS*, 11:183; *SUD*, 69).

The despair of the "Diapsalmata" would be well understood as the intensified, demonic despair of growing self-consciousness, and this demonic despair—of willing to be oneself in despair—is held to be its most intensive form (*SKS*, 11:187; *SUD*, 73).

There are other forms of despair that Aesthete A does not manifest. For example, his is not the despair characterized by religious aestheticism. He is not a poet of the religious (as is Johannes de Silentio, formally, in *Fear and Trembling*, someone who understands something of the religious and of a God relationship but still stands outside it).

In conclusion, let us return briefly to the nineteenth-century young man whom I attempted to translate into twenty-first-century terms. We have seen his problem. The portrait of Aesthete A is of a character dancing sometimes wildly, sometimes wearily, on the edge of the abyss. Kierkegaard, through his pseudonyms Vigilius Haufniensis and Anti-Climacus, would offer him *The Concept of Anxiety* and *The Sickness unto Death* as manuals that could help him further understand his problem and point him in the direction of a cure.

Would we recommend the same for our twenty-first-century version of the brash young intellectual seeking to find himself in our perhaps even more confusing world? Would we (with Kierkegaard's sense of seriousness) "seriously" offer this updated young man *The Concept of Anxiety* and *The Sickness unto Death* as aids? I think *not.* Not only are both bound to nineteenth-century culture and a theological-philosophical tradition that is (unfortunately) less known and valued, but also that intellectual tradition is full of presuppositions that are no longer shared.

For Vigilius Haufniensis's notion of original or inherited sin, while freed from the historical interpretation as simply the sin (and the consequences of that sin) passed on to all the descendants of Adam, is still bound in the fine web of speculative Christian doctrine spun from the thin air of biblical narrative by a series of church fathers and given its definitive form by an intellectually dexterous Saint Augustine. The Christian doctrine of original sin, we now realize, is neither historically nor literally true. Yet it is profoundly true all the same, at least in the sense that it contains profound truths about the human condition that are overlooked at our own peril. For something remains very wrong among the estimated 105 to 120 billion descendants of Mitochondrial Eve.[19]

What can we offer our twenty-first-century young man instead? Should it be Prozac or Ritalin or some more subtle concoction of pills? Would that hold him in check until he matures? Or should we offer him *The Sickness unto Death,* or an attempted secularized version thereof, such as one finds implicitly in Heidegger's *Being and Time*? *Dasein*'s *Geworfenheit, Verfallenheit,* and encounter with *Angst* and his search for authenticity had their attractions as concepts in the early and mid-twentieth century, and some of them may still linger in the twenty-first. But *Being and Time* too may well be almost a dated work by now. To offer him Sartre or Camus might in one sense bring him up to the 1950s, but neither *Nausea* nor *The Plague* (nor *The Myth of Sisyphus*) admit of any passing a strictly secular and nontranscendent horizon. From the English-language realm, there is reason to consider Thomas Merton's *The Seven Story Mountain,* also from the 1950s but ultimately sharing in the same religious worldview with Kierkegaard and recounting a search that is not at all unlike that of Aesthete A.

If we seek a twenty-first-century way to reformulate these old truths, in light of the postmetaphysical prophecy of Nietzsche's Zarathustra that has largely come to pass, and of the apparent facts of neo-Darwinism, how shall we reformulate these insights? To date, those who have sought to do so in a totally secular way have not succeeded. Do we perhaps need a more Athanasian Kierkegaardian, in contrast to our more Augustinian Kierkegaard himself, capable of steering us at least away from the language of guilt and punishment and, if one keeps the image of restoration, at least emphasize the restoration of the God image in our shattered-feeling humanity? But that would be to await an intellectual repetition of Kierkegaard, whereas as he himself instructed us through Constantin Constantius, there is no such aesthetic, intellectual repetition to be hoped for. Thus we must hope for an entirely new conceptual breakthrough.

Meantime, the one work that I believe one can still offer our twenty-first-century young man, to good effect, would be *Either/Or* itself. Not a cure, not even a full analysis, but a warning and perhaps the shock of recognition in seeing himself in the not-too-distant mirror image of intellectual and spiritual lostness. Depending on how culturally precocious our young man is, he may have to widen his cultural horizons by taking in a few evenings of Mozart opera in order to fully appreciate the text. But he can still discover himself in the poignant cries of the "Diapsalmata," in the heady irony of "The Rotation of Crops," in the maudlin self-pity of "The Unhappiest Man," and of course stimulate his fantasy life by a reading of "The Seducer's Diary," as many a contemporary student has done.

Thus, of the psychological works of Kierkegaard here briefly considered, it is *Either/Or,* his first proper publication, that best stands the test of time, that stands the best chance of speaking across almost two centuries about persisting phenomena in the human condition and the persistent inkling that we have it in our power to do something about it. Whether we emerge as twenty-first-century Pelagians or semi-Pelagians in our theory is far less important than what emerges in our praxis—unless of course one still believes, as orthodox Christians once did and many still do, that correct theory or doctrine can actually affect praxis.

5

Narcissism: Kierkegaard and Freud

> He has a keener eye for truth than other people who are not melancholic. When in his heightened self-criticism he describes himself as petty, egoistic, dishonest, lacking in independence, one whose sole aim has been to hide the weaknesses of his own nature, it may be, so far as we know, that he has come pretty near to understanding himself; we only wonder why a man has to be ill before he can be accessible to a truth of this kind.

For anyone not familiar with it, the quotation above might seem to be about Kierkegaard's Aesthete A but is really a patient of Sigmund Freud's in turn-of-the-century Vienna.[1] Both author-analysts are nonetheless interested in very similar symptoms, their underlying causes, and their intentionality. Kierkegaard and Freud share an interest in many of the same symptoms and in their underlying cause. Narcissistic symptoms in themselves are only a starting point. For the problem is deeper than narcissism or even melancholia and has to do with the nature of desire itself.

As we have already seen in *Either/Or*, part 1, Kierkegaard confronts the reader with a self-concealing anonym, obsessed and preoccupied with himself yet intensely dissatisfied with himself; imprisoned in himself and by himself and bursting uncontrollably out of himself. In the words (but not the meaning) of the poet Ovid, *Odi et amo*, he hates and he loves, but it is himself. In his obsession with himself and in his own self-dissatisfactions, we suspect that his passion contains not only self-hatred but self-love as well. However, the object of his hate and equally of his love is obscured to him by the opacity of his desire. Moreover, his essays into love go beyond the theoretical. For "The Seducer's Diary" is the theory fictionally played out.

Either/Or is frequently in conversation with the great books—with Plato (*The Symposium*, in particular), Augustine (*Confessions*), Goethe

(*Faust*), and Hegel (*Phenomenology of Spirit*), among others. At the same time, it and Kierkegaard's aesthetic writings overall frequently seem to anticipate or complement in advance Freud's pioneering work while firmly rooted in their own times.[2] Like so many eighteenth- and nineteenth-century works, it is written in the shadow of Goethe's *Faust,* which seemed to sum up the striving post-Reformation Germanic soul. But it is also a book written in the shadow of Hegel's *Phenomenology,* echoing its categories and terminology even as it tries to turn Hegel's universal character inside out and examine a concrete individual spirit instead of the spirit of the times. Aesthete A is both a *Danish* Faust and a *Danish* Don Juan, a synthesis of two medieval myths contemplated against the music of Mozart in a tragicomedy played out in the empty theater that is *Either/Or.* There, Aesthete A is alone with himself, or rather with his nineteenth-century ego in search of a self. And we, as twenty-first-century egos, are the scribbling voyeurs and *auditeurs* to his public soliloquies on what a self is not.

Anonymous author A evidently is an exhibitionist, even if he has supposedly hidden his manuscript in an antique writing desk. Victor Eremita's literary detective story serves only to focus our attention on the elusive author. Aesthete A is a literary fiction, but he is believable and we recognize a common, if contorted, humanity in him. Kierkegaard has provided in him a treasure trove of insights about a nineteenth-century bourgeois ego stumbling, thrashing, driven by a force he powerfully feels but only intellectually seeks to master. He ventures an interpretation of his inner and outer lives, even as he would seem to reject applying their lessons. He is not and cannot be Everyman, but we know ourselves in him nonetheless.

He makes a powerful impression, and, by degrees, it is one of narcissism. The term "narcissist" is not without its own problems. One ought to be as clear as possible about the term before applying it. The term, as currently used, derives from a turn-of-the-twentieth-century concept of psychoanalytic culture. Sigmund Freud credits Paul Naecke with coining it in 1899.[3] Freud's essay "On Narcissism" established it as a psychoanalytic category, and a succession of works on the subject has given it a central role in understanding the development of the subject.[4]

Freud on Narcissism

In his now classic essay "On Narcissism" (1914), Freud, taking his point of departure from analysand symptoms, theorizes that in such withdrawn, self-absorbed patients "the libido that has been withdrawn from the external world has been directed to the ego and thus gives rise to an attitude which may be called narcissism" (*SE*, XIV:75). Moving on to discuss the libidinal development of other persons, he observes that "in their later choice of love-objects they have taken as a model not their mothers but their own selves. They are plainly seeking *themselves* as love-objects, and are exhibiting a type of object-choice which must be termed 'narcissistic.'" (*SE*, XIV:88).[5]

Narcissists are to be understood therefore as directing libido—defined as the dynamic manifestation of the sexual in mental life—back toward themselves instead of outward.[6] Without becoming involved in speculation about the reasons (the narcissistic wound, etc.), we can note that Freud understands narcissism as itself part of a larger process of identifying a satisfying love object. For whatever reason the *normal* choice does not take place, an attempt is still made to find an object, even oneself. The symptoms that have developed are the consequence of the false choice of oneself as that love object.

Freud sums up love "according to the narcissistic type" as a person loving "(a) what he himself is (i.e., himself), (b) what he himself was, (c) what he himself would like to be, (d) someone who was once part of himself" (*SE*, XIV:90). Obviously, in this definition love of another may still be narcissistic and perhaps is always partially so.

More recent psychoanalytical writers fill out the description. In all of them, we see Kierkegaard's Aesthete A lurking, either as a hurting and hurt-inflicting narcissist or as a yearner for a transcendent source of satisfaction. C. Fred Alford defines narcissism as the human condition itself. "What is sick or healthy, regressive or progressive, is how individuals come to terms with their narcissism, understood as a longing for protection, wholeness, and control over self and world." Alford later defines progressive narcissism as the desire to associate with something transcendent, better, more beautiful, and comments that some are able to draw on the feeling of earlier or original narcissistic perfection as a signpost pointing to the transcendent.[7] This begins to sound like not only the symptoms but also the underlying problem of Aesthete A. However, Alford's progressive narcissism sounds even more like the heightened problem of the young man in *Repetition.* In contrast to Aesthete A, *Repetition*'s young man is indeed in love with another and seeking to get himself back (as freedom), but he convinces himself (erroneously?) that he has to sever the human love tie in order to come back to himself. In contrast, Aesthete A is entirely taken up with himself, even if he cannot contain himself, and consciously interacts with others only as a diversion.

Otto Kernberg, considered one of the principal recent theorists of narcissism, has an operative definition of narcissism that would include only the unhealthy, unadapted subset of narcissists in Alford's wider, universal definition.[8] Kernberg writes, in language clearly applicable to Aesthete A as well,

> I describe patients with narcissistic personalities as presenting excessive self-absorption usually coinciding with a superficially smooth and effective social adaptation, but with serious distortions in their internal relationships with other people. They present various combinations of intense ambitiousness, grandiose fantasies, feelings of inferiority, and overdependence on external admiration and acclaim. Along with feelings of boredom and emptiness, and continuous search for gratification of strivings for brilliance, wealth, power and beauty, there are serious deficiencies in their capacity to love and to be concerned about others. This lack of capacity for empathic understanding of others often comes as a surprise considering their superficially appropriate social adjustment. Chronic uncertainty and dissatisfaction about themselves, conscious or unconscious exploitiveness and ruthlessness toward others are also characteristics of these patients.[9]

He adds that such patients "present an unusual degree of self-reference in their interactions with other people" and have a shallow emotional life.

> In general, their relationships with other people are clearly exploitative and sometimes parasitic. It is as if they feel they have the right to control and possess others and to exploit them without guilt feelings—and, behind a surface that very often is charming and engaging, one senses coldness and ruthlessness.[10]

He notes in addition that their lives are characterized by restlessness and boredom.[11]

Melancholia and Narcissism

Kernberg provides a near checklist for personality traits exhibited in the "Diapsalmata," and what little is lacking in narcissism will be supplied by "The Rotation of Crops" and "The Seducer's Diary." But at the same time, Aesthete A is more than the embodiment of Kernbeg's list. For he distinguishes himself from the outset by his suffering, which we recognize from his very first entry as intense and real:

> What is a poet? An unhappy person who conceals profound anguish in his heart but whose lips are so formed that as sighs and cries pass over them they sound like beautiful music.[12]

He is, however, preoccupied with himself from the first entry to the last. One entry after another betrays his gloom, which he terms his *Tungsind* and which Judge William perceives as his central problem, as well as the problem of the age (*SKS*, 3:32; *E/O*, 2:23).

> I am as timorous as a *sheva*, as weak and muted as a *dagesh lene* . . . and yet as uncontrollable as a pasha with three horse tails, as solicitous for myself and my thoughts as a bank for its banknotes, as reflected into myself as any *pronomen reflexivum*. (*SKS*, 2:30; *E/O*, 1:22)

All of this might suggest melancholia, rather than narcissism, but the two are connected, as Freud theorized and Kierkegaard demonstrated. In fact, the foregoing is almost a classic description of what Freud means by "melancholia" in his "Mourning and Melancholia": libido withdrawn from an external object and placed back onto the ego itself, combined with a sense of deflation. Freud writes,

> The distinguishing mental features of melancholia are a profoundly painful dejection, cessation of interest in the outside world, loss of the capacity to love, inhibition of all activity, and a lowering of the self-regarding feelings to a degree that finds utterance in self-reproaches and self-revilings, and culminates in a delusional expectation of punishment.[13]

Freud comments that melancholiacs frequently exhibit the trait of "insistent communicativeness which finds satisfaction in self-exposure" (*SE*, XIV:247), which sounds precisely like Aesthete A. But, for Freud, self-reproaches are really reproaches against a loved object that have then been redirected onto the patient's own ego (*SE*, XIV:248). Even self-dissatisfaction is thus another aspect of narcissism. Why and how does a melancholiac become his or her own love object and a narcissist? In Freud's view, object cathexis (i.e., the investment of libido in an external object) regresses into narcissism when object love is frustrated and the person makes his own ego into his substitute love object (*SE*, XIV:249). Freud associates this kind of melancholia with narcissism. If we are as yet unsure of the narcissism of A, his melancholia would seem firmly established. Freud also observes "the emergence of mania after the melancholia has run its course" (*SE*, XIV:258), and we have ample evidence of this in the manic aspects of A's personality.

The Symptoms of Aesthete A

The outcries of Aesthete A in his "Diapsalmata" indicate that he has withdrawn from the outside world and into himself, but for reasons that are not specified. We recognize that he has been powerfully disappointed, even if we are unclear about the details. The immediate results are equally clear: "I don't feel like doing anything" (*SKS*, 2:28; *E/O*, 1:20); "When I get up in the morning, I go right back to bed again" (*SKS*, 2:35; *E/O*, 1:26), writes this Danish Oblomov. "I live like one besieged, but lest I be harmed by sitting still so much, I cry myself tired." "My sorrow is my castle" (*SKS*, 2:30; *E/O*, 1:21). "My [*Tungsind*] is the most faithful mistress I have known" (*SKS*, 2:29; *E/O*, 1:20).

Attending his inactivity (but also his restless activity) are his twin mistresses, boredom and emptiness. "How sterile my soul and my mind are, and yet constantly tormented by empty voluptuous and excruciating labor pains!" (*SKS*, 2:32; *E/O*, 1:24). "On the whole, I lack the patience to live . . . my eyes are surfeited and bored with everything, and yet I hunger" (*SKS*, 2:33–34; *E/O*, 1:25). "How empty and meaningless life is" (*SKS*, 2:38; *E/O*, 1:29). "How dreadful boredom is—how dreadfully boring . . . the only thing I see is emptiness, the only thing I live on is emptiness, the only thing I move in is emptiness" (*SKS*, 2:46; *E/O*, 1:37).

The discourse on boredom in "The Rotation of Crops" is in the mood of irony rather than melancholy. But even in their witty, ironic form, we cannot doubt that the words are transformed cries of boredom and pain. Boredom is the root of all evil, repeats Aesthete A, and informs us that it is also the root of all motion, most notably the power of repulsion.[14]

The withdrawn, isolated Aesthete A is not beyond desire but for the moment is beyond love. "I have always made it appear, especially when I was touched most deeply, as if my heart were closed and alien to every feeling" (*SKS*, 2:49 *E/O*, 1:40). "My soul is dull and slack; in vain do I jab the spur of desire [*Lyst*] into its side" (*SKS*, 2:50; *E/O*, 1:41).

In the "Diapsalmata" there are already more than a few indications of the haughty and disdainful attitude that we see justified in "The Rotation of Crops" and executed in "The Seducer's Diary." "I laugh, for I despise people, and I take my revenge" (*SKS*, 2:49; *E/O*, 1:40).

The withdrawal of Aesthete A from the world is a withdrawal born of disappointment. And if he is disillusioned ("What is youth? A dream. What is love? The content of the dream" [*SKS*, 2:51; *E/O*, 1:42].), he would dearly love to have his illusions back and to have them work. But he knows that they do not work, and he already suspects that they cannot. Hence he wishes for possibility: "My soul has lost possibility. If I were to wish for something, I would wish not for wealth or power but for the passion of possibility, for the eye, eternally young, eternally ardent, that sees possibility everywhere. Pleasure disappoints, possibility does not" (*SKS*, 2:50; *E/O*, 1:41).

Kierkegaard's character A is thus at the edge and on the edge: beyond mere disillusionment and feeling the negative limits of all that is. What shall we make of his self-confessed symptoms? We shall never know what constituted his narcissistic injury, what his parental relations were like, how he weathered the Oedipal crisis (badly, one would assume). In addition and more important, Kierkegaard does not care about any of these Freudian categories, and it distorts his book if one overemphasizes them.

We concentrate instead on the surface symptoms of manipulation, coolness, and indifference, as well as his self-understanding as a clue to who he is and what his problem is.

While the term "narcissism" never occurs in *Either/Or*, there are suggestions of it all the same, as, for example, when Aesthete A writes, "I have only one friend, and that is echo. Why is it my friend? Because I love my sorrow, and echo does not take it away from me" (*SKS*, 2:42; *E/O*, 1:33). One almost looks for the capitalized "Echo" here, at last acknowledged by her Narcissus.[15] Johannes the seducer writes, narcissistically, to Cordelia, "I have found in myself the most interesting person among my acquaintances" (*SKS*, 2:389; *E/O*, 1:401), and confesses, "I am in love with myself, people say of me" (*SKS*, 2:392; *E/O*, 1:404).[16]

The decisive quotation for further inquiry may, however, be the following:

> Am I the lover
> Or beloved? . . . Since *I*
> *Am what I long for*, then my riches are
> So great they make me poor.

The writer is not Kierkegaard but the Roman poet Ovid, and the speaker is the mythological Narcissus.[17] If Aesthete A's love object is also himself, his riches might be impoverishing him. In answering Narcissus's rhetorical question ("Am I the lover or beloved?"), various parts of *Either/Or*, part 1, have much to say.

From Narcissism to Desire

The undisputed melancholy and suspected narcissism of Aesthete A and of his fictional avatar, Johannes, lead then to an exploration of desire and its object. "Desire" is a word that, in English, is full and that in Danish is expressed in a range of degrees and corresponding terms.

Indeed, desire, so very central to contemporary psychoanalytical thinking, particularly of the school of Jacques Lacan, seems to be yet another term and category in which Kierkegaard anticipates postmodernism. Moreover, it is a term that brings together central themes of *Either/Or.* The work begins, it will be recalled, with a meditation on whether there is a difference between the outer and the inner. Desire, as an upsurge of subjectivity into the world, is the place where outer and inner meet. And what transpires in desire will be of great significance for any possible reconciliation of outer and inner. The implicit background of the "Diapsalmata" would seem to be that Aesthete A is adrift in the outer. He is empty and lacks something, and he has been seeking to act out that lack externally. When we meet him, he is returning to the inner only to confront his inner lostness as well. *Either/Or,* part 1, is his articulation of the failure of the outer to satisfy his inner lack.

Aesthete A becomes part of a long conversation in Western thought with regard to both the "real" object of desire and to the effects of desire and the desirable upon the subject of desire him- or herself. If one sees shades of the *Phenomenology* of Hegel in the background of *Either/Or* and recalls that for Hegel "self-consciousness in general is desire [*Begierde*]," we should not be at all surprised to find desire as a central self-conscious theme for a character moving toward self-consciousness and engaging in a kind of exhibitionism of consciousness. Hegel in turn points to his own antecedents, most notably Spinoza, who wrote that *cupiditas* (appetite) is the essence of man.[18]

Aesthete A is a better Hegelian than either he or Kierkegaard would ever admit, and *Either/Or,* part 1, is in large part an exploration of his desire, a description and tale of the opacity of his desire as it seeks illumination about itself. If Hegel's *Phenomenology* has been cited as a "bildungsroman," *Either/Or,* part 1, is also clearly part of the genre.[19] Yet both are works about desire and deception and about the "systematic pursuit and misidentification of the Absolute."[20]

Excursus: Kierkegaard's Vocabulary of Desire

Kierkegaard's texts employ at least five Danish words that denote desire. Two examples from other works by Kierkegaard indicate the range of vocabulary and its importance in considering Kierkegaard's concept of desire. The English translations, both old and new, are problematic in this respect.[21]

Kierkegaard's vocabulary includes the following Danish words expressing aspects of desire: *Ønske, Laengsel, Begjering, Lyst,* and *Attraa. Ønske* is usually rendered "wish" and *Laengsel* "longing." *Begjering* is frequently rendered "yearning" or "craving," but *Lyst,* which can mean the simplest of desires, can equally mean "craving" or sensual desire in some contexts.[22] Where several of the words occur close together, the inadequacy of the translations becomes especially apparent. For example, the "Exordium" in *Fear and Trembling* has "his soul had but one wish [*Ønske*], to see Abraham, but one longing [*Laengsel*], to have witnessed that event. His craving [*Begjering*] was not to see the beautiful regions of the east. . . . His craving [*Attraa*] was to go along on the three-day journey. . . . His wish [*Ønske*] was to be present in that hour when Abraham raised his eyes and saw Mount Moriah in the distance" (*SKS,* 4:105; *FT,* 8).

In "Two Upbuilding Discourses," of 1843, *Ønsker, Begjeringer, Lyster,* and *Attraaer* are found together, in apparently ascending order: "Is it not true that [life's earnestness] taught you that your wishes [*Ønsker*] would not be fulfilled, your desires [*Begjeringer*] would not be gratified, your appetites [*Lyster*] would not be heeded, your cravings [*Attraaer*] would not be satisfied?"[23] What seems clear is that *Attraa* is used by Kierkegaard for the strongest form of desire, sensuous or not. Moreover, *Attraa* is the Danish word Kierkegaard uses to translate desire (*epithumia*) in Plato's *Symposium.*[24] *Attraa* is desire in double strength, which may be either sexual/sensuous or religious.

Desire language in the "Diapsalmata" of *Either/Or* is limited to the terms *Begjere* and *Lyster,* and Aesthete A complains about the paltry desires of the age: "Indeed, how many are there in our day who truly dare to wish, dare to desire [*begjere*]?" (*SKS,* 2:30; *E/O,* 1.22). This entry is followed by a reference to desire in folk literature and a comment on the latter's significance:

> The tremendous poetical power of folk literature is manifest, among other ways, in its power to desire [*begjere*]. In comparison, desire [*Begjer*] in our age is simultaneously sinful and boring, because it desires what belongs to the neighbor. Desire in folk literature is fully aware that the neighbor does not possess what it seeks any more than it does itself." (*SKS,* 2:30; *E/O,* 1:22)

We have no inkling here, however, what desire truly seeks.

Later Aesthete A complains that the times are without passion. "[People's] desires [*Lyster*] are staid and dull, their passions drowsy" (*SKS,* 2:36; *E/O,* 1:27–28). Further on, he complains, "My soul is dull and slack; in vain do I jab the spur of desire [*Lyst*] into its side" (*SKS,* 2:50;

E/O, 1:41). *Lyst* and *Begjer* are linked again in "The Rotation of Crops" when the author complains about that subspecies of the boring who bore others: "Certainly this class of animals is not the fruit of man's appetite [*Begjer*] and woman's desire [*Lyst*]" (*SKS*, 2:278; *E/O*, 1:288).

But in "The Immediate Erotic Stages," *Attraa* is the term, and it is in this essay that Aesthete A sketches his triadic theory of desire's stages—dreaming, seeking, desiring—(with a somewhat forced triadic subdivision of the third),[25] which Aesthete A conveniently groups in his discussion around three Mozart operas.[26]

Don Giovanni is the third operatic figure in a rising hierarchy of desire, and yet his desire is not yet fully awakened. For the status of the object of desire is still very much in question, called into question by his indifference.[27] Despite his reflexivity and relative advance beyond the Page and Papageno, his desire remains opaque, and one can seriously ask whether in fact he truly desires the apparent objects of his desire.

In Hegel's terminology, his desire as the synthesis of the preceding stages (namely, dreaming desire and awakening desire) should be desire that is *an-und-für-sich*, in and for itself and thus complete. In a Hegelian depiction, we should expect to find in him desire that has been explicitly separated, or "other" now restored to the original unity of the subject of desire with the object of desire. However, this is very evidently *not* the case. Aesthete A writes that the third stage is the unity of the previous two stages because "in the particular, desire has its absolute object; it desires the particular absolutely" (*SKS*, 2:90; *E/O*, 1:85), but it is not yet the summit of desire.

But Kierkegaard's comment does not ring true, and Kierkegaard's own analysis of Don Giovanni does not seem to support it. For Don Giovanni, he would have us believe, arbitrarily elects an individual representative of total femininity (*SKS*, 2:103–4; *E/O*, 1:100): he targets a particular woman as "Woman." That it can even be termed "arbitrary" is questionable, since Don Giovanni is evidently a compulsive womanizer. Don Giovanni does not will and choose freely; he is the prisoner of his own compulsion. Moreover, the ostensible object matters little to him and a substitute can readily be found, as happens in his serial seductions. In no sense is any object for Don Giovanni absolute. One may even question whether they can be called the objects of his desire rather than merely symbols and stand-ins for the unrecognized Object.

Don Giovanni is the exemplification of the incompleteness of the theory of desire in "The Immediate Erotic Stages." For what is missing in the theory is the *satisfaction of desire*, in desire's attainment of its (absolute) object. Of course, this is missing from the entirety of *Either/Or*, in theory and in practice, and that is very much to the point. The third and so-called awakened stage of desire has merely seized on an object at hand. Where this seems to work at all, it is a matter of a subject's having identified an illusory absolute that he can live with, at least for a short while.

Johannes of the "Diary" would seem to apply the theory of "The Immediate Erotic Stages" and to embody the higher synthesis of Faust and Don Giovanni, of which the essay spoke. Johannes's reflexivity allows him to be the seducer, whereas Don Giovanni's lack of reflection and consciousness merely gave seductive power to his sensuous, animal desire but not to himself as an individual. Yet even in Johannes's reflexivity and manipulative awareness that is so demonic, we cannot imagine him but at the extreme of the theory developed by Aesthete A and as the exemplification of its bankruptcy. For, in him, desire is *not* satisfied either, despite the higher intellectual form it takes.

While we perceive Johannes as a figure of desire, the term does not play a role in the "Diary" in a major way. However, in the long entry of June 7, he writes of watching Cordelia at the window in the evening:

> In these nocturnal hours, I walk around like a ghost; like a ghost I inhabit the place where her dwelling is. Then I forget everything, have no plans, no reckonings, cast understanding overboard, expand and fortify my chest with deep sighs, a motion I need in order not to suffer from my systematic conduct. Others are virtuous by day, sin at night; I am dissimulation by day—at night I am sheer desire [*lutter Attraa*]. If she saw me here, if she could look into my soul—if. (*SKS*, 2:342; *E/O*, 1:352)

But while he is a reflective seducer, he is not a reflective *desirer*: he reflectively observes his own seducing, but not his desiring. If there is such a being as the reflective desirer, then the theory needs to admit of one more stage as well. While Johannes would seem to be the exemplification of the third stage of desire in "The Immediate Erotic Stages," he is the exemplification of the inadequacy of the theory. For if the theory held up, Johannes as awakened desire would desire Cordelia and find satisfaction of his desire in her. And yet it is precisely this that we cannot believe. Cordelia Wahl is, to be sure, the object of his choice (*Wahl*). Her surrender to him, that is, making him the object of her own desire, is Johannes's demonically calculated goal and achievement. Yet it would be rash and naive to construe Cordelia herself as the object of his desire. The true object of his desire eludes him and eludes us, at least within *Either/Or*. In this the work leads us beyond itself as the object slips away, is deferred, as deconstructionists would put it, and with it the meaning of the work.

For Cordelia never was the libidinal object for Johannes. His conquest of Cordelia was the fulfillment of his idea of himself as the reflective seducer. The essence of his conquest is that he has managed to become loved and desired without himself having loved or really desired Cordelia in an erotic sense. He desired that she desire him, and in this he has succeeded, but at a price to both of them. This is the Hegelian master-slave dialectic in the arena of love: Cordelia is taken captive, but the presumed master is not free. Like the master in Hegel's dialectical portrayal, Johannes has less chance of obtaining freedom than Cordelia does. For something may yet intervene for Cordelia to free her from her master. Johannes's master, on the other hand—his own objectless desire—will be much harder to throw off.

But if, as Sartre says, the desirable moves the desiring, then we must look beyond Cordelia for the cause of his movement.[28] "The Rotation of Crops" might suggest that it is mere boredom, ennui, that sets him in motion, but that explanation seems inadequate. If it is his own idea of himself that moves his desire, then the desire operating in his apparent seduction is narcissism and *he* as idealized image to himself is the beloved. In short, narcissism.

There is an image at the beginning of the "Diary" in which Johannes sees Cordelia in a mirror (*SKS*, 2:305; *E/O*, 1:315–16). The scene almost requires a second mirror in which we would behold Johannes at the moment of choice catching a glimpse of his idealized seducer self in the second mirror while he contemplates the image of Cordelia in the first. For Johannes's pursuit of Cordelia is really the pursuit of his own image as seducer. And yet when he has come as close to actualizing that mirror image as one can imagine, what has he achieved? "My riches are so great they make me poor"—precisely Narcissus's sentiment in *Metamorphoses*, translated into the self-pitying Danish of the "Diapsalmata." His desire to fulfill his image as seducer can lead us to speculate that this is itself only a reflection of a deeper desire to get himself back, to recover himself—a theme played out less obscurely (but by no means straightforwardly) in *Repetition*.

Significance and Centrality of Desire in *Either/Or*

By the end of *Either/Or*, part 1, Aesthete A and his literary creation Johannes the seducer have not found an abiding and satisfactory external object of desire. As both narcissist and seducer, his identification of an object of desire has continuously been a misidentification. Both Cordelia and he himself are unsatisfactory substitute objects for him. If there is a possible object that will fully satisfy desire, it remains unattained, indeed "lost."[29] There is no suggestion in *Either/Or* proper that Aesthete A recognizes a lost object in the background of his search or as in any perceptible way setting his desire in motion. Nor is this contained in part 2, where Judge William will urge Aesthete A to choose himself and to choose himself in relation to another, to rise above selfish individualism to the ethically fulfilled self of a married relationship. In any event, Aesthete A would already seem to be beyond the advice of William and also beyond the proffered solution. The ongoing analysis of aesthetic existence in Kierkegaard's works will eventually make clear, at least in *The Sickness unto Death*, that the problem of Aesthete A and of a Johannes revolve around the Lost Object, who is nothing other than God and from whom he has been severed.[30] Kierkegaard's notion of an original wholeness, before an original sinning, is remarkably similar to the late twentieth-century Lacanian notion of an original but imaginary wholeness from which one has been separated and to which one longs to return. In Lacan's school of thought, the individual, "castrated" and scarred by the radical sign of finitude after the imagined union with the mother, is severed, seeks an impossible object and the satisfaction of impossible desire in a chain of possible objects.[31] This analysis would seem to apply to Aesthete A and his avatar, Johannes. It might in fact make sense to many of the predicament of Aesthete A.

Aesthete A certainly suggests that he has run the gamut of possible love objects, including himself. Modern psychoanalytic theory may underline how universal the problem of Aesthete A actually is, how powerful the dynamism of desire, how inadequate the theories that seek to account for it. Yet Kierkegaard does not stop where the postmodernists do. For he does believe in an Aristotelian "final cause" (or goal) of desire. And if there are similarities and anticipations of post-Hegelian movements in Kierkegaard's thought, there are clearly differences, and this is the most radical. For him, the analysis such as offered by a Freud or Lacan, by a Sartre or Derrida, would be an analysis cut short, because it would condemn a subject to meaningless desire when there is good reason to believe, and experience, meaningful desire. For Lacan, for example, the shifting objects of desire (viz., the other) stand for, but never satisfy for, the unattainable Other that is the true object of human desire.[32] The solution that Lacan and others offer is various forms of resignation to the absurdity of human desire that seeks restoration of an imagined primordial unity rather than a real one. For his part, and a century earlier, Kierkegaard seems fully aware of the shifting nature of desire and of the elusiveness of meaning. Although he precedes Lacan, he would be unmoved by Lacan's rejection of the Platonic model of restored union with the Other that has molded Western thinking. Kierkegaard might appreciate the new sensitivity to language and the additional skepticism about conceptualizing found in postmodern writers. For him, the surmounting of the limitation of words and concepts comes in experience. *Either/Or*'s exploration of desire, and its own theorizing, would seem to point toward experimentation and experience rather than toward more ideas.

If we take his nineteenth-century analysis seriously, instead of indulging in the Nietzschean temptation to consign it to the dustbin of Western metaphysics, the alternatives would seem to consist in either personal exploration of the restless heart (Augustine) or else an attempt to grasp what the Buddhist tradition means in its discourse about the stilling of desire.

Kierkegaard, as has been noted, belongs to the tradition of understanding desire that goes back to Plato's *Symposium.* Moreover, Kierkegaard's exploration via Aesthete A seems influenced by Aristophanes's enormously influential mythic statement of human desire for its other(ed) half. If so, Kierkegaard's work seems to be pointing to the much-neglected opening moment of Aristophanes's tale when the original beings are propelling their odd shapes toward the heavens. For Kierkegaard, this is what desire was originally about, and what it is still about: metaphorical assent to the heavens. The desire for the original state is not desire for one's other half but rather desire to get back beyond such desire and therefore become capable of resuming the assault upon the abode of the gods.

6

Repetition Compulsion

> I would ask you to re-read Kierkegaard's essay on *Repetition*, so dazzling in its lightness and ironic play, so truly Mozartian in the way, so reminiscent of *Don Giovanni*, it abolishes the mirages of love.
>
> —Jacques Lacan, *The Four Fundamental Concepts of Psychoanalysis*

Repetition (1843) is one of the most admired of Kierkegaard's more properly literary works. Yet while some find it poetic and charming, others see it as opaque and puzzling. Despite its literary merits, it is frequently overlooked in the enthusiasm for its better-known twin, *Fear and Trembling*, published on the same day. It is also often overshadowed by the two massive tomes and fellow quasi novels *Either/Or* (published earlier in 1843) and "'Guilty?'/'Not Guilty?'" of *Stages on Life's Way* (1845). *Repetition* stands as a middle point between them and in the development of the notion of a religiously directed melancholy, but it is also distinctive in many important ways. Given the serious playfulness that characterizes so much of Kierkegaard's writings, it would be not at all surprising to find *Repetition* full of repetitions. And, of course, it is—from the title, which is repeated at the beginning of the epistolary part 2, to narrated aesthetic repetitions, to ironic-dramatic repetition, and even a repetition external to the work that intrudes into it. Last but not least is the fledgling concept of repetition itself that the book is nominally about.

One of many questions raised by the title turns on all the *other* repetitions in the book—implicit and explicit, subtle and not so subtle—and their relation both to the concept "repetition" and to the other things that the book may also be about, perhaps even beyond the conscious knowledge and intention of the author.

The aim here is to consider *Repetition*'s own repetitions as a point of entry and possible clue to the meaning(s) of the work. For *Repetition* is a literary rebus in the full Freudian sense and thus well ahead of its time. Its tantalizing ambiguities, obscurities, and simple loose ends call the reader back for one more try at its multiple levels. Moreover, its similarities to Sigmund Freud's *Beyond the Pleasure Principle* (1920) are sufficiently striking to tempt a naive reader of Kierkegaard's work, unaware of its 1843 publication date, to the erroneous speculation that *Repetition* might be a literary reworking of Freud's exploration of repetition automatism. Whenever one introduces the Viennese psychoanalyst's name, one raises a host of Freudian associations, including considerations about the unconscious of Kierkegaard and of the text. Both are intriguing subjects of speculation, for which Kierkegaard has furnished considerable material. However, they cannot be allowed to obscure the text. For it is clear that the author behind the pseudonym has a definite sense of what he wishes to be communicated. Yet many are not sure what it is, and in puzzling it out, one may even begin to think that one has noticed things that the author has not. This raises interesting questions about how much the author is in control of his text. Kierkegaard seems not unaware of unconscious slippage by an author and warns a writer against drawing upon one's own experience only to end up in what he terms mere private talkativeness.[1] Yet we can also legitimately ask how well Kierkegaard was able to follow his own advice and how fully he remained in control. For he ultimately allowed unanticipated external events in his own life to alter the ending of this purportedly fictional work.

The whole work is a huge puzzle, a source of fascination for some, a source of frustration for others. The title, subtitle, and purported principal theme of investigation are confounding, and the confusion is only compounded by the invocation of Platonic recollection and a digression on theatrical farce in Berlin. It is Kierkegaardian indirect communication perhaps taken to an extreme.

Some impatient readers of the work give up, sometimes too easily. Since the text is undeniably complex, we may be grateful for helps and hints from various interpretive quarters. The many schools of text interpretation that have arisen since 1843 render the text more interesting still, in light of their various approaches to a text. Indeed, it may have been the case in 1843 that one simply read a book (if ever there was such a thing). Nowadays the self-respecting intellectual *labors* through one, with the weight of interpretive consciousness and a plenitude of interpretation theories.

To its credit, *Repetition* stands up very well under structural, intentional, psychoanalytic, deconstructionist, and reconstruction methods.[2] In this writer's view, it profits from them all, while in its ironic playfulness it eludes reductionist attempts. *Repetition* remains perplexing and by no means does this writer claim to have solved all its puzzles or exhaustively answered all the questions that careful reading casts up. The book's final meaning of "repetition" (*redintegratio in statum pristinum*) is stated forthrightly in any event. That much is rather simple, at least in Latin, which speaks of "reintegration into [one's original] pristine state."

Structurally, *Repetition* has two parts, signaled informally by the repetition of the title. Yet there are many unindicated subdivisions. Themes shift markedly, although not without purpose. And the shifting, pitching quality of the work, particularly of the first part, may well account for the off-putting quality that some readers experience.

The first part begins the speculations and observations of the narrator, Constantin Constantius, a self-described nineteenth-century experimenting psychologist of a literary-philosophical cast. Constantin intermingles musings on the announced new category "repetition" with the engagement story of a young man he claims to have met a year before. This is the young man who, we shall see, like Diogenes, proves by his own actual motion the reality of a concept, which speculators like Constantin only muse about. In short, whereas Constantin merely thinks repetition and much of the time is never quite sure what it is, the young man will simply live it.

A fourteen-page "digression"—a combination of aesthetic appreciation of farce and personal recollection—interrupts the journey and narration. (Meantime, as the reader discovers, the young man's love story—which a reader would normally presume to have been concluded before the book began—will actually continue to unfold during the writing of the book and radically alter the ending.) There is, however, more structure than the foregoing might suggest. In fact, part 1 can readily be divided into six sections:

1. Prologue on repetition
2. Narrative about the young man
3. Second prologue on repetition
4. Journey to Berlin
5. Digression on and recollection of farce
6. Passionate recollection of failed repetition

All six sections are written by Constantin, who presents himself as an older and wiser figure. But the sequence suggests anything but serenity. Sections 1 to 4 shift themes abruptly. It is notable that section 3 is a return to (a repetition of) the discussion of "repetition" in the first section.

Part 2 finds Constantin home, leading a dull (repetitious) life when letters begin arriving from the young man. This second part is largely epistolary, with commentary by Constantin. The troubled love story that the letters relate is a further exploration of repetition (although the young man almost certainly never intended to contribute to a book by Constantin).[3] Yet Constantin's narrative and observations are framed around the young man's story, whose letters alone constitute approximately forty pages of the book's one hundred. Constantin's two narratives about the young man's story (section 2 of part 1 and section 1 of part 2), as well as his intervening observations and his epistolary conclusion, contribute additional mass to the love story. And yet the work is finally *not* about the love story as such: it is about repetition, as it says it is.

As already noted, developments in the story will eventually carry the exploration and the book further than its author realized when he began. The five sections (building on the numerical sequence above) of part 2 include the following:

7. Second narrative by Constantin
8. Approximately forty pages of letters by the young man to Constantin, his "silent confidant"
9. Observation by Constantin
10. May letter of the young man
11. Constantin's August letter to readers[4]

With the resumption of the tale of the young man, begun in the second section of part 1, part 2 becomes perhaps an elaborate repetition itself. However, it is a repetition of a relationship between the young man and Constantin that seemed over when the young man vanished at the end of part 1. In part 1, the young man was himself a kind of recollection on the part of Constantin. Through his letters in part 2, he emerges as a living personality struggling against his relationship with a nameless young girl and struggling too in his relationship with his seductive confidant, Constantin. We never learn the real problem between the young man and the young woman. Indeed, this is the "blank page" figuratively inserted into every volume of Kierkegaard's aesthetic works, a repeated absence that invites endless speculation. The fact that we do not know, and probably never will know, the real reason for his break with his fiancée, Regine Olsen, may force us to focus on its effects, which are ultimately more significant. However, we learn the essentials: his relationship to the young girl leads him to define, at least negatively, the object of his desire. Simply stated in words that never appear in the text, "It is not she."[5] Of this relationship we know little and it will *not* be repeated. In contrast we learn much more about the relationship between the young man and Constantin, ostensibly the secondary drama and formal occasion of the narrative. The young man breaks with Constantin as well, but he takes up the relationship again, repeatedly in fact. For Constantin's narratives and the young man's letters constitute a chronicle of their own relationship as well. From these sources we learn that their exchanges are closer to dialectic than to dialogue. Each in speaking is preoccupied with himself, hears and observes the other warily. And in the end each seems to have a mediating influence upon the other. What are they each up to? Constantin's narrative is on one level the tale of the young man's distancing himself from his would-be adviser. As Constantin tells it, the young man's outpouring of his soul, into which Constantin lured him through café conversation, first took place in office visits. Soon the young man insisted on dawn meetings at the harbor. Then he disappeared. In part 2, he reappears, but at a letter's remove (and without return address). The young man would seem to be seeking a "talking cure" by pouring himself out to his silent listener. Indeed, theirs is at times an impersonal, almost clinical relationship, as the young man himself senses. During the long and one-sided epistolary phase, the physically distant Constantin never gets to address a word directly to the young man, not even the famous "Go on" of the silent Freudian analyst. While Constantin is the recipient of these letters, we may wonder to what extent he really is the addressee of these near "Dear Diary" recollections.[6] In a real sense, and in the phrase of *Either/Or*'s "Diapsalmata," the young man's letters are really *ad se ipsum*—at least *for* himself if not *to* himself. Constantin serves as a point of focus for the young man, someone to tell the story to, as the young man himself says.

The young man's first letter in part 2 (August 15) records his considerable ambivalence about Constantin: he needs him and yet resents his need of him. Much like a patient in psychoanalysis, he idealizes the analyst Constantin, whom he both admires and resents as one who has "subjugated to such a degree every passion, every emotion, every mood under the cold regimentation of reflection!" and as someone always alert, always conscious, never vague and dreamy (*SKS*, 4:59; *R*, 189). "You know about everything, do not get mixed up," he writes in reproachful admiration (*SKS*, 4:58; *R*, 188). He demands Constantin's silence yet resents all the secrets Constantin must know. But just as he marvels at the "indescribably salutary and alleviating" effect of talking to Constantin, which he likens to talking with himself or "with an idea," he dismisses Constantin as "mentally disordered" for being so cool and collected. He deems Constantin's power to make him seek his "approving smile and its ineffable reward" to be "demonic." The reader knows from Constantin's own narrative that he is neither all-seeing nor mad, and Constantin defends himself from both sets of charges as well. (A Freudian would probably regard these remarks as symptoms of the important transference phase of an analysis.) The young man keeps withdrawing from and returning to Constantin, a repetition that changes in form as well as content. (Perhaps Constantin's apparent attempt to reduce the young man to fiction is his form of retaliation for rejection.)

The name of the pseudonymous author of the work is also a repetition, at least as a root. The "constant" of Constantin Constantius is thereby emphasized. It is the basis not only for the construction of a pseudonym's name but also for his disposition and simultaneously for the naming of a pole of constancy, over against which stands the nameless and wavering young man.[7]

Both parts of *Repetition* are overwhelmingly "I"-centered, regardless of the "I" speaking. In fact, the use of the first-person singular pronoun *jeg/Jeg* 731 times in a book of approximately one hundred pages is remarkable.[8] Not only is the pronoun constantly used throughout the short book but also it is much used whether by Constantin as narrator and observer or by the young man as letter writer. Given the genre of letter writing, an abundance of first person pronouns is not unexpectable but exceeds normal expectations. The young man's epistles account for a total of 319 instances of the pronoun, or approximately 43 percent of its occurrences. As a result, *Repetition* is the most egocentric of the entire Kierkegaardian body of work. Only *The Point of View for My Work as an Author,* a nonpseudonymous work, rivals it; and among the pseudonymous works, *Stages on Life's Way* is a close second (further suggesting parallels between the works), followed by *Prefaces* and *Either/Or,* part 1. Yet *Repetition* takes first place. In fact, a range of McKinnon text-study programs place the first person pronoun at the center of the book.[9] The reader too cannot fail to get the point. In short, the book is extraordinarily ego-centered. Yet the work is not simply egotistical. For ultimately the work is not about the "I" of the young man, or the "I" of Constantin, or the "we" of their strained relationship. For despite Constantin's self-preoccupation as analyst and the young man's self-preoccupation as suffering lover, the book's preoccupation is a higher one, namely, about a higher self.

There are numerous dramatic repetitions in the exploration of the category in part 1, and they would seem trivial were they not part of the negative definition of the concept of repetition. Constantin, for example, goes back to Berlin and seeks to repeat his experience there. At the lodging house, there has been a marriage. At the theater, the same seat is not available; the lead actress is not playing. Constantin, who had sought an aesthetic repetition of his Berlin experience, recalls his childish despair of repeating an experience whose pleasurability, he now realizes, consisted largely in its novelty and is therefore ipso facto unrepeatable.[10] In addition, he is deprived of the reassurance he had sought in the repetition and is distressed. Ostensibly it had all been part of an experiment, an exploration of the possible meaning of repetition. (But how odd for a book to start with a word, its own title, and to try to find the content that will be adequate to it. As such, it is a book in search of its own title's meaning, a literary identity hunt.) Ironically, Constantin's repeated failure to achieve repetition constitutes a principal disproof of the category for him. By the time he has become narrator, Constantin has recovered from his experiment but is by no means master of the situation. Nor is he master of the young man, who maintains some control over their relationship by repeated disappearance, withdrawal, and keeping his distance.

In the young man's letters, Job is appealed to and invoked, repeatedly, as a figure of repetition. His September and November letters open with an invocation of Job. ("Job! Job! O Job! Is that really all you said, those beautiful words: The Lord gave, and the Lord took away; blessed be the name of the Lord?" and "If I did not have Job! It is impossible to describe all the shades of meaning and how manifold the meaning is that he has for me."[11]) Job is symbolically important, however, not just for the fact that he got everything back (thereby literally fulfilling the meaning of the Danish term for "repetition," *Gjen-tagelse*, "getting back") but also for the fact that he gets everything back double. He is even more important for the fact that, against all skeptics, Job knew he was in the right. Whether or not able to persuade others or even put it into coherent terms for himself, he is nonetheless convinced that he has done the right thing.

The October letter, which is reminiscent of the self-alienation of the "Diapsalmata" of *Either/Or*, links the young man to Job, without this time mentioning him by name, as it declares, "Even if the whole world rose up against me . . . I am still in the right."[12] The theme is repeated in an explicit reference to Job in the December letter: "The secret in Job, the vital force, the nerve, the idea, is that Job, despite everything, is in the right" (*SKS*, 4:75; *R*, 207). The January letter explicitly links Job and repetition. This is in fact the first time that the young man uses the term ("Job is blessed and has received everything *double.*—this is called a *repetition*" [*SKS*, 4:79; *R*, 212]).

The significance of the repeated allusions to Job is, as the young man acknowledges, multilayered. He appeals to Job as a figure of justification vis-à-vis the presumption of guilt. He also appeals to Job as an inspiration and figure of hope for getting everything back double. The book of Job is full of ironies, and the young man's appeal to it will be ironic too. For author Kierkegaard purportedly began the work, as well as *Fear and Trembling*, with some hope of getting Regine Olsen back. Yet when the young man's restoration occurs, he no more gets back exactly what he lost than did Job. For Job, although subsequently blessed with new offspring and wealth, did not of course get his dead children and destroyed property back. Only his public honor was restored—and enhanced. Kierkegaard's and the young man's hope may have been similar in terms of public opinion, but the real restoration here is ultimately restoration of self and of freedom from the captivity of desire.

But in the appeal to Job is also the inkling on the young man's part of the religious dimension of his problem, something that Constantin, while not himself a figure representing the religious, is more explicit about. (There is, additionally, a parallelism between *Repetition*'s invocation of Job and *Fear and Trembling*'s invocation of Abraham, equally between the contrasting philosophical figure for each book, the unnamed Hegel in the former, Socrates in the latter.)[13]

The young man's January letter repeats the reference to repetition but links it to a thunderstorm. ("I am waiting for a thunderstorm and for repetition" [*SKS*, 4:81; *R*, 214].) The thunderstorm motif, itself a reference to Job, will be repeated until a thunderstorm of a different sort occurs, when the clouds break as it were and he is free in a sense that was totally unanticipated. Constantin complains about his patient in the "Incidental Observation" that follows the text of the January letter:

> He is suffering from a misplaced melancholy high-mindedness that belongs nowhere except in a poet's brain. He is waiting for a thunderstorm that is supposed to make him into a husband, a nervous breakdown perhaps. (*SKS*, 4:83; *R*, 216)

There is one additional sense of *Repetition*'s repetitions to consider. For *Repetition* is itself also a repetition—repetition of the love story that turned Kierkegaard into a poet and that haunts his works (and that will provide the basis for the Freudian speculations below). For the story of an engagement appears in *Either/Or*, part 1. *Repetition* in a sense repeats that and then is repeated in *Fear and Trembling* and *Stages on Life's Way*. The last named is the most significant repetition. Not only does *Stages on Life's Way* contain a diary-novella ("'Guilty?'/'Not Guilty?'") that parallels the epistolary section of *Repetition*, and not only is the problem of melancholy repeated in a higher key, but also Constantin Constantius and the young man both reappear as characters in "The Banquet" (and this, as noted above, in spite of Constantin's apparent attempt to dismiss the young man as his own fiction in the final pages of *Repetition*). But in "'Guilty?'/'Not Guilty?'" the parallels—if not quasi repetitions—are most striking. For not only is the theme of a broken relationship repeated, along with the mood of melancholy and the suggestion of a religious grounding of the problem, but key elements are mirrored as well: the young man of "'Guilty?'/'Not Guilty?'" is an equally unnamed but Latin Quidam, the new silent onlooker is a Frater Taciturnus, and the written recollections have become a diary instead of letters. In short, everything has become more explicit, without of course being revealed. Moreover, the subtitle of "'Guilty?'/'Not Guilty?'" is "A Passion Narrative, a Psychological Experiment" and echoes (if not repeats) *Repetition*'s subtitle, "A Venture in Experimenting Psychology." *Repetition* is thus itself both repetition (of *Either/Or*) and to be repeated (in *Stages on Life's Way*).

Repetition is repetition in yet another sense as well. To explore it one must move beyond Constantin Constantius's psychology and on to twentieth-century psychoanalysis. For here one finds a sense of repetition that Kierkegaard does not consciously engage, even if he personally demonstrates it: namely, repetition compulsion or "repetition automatism," that is, repetition as the manifestation of some deeper compulsion to repeat. For a survey of its fuller meaning we turn to Freud.[14] (What follows is not a thorough-going account of Freud's work so much as a highlighting of points of contact with *Repetition*.)

In 1920, Freud published his own reflections, meditations, and speculation on repetition in *Beyond the Pleasure Principle*, the last of his "meta-psychological" works (and one that many Freudians accordingly shy away from). But, before that, he had published, in 1914, an essay titled "Remembering, Repeating and Working-Through"[15] in which he described repetition of an action as a second type of remembering and where, speaking of a patient, he wrote, "He reproduces it not as a memory but as an action; he *repeats* it, without of course, knowing that he repeats it." Freud remained fascinated with the role of repetition and what he increasingly saw as a compulsion to repeat.

Beyond the Pleasure Principle begins as an investigation of the assumption of psychoanalysis that "the course taken by mental events is automatically regulated by the pleasure principle" (*SE*, XVIII:7). Freud was struck by the fact that there is a motive force that is beyond the pleasure principle, that patients evidenced a compulsion to repeat that clearly could not have pleasure as its motive. What would the meaning of actions be that seemed directed at neither the production of pleasure nor the avoidance of unpleasure? But first Freud looked at a range of repeated actions, including, by the way, attempts at repetition of a theatrical experience.

Among repetitions, dreams are one form in which situations are "reenacted." The child's game of *Fort/Da*, or disappearance and return (peekaboo), is another, in which the child repeats and transcends the distressing experience of the mother's disappearance by repeating it as a game. Children repeat both pleasurable and unpleasurable experiences as a game, Freud noted, and so surmount both by abreacting the strength of the impression made by an original experience (*SE*, XVIII:16–17). "Abreacting" will provide a strong clue to the motive of repetition.

Freud's practice provided other forms and examples of repetition. He remarks that the physician's interest in psychoanalytic practice is to force as much as possible into the channel of memory and to allow as little as possible to emerge as repetition (*SE*, XVIII:19). But Freud acknowledges that in his psychoanalytic practice he has observed patients "remember" or call up events from the past by repeating such repressed material as a contemporary experience.[16] If one takes this observation seriously, Freud notes, then there really are some grounds for thinking "that there really does exist in the mind a compulsion to repeat which overrides the pleasure principle" (*SE*, XVIII:22).

The suggestiveness of Freud's thoughts on repetition for an interpretation of *Repetition* should already be clear, not so much in terms of Constantin or the young man but of Kierkegaard himself. For while Constantin's return to Berlin is not a repetition compulsion but a simple repetition experiment, *Repetition* seems in part to be indeed the product of a repetition compulsion on the part of Søren Kierkegaard. In repeated narratives of a mysteriously impossible love between a young man and young woman that run the course of his aesthetic authorship, Kierkegaard sometimes seems fixated on an uncompleted personal episode and to be working through its trauma by poetic-literary reenactment.

Freud went on to speculate about the relationship of the pleasure principle to freeing the mental apparatus entirely from excitation or else to keeping it as low as possible. The same line of thought leads him to speculate that the dynamism underlying both the pleasure principle and the compulsion to repeat is a desire to return to an original state. He does not use Constantin's Latin *redintegratio in statum pristinum*, but he says the same thing: underlying repetition is the desire to return to an original state. To keep matters clear, it must be immediately pointed out that Kierkegaard and Freud most certainly do not have the same original state in mind. For Freud it is a matter of returning to an original inorganic state, namely death, and thus repetition compulsion is about the death instinct (which is beyond the pleasure principle). For Kierkegaard (and as intimated by Constantin), the original state will be the *status pristinus* before original sin. For fallen humankind (in Kierkegaard's very orthodox Christian thinking), this translates as God relationship restored (and enhanced) by the incarnation and atonement of the Son of God. Freud and Kierkegaard run along parallel banks, but there is no convergence. If the longing for death that Freud discerns has a parallel but unstated category of longing for eternal life in Kierkegaard's thought, this is not at all to suggest that they are really the same. To go any further, one would have to reduce the one to the other, which would be unfair to both.[17]

If it is true that in the pseudonymous Constantin's *Repetition* we have a Kierkegaardian recollection and Freudian repetition, Kierkegaard's conscious thoughts still dominate the book and his own Christian metaphysical beliefs definitely diverge from the meta-psychological speculations of Freud. In short, the possible Freudian repetition in Kierkegaard's *Repetition* does not undercut the deeper meaning of the final work, even if one views its composition in relationship to a self-inflicted trauma on the author's part. Consideration of Freudian repetition and of the possibility of Freudian repetition in Kierkegaard himself may even indirectly underline the significance that Kierkegaard gave to repetition. For the work also manifests Kierkegaard's determination to overcome his ill-fated love affair and to point in the direction of the religious, to which unsublimated love has frequently been a distraction.[18] The meaning of Freudian repetition for Kierkegaard's concept of repetition is that there is no repetition by simply ignoring or forgetting—or repressing—experience. One can ultimately transcend one's starting point, but only if one sets out from it.

Real, existential repetition, toward which the book points in its exploration of itself as a word and concept, occurs, as we know, in the work. In fact it intervenes dramatically in the composition of both *Repetition* and *Fear and Trembling* Kierkegaard's own ruptured romance and engagement clearly stand in the background of the work. For the greater part of the composition time of the work, Kierkegaard wondered about the possibility of "getting back" (*Gjen-tagelse*) Regine Olsen. A dramatic and ironic repetition intervened when an engagement occurred again, only not with Søren Kierkegaard but with Schlegel (Regine's original intended fiancé before Kierkegaard wooed her). Because of that unanticipated event, Kierkegaard tore up the last pages of the original draft and substituted the current ending.[19] Reality thus intervened in the composition of fiction. The troubled young man gets himself back when he is freed of the mistaken object of his desire. He does not achieve full *redintegratio in statum pristinum*—the religious-level repetition that the work points toward—but it is at least an aesthetic and partial repetition and, ironically, precisely what Constantin had despaired of in part 1. In his May 31 letter the young man declares, "I am myself again. Here I have repetition; I understand everything, and life seems more beautiful to me than ever. It did indeed come like a thunderstorm" (*SKS*, 4:87; *R*, 220). At this point, the young man poetically-ecstatically fills in the content to Constantin's new philosophical category of repetition: "Is there not, then, a repetition? Did I not get everything double? Did I not get myself again and precisely in such a way that I might have a double sense of its meaning?" And he goes on to declare that "only repetition of the spirit is possible, even though it is never so perfect in time as in eternity, which is the true repetition" (*SKS*, 4:88; *R*, 221).

The elements of a concept are now all in place. Repetition is understood as the restoration of oneself, most perfectly in a religious sense and therefore in eternity, where Christian salvation is fully achieved. Yet if the young man has himself back in some sense, he does not mistake the repetition of freedom he has experienced for the religious repetition toward which it is pointing (and which Kierkegaard's subsequent writing will define as freedom from sinfulness and as restoration of the God relationship).

The foregoing would suggest that the full meaning of repetition is beyond the work. This is very true, as Kierkegaard and Constantin were both aware. It is also true in at least two other senses. First of all, Kierkegaard, through Constantin, posits a concept whose actualization is existential rather than conceptual. In contrast to the Hegelian system, it is not when one gets to the concept (*Begriff*) that one has attained the full meaning but in existence. Real repetition is beyond the concept. But even the concept is beyond the work. For *Repetition*, which logs the melancholy of the young man, penetrates to his deeper problem and to the deeper nature of his desire and then points beyond him. Constantin Constantius sees this much and identifies the religious nature of the young man's problem while commenting for himself, "I am unable to make a religious movement" (*SKS*, 4:57; *R*, 187). In doing such, the work goes beyond itself. It never suggests that the unexpected, ironic repetition (of personal freedom) experienced by the young man is the *full* meaning of repetition. It is in fact quite clearly otherwise. Constantin is aware that the deeper problem of the young man ultimately requires more than the courage to get free of the young woman. In an inkling of the depth toward which the love affair points, Constantin remarks, "If this is the way it is, then there is nothing left for him except to make a religious movement" (*SKS*, 4:54; *R*, 183).

What is this enigmatic little book about then? About repetition, of course, but also about movement and *motion*. The term figures in the opening sentence of the book: "When the Eleatics denied motion . . ." For *Repetition* begins with the problem of motion and ends with the problem of *making the movements*. For it is in that that full repetition consists—what the *Papirer* refer to as "second repetition," namely, sin (or shattered selfhood in relationship to God) and the problem of overcoming it.[20] A draft passage of *Repetition* in the *Papirer* states,

> The true repetition is eternity; however, that repetition (by being psychologically pursued so far that it vanishes for psychology as transcendent, as a religious movement by virtue of the absurd) . . . as soon as the issue is posed dogmatically will come to mean atonement.[21]

Repetition is about motion, then. And it is the motion already under way in the young man that originally captivated Constantin. His interest in and willingness to sympathize and even suffer with the young man are based on the recognition that "in his love the idea was indeed in motion" (*SKS*, 4:18; *R*, 140). And "the idea" he further acknowledges is far more exacting than even a beautiful woman (*SKS*, 4:18; *R*, 141). Constantin repeats this assessment in his second narrative about the young man's love story when he defends his interest in the young man—what he calls his "objective theoretical interest in people" in general but particularly "in everyone in whom the idea is in motion!" (*SKS*, 4:51; *R*, 180). Constantin implies thereby that this is not a visible universal condition. Against Hegel's *Phenomenology of Spirit*, Constantin is trying to make the point of the significance of the movement of spirit on the individual level, rather than on the global, world-historical plane.[22] Yet if he is interested in and focused on the individual spirit, he cannot get away from the philosophical and Christian language that would suggest that "the spirit" or "the idea" is the one same spirit and idea moving in each and therefore transcending individual ego. The "I" of Constantin and the "I" of the young man are, in varying degrees, aware of the idea in motion and propelling the young man beyond "the borders of the wondrous" into the realm of the religious. And, after unexpected freedom from the young girl, the young man declares in his May 31 letter, "I belong to the idea" (*SKS*, 4:88; *R*, 221). Henceforth he recognizes a transcendent source of his identity and a transcendent goal. The young man may or may not make the movement, and Constantin himself says he is unable to do so. But this, in Kierkegaard's thinking, is ultimately a matter of will, supplemented decisively by grace. Repetition is thus about both restoration and desire, not of course restoration of the young woman nor desire for *her*. Both Constantin and the young man realize that. Constantin additionally recognizes that true repetition in the fullest sense is not mere aesthetic repetition, that is, merely restored emotional freedom such as the young man experienced. The young man's repetition experience defined his desire only negatively, refining it into the recognition that it was "not she" and not woman. True repetition is a desire for a getting back of the Other, restoration of the God relationship. It is desire for the transcendent Other but, paradoxically, desire for restoration of a relationship that one cannot remember actually having.

What, then, is repetition? If we apply the lesson of the young man's experience (namely, "It is not she") to the unasked question ("What is the true object of the young man's desire?"), we may conclude that the answer has been there from the beginning: repetition as the self restored to a "timeless" perfection that is dependent upon time, namely a perfection lost in the past and to be recovered in the future. What are all the repetitions? They are part of a riddle that defines the concept "repetition" negatively and sketches it positively, all the while insisting in its jests on its own earnestness about the existential significance of the concept. The various kinds of repetition in the eponymous novella are a lot of deliberate commotion about a particular motion. The commotion draws one into the book and into its games but also propels the reader beyond the book where that motion is to be made, if any place. The work never establishes that religious repetition is real but only that it is not to be had in philosophy or in fiction, or even in a philosophical fiction like *Repetition* itself. As such, *Repetition* rings contemporary and holds up well with new literary theories. For not only is it an intriguing psychoanalytic rebus but also a deconstructionist's delight with a meaning repeatedly deferred.

In works written subsequent to *Repetition*, Kierkegaard continues to sketch the movements of the human spirit back to the religious *redintegratio in statum pristinum* postulated in *Repetition*. Other terms are introduced, but "repetition" does not disappear. The final point—or experiential reintegration—that Kierkegaard ultimately had in view is not only beyond *Repetition* but also beyond his own aesthetic writings. No description of religious completion is found in the works, although further points along the way are indicated and discussed in his nonpseudonymous religious discourses. The ending of *Repetition* is thus not the last word about repetition. Repetition as lived by the young man and conceptualized by Constantin goes well beyond the novella and is beyond the pleasure principle as well. And there can be no doubt that Kierkegaard at least would think of it as conceptually going beyond Freud's future work also.

Kierkegaard's impetuous engagement to Regine Olsen and then his laborious breaking of the engagement undoubtedly constituted an emotional trauma in Kierkegaard's life, as understood by contemporary psychology. His writings record not only his working out of the affair but also his literary transformation and elevation of it. As such, it is finally more than Freudian repetition, while certainly it is also an abreaction along Freudian lines. The elevation continued two years later in the large novella "'Guilty?'/'Not Guilty?'" that forms the largest part of the 1845 pseudonymous *Stages on Life's Way*, where the darkening spiritual crisis is explored.

7

Melancholia and the Religious: Beyond Repetitions

> In the Middle Ages a person saved his soul by telling his beads a certain number of times; if in a similar manner I could save my soul by repeating to myself the story of my sufferings, I would have been saved a long time ago.
>
> —"Quidam's Diary": Midnight, 14 June

> The reader who has read Constantin Constantius's little book will see that I have a certain resemblance to that author but nonetheless am very different.
>
> —Frater Taciturnus's "Letter to the Reader"

When a writer keeps repeating a story line, can he eventually convince the reader—or perhaps himself—that things had to develop in the way that they did? This is the almost inescapable question that emerges in contemplating the many variations of doomed engagement in Kierkegaard's pseudonymous writings.

In "'Guilty?'/'Not Guilty?'" Søren Kierkegaard pseudonymously once again recounts an unhappy love story just as he did in major portions of *Either/Or*, part 1, and *Repetition*. But in this work there are distinctive differences, despite striking similarities. In this large section of *Stages on Life's Way* (1845) that is really a stand-alone novel, he expanded a theme begun at the end of *Repetition*, namely, crisis in normal human existence as religious potential emerges in the personality. This particular crisis is that of a character blocked by enclosing reserve from normal human fulfillment in a conventional love relationship. The sweet melancholy of *Repetition*'s young man has now become a gloomy melancholia. However, while the story suggests that a combination of a dawning spiritual interest and enclosing reserve are the joint causes for the failed romance, there is really no reason for the reader to think that there is any necessary connection at all between enclosing reserve and the spiritual and religious. This story's suffering is in great part self-inflicted and also totally unnecessary to the fulfilling of a felt religious destiny, despite the narrator Frater Taciturnus's insistence to the contrary. But we will have to wade through a sea of repetitions to establish this point.

Kierkegaard appears in this work still to be extricating himself from his ill-considered engagement to Regine Olsen in 1841, in the same kind of repetition compulsion suggested in chapter 6. Kierkegaard's ongoing emotional problems of the time may affect the fact and the composition of "Quidam's Diary," but Kierkegaard's private life is not what the work is formally or ultimately about. Instead, it is about beginning to understand the religious dimension of the personality as revealed in a conflict between aesthetic and ethical categories, especially the clash between a romantic notion of elusive perfect love and the sober idea of a universal duty to marry. Many readers of Kierkegaard are so struck by the repeated love story that they mistakenly believe that Kierkegaard remained obsessed with it throughout the remainder of his short life. Despite continued exploration of the repeated love tale in the pages to follow, it cannot be emphasized enough that Kierkegaard, at least theoretically and theologically, did indeed reconcile earthly love and the religious by the time that he published *Works of Love* in 1847.[1]

Not only do the similarities and parallels between the 1843 novella and the 1845 novel provide further evidence of a literary repetition compulsion on the part of Søren Kierkegaard, but also Quidam himself seems to have some sense of this.[2] If indeed "'Guilty?'/'Not Guilty?'" is something of a literary repetition compulsion, one may question whether Kierkegaard really enjoys the sovereign control over his pseudonyms and the direction of the authorship that his 1848 composition *The Point of View for My Work as an Author* would suggest. For example, does his unconvincing theory of a religious crisis and development inextricably linked to enclosing reserve not ultimately work against him (viz., portraying the dynamism of the emerging religious) as it draws the reader's attention back to the pathos of the love affair itself? The repeated insistence that the religious has made normal human love impossible repeatedly fails to persuade. But while Kierkegaard's personal life seems to intrude into the text, in the end, his personal problems do not block his creative transformation of experience or negate the more important meaning that the work seeks to impart. In sum, if his tactic of retelling a love story in order to call attention to the religious does not work to explain away his or similar conduct, that does not per se invalidate his theory of religiously directed melancholia (*Tungsind*) and personal crisis sparking deeper religious subjectivity.

The problem in Kierkegaard's presentation arises when Taciturnus adds enclosing reserve as an essential element in the link of melancholia [*Tungsind*] with the religious, suggesting that inescapable isolation and the inability to sustain an earthly love form a unit with the religious. His insistence on linking enclosing reserve to the religious never amounts to a formal argument, and it can even lead the reader (and especially one familiar with previous versions of the love story) to suspect that the religious is being invoked as a dramatic, (self-)justifying cover for an isolating and debilitating personal reserve that is totally independent of the religious. Quidam would have us accept his retelling of the story as a (romantic) embrace of a once-and-still beloved, through the medium of recollection. Thus, religious impulse and love both survive in some form, and there is some kind of reconciliation after all—but only in the pseudonymous speaker's mind! Indeed, this line of interpretation would bring us back to the aesthetic categories of *Repetition* or even to the young man (Aesthete A) of *Either/Or*, part 1. But Quidam is beyond the sweet, idle melancholy of that young man and well into the religious crisis that Constantin foretold for the young man of *Repetition*. In his brooding melancholia, Quidam attempts to justify himself to himself (guilty?/not guilty?). His answer does not satisfy himself after all, and the answer should not satisfy us. Nonetheless, it contains insights into his predicament and complex psychology.

Overview of the Diary

"'Guilty?'/'Not Guilty?'" purports to be an anonymous diary fished out of Søborg Lake by Frater Taciturnus, stitched together by Hilarius Bookbinder along with the other manuscripts that constitute *Stages on Life's Way*, and then brought to the public. Its purported publication history is a tale of literary and psychological distancing, from Frater Taciturnus, who is not quiet, from Hilarius, who does not laugh, and from Søren Kierkegaard, who is more than a little severe (Severinus) with the central character.[3] It is a noisy narrative of "Someone's" (Quidam) self-torment, vacillating between self-accusation and self-justification, a tale of gloom and foreboding. Not a happy business at all. While not the best of Kierkegaard's literary works, it has moments of literary sparkle and psychological brilliance.[4]

"'Guilty?'/'Not Guilty?'" constitutes almost two-thirds of the mass of *Stages on Life's Way*.[5] Within "'Guilty?'/'Not Guilty?'" the morning and midnight diary entries ("Quidam's Diary") form two-thirds of the novel, with the remaining portion being a nearly hundred-page-long letter to the reader. The morning and midnight diary entries are placed in a kind of counterpoint. As in musical counterpoint, the whole can be less interesting when reduced to its parts: when the upper and lower "lines" are played separately. Nonetheless, the experiment is worth making. For the separate morning and midnight diaries, now intertwined, are supposed to report different years and different stages in the intensification of religious crisis. The morning entries actually stand alone quite well as a separate composition.[6] In contrast, the midnight entries, read alone, are unrelieved gloom and a tune that one would soon tire of. The ending section, Frater Taciturnus's long "Letter to the Reader," is reminiscent of the long-winded letters of Judge William in *Either/Or*, part 2.[7]

"'Guilty?'/'Not Guilty?'" is more than a recapitulation of the psychology of *Repetition.* It is a clear, deliberate advance beyond it and the psychology of *Either/Or* as well. The differences, even expressed in parallels, point to this.

"'Guilty?'/'Not Guilty?'" could at first glance seem to be a diary reworking of *Repetition*, with the emotionally distant Quidam now as subject and author, overheard by the "Silent Brother" (Frater Taciturnus), who is a more stable ("constant") listener than Constantin and does not intrude himself constantly into the story. But it is not. For between them there is no relationship (of confiding, fleeing, reconciliation) such as characterizes the almost clinical relationship of "analyst" Constantin and "patient" young man in *Repetition.* The Latinate Quidam writes only to himself about the unnamed Quaedam (feminine Someone). If one takes the epistolary novella *Repetition* and the diary-novel "'Guilty?'/'Not Guilty?'" as mirrored images of the love story, the latter must be regarded as "through a glass darkly," and this is nowhere more darkly reflected than in the term *Tungsind* (melancholia) that characterizes the latter work, in contrast to the *Melancholi* (melancholy) that marks *Repetition.* To rejoin the music metaphor, if *Repetition* is the love story in the key of *Melancholi*, "'Guilty?'/'Not Guilty?'" is the love story in the key of *Tungsind.*

Linkages abound. The title for "'Guilty?'/'Not Guilty?'" comes from *Repetition* itself, where the October 11 letter of the young man asks, "How did it happen that I became guilty? Or am I not guilty?" (*SKS*, 4:68; *R*, 200.) What was only a rhetorical question in the novella has become the haunting question of the novel. The subtitles of both works are also close: "A Venture in Experimenting Psychology" (*Repetition*) and "A Psychological Experiment" ("'Guilty?'/'Not Guilty?'").[8]

The pronoun "I" is "overused" in both books and is excessive even by letter and diary standards.[9] In fact, *Repetition* and *Stages on Life's Way* are literally the most egocentric books in the aesthetic body, even though neither "I" is ever named. ("Young man" and "Quidam" are as close as we get, the latter, as has been observed, only an indefinite pronoun.) Each young man's entries are for a seven-month period (August to February in *Repetition*; January to July in "'Guilty?'/'Not Guilty?'").[10] Constantin tells the story of a young man's engagement a year before; the morning diary tells of Quidam's engagement a year previous. Both works end with concluding letters by the editor, who meantime has tried to reduce the engagement chronicler to a fiction. *Repetition* is ambiguous about whether the young man is ultimately a fiction, whereas Frater Taciturnus's "Letter" portrays Quidam as his literary product.

Repetition is about a love story still unfolding. We expect the past tense (since it too is the story of a year ago), but as it unfolds into the concluding pages (and beyond) of the book, we get the present. The morning diary of "'Guilty?'/'Not Guilty?'" is about the previous year. Where we expect a declared diary entry to be about that day (the meaning of "diary" after all), we get a "diary" of the past in the present tense. For the morning diary is really a recollection of events of a year ago and a discernment of their meaning a year later, on the day of the diary entry. The brooding midnight entries are about the enduring effects felt a year later.

Each book alludes to the religious character of the base problem of each young man. In *Repetition* it only begins to break through; in "'Guilty?'/'Not Guilty?'" it is the very starting point. For the "Diary" begins with the foreboding melancholiac (*tungsindig*) recognition that the religious is at the bottom of Quidam's problems. *Repetition* was about *redintegratio in statum pristinum*, which is how it defines repetition. Taciturnus tells the reader at the end of "'Guilty?'/'Not Guilty?'" that he has Quidam expect everything to end in a *restitutio in integrum*, or restored self-unity (*SKS*, 6:401; *SLW*, 434), which is fairly synonymous.

In both works, Kierkegaard's implied thesis is that a love wound shatters life lived in aesthetic categories only and, by degrees, necessitates confrontation with a higher possibility, namely, the religious. But whereas this message is announced in *Repetition*, it is boomingly declared in "'Guilty?'/'Not Guilty?'"

Key differences emerge in the "Quidam's Diary." It is even more solipsistic than *Repetition*. For *Repetition* was at least addressed to another, and the relationship between the young man and Constantin provides some relief from the ever-present "I." In the "Diary," there is no such other. Neither the author nor the reader has any relief from the self-torturer who writes in the morning about today a year ago (in a misrelation to time?) and then at midnight about his state of mind that day, when the day is done. In the morning, he narrates his way out of a precipitous engagement a year ago, but as if it were today. At midnight, he stews over the aftermath a year later. This is a fuller and darker sketch of the divided self first sketched in *Either/Or*, part 1. The "Diary" is a kind of literary schizophrenia. All of this only highlights the crisis—the vague, religious crisis—that has been heating up (since the "Diapsalmata") and is now coming to a critical point.

Morning Entries

The morning diary purports to be the "reminiscence diary" of Quidam, written a year after the events narrated (although, with only one exception, in the present tense). In counterpoint to it is the much larger midnight diary, which is "really" today.

Thus the diary's interlaced and confusing chronicle of unraveling romance and enduring aftereffects mirror the misrelation to time first presented in *Either/Or*, part 1. Technically, the morning and midnight diaries begin in year two, five months after the July rupture in year one. But, even the "one year ago" recollections of the morning diary are not the actual beginnings, for he admits to having seen her a full year before the morning-chronicled love pursuit took place, and perhaps that should be the true year one. By the time the diary ends, we cannot feel that the story is over. In fact, we might expect a sequel, in January of year three, that begins, "Two years ago . . ."! For the essential problem, whatever it is, is still unresolved, even if implosion seems imminent. As if to suggest this very point, the ending entry on July 7 predicts, "The third of January the unrest begins again" (*SKS*, 6:367; *SLW*, 396).

Meantime, the first entry, that of January 3 in year two, sets out the essential problem, both as it existed "then" (a year ago) and as it exists "today": a young man of powerful religious sensitivity is afflicted by a melancholia (*Tungsind*) that is linked to his religious nature and the unspecified religious direction in which it impels him. It is a lonely, individualizing problem. Meantime he struggles with the more conventional universal-human possibility of marriage. The religious impulse and the romantic instinct are held to be in conflict: "Should a soldier stationed at the spiritual frontier marry? Does a soldier stationed at the frontier, spiritually understood, dare to marry—an outpost who battles, night and day . . . with the robber bands of a primordial [*Tungsind*]?" (*SKS*, 6:183; *SLW*, 195).

One does not need the midnight entries to see that the relationship is doomed from the beginning. But underlining the doomed quality of the relationship is the midnight entry of January 5 on quiet despair.

Quidam's relationship to the young girl is a kind of macho romanticism that proves itself, in hindsight, to be inadequate.[11] She does not understand him, as he recognizes. This was the problem all along. He sees that it makes a married relationship impossible. It never occurs to him that his problem with marriage might be the unrealistic romanticism that leads a young man to single out a young lady who is allowed to be nothing more than the projection of sweet love fancies. It never occurs to him that he is a victim of the unreal social ideas of his age concerning romantic love. The ideas of a bygone age might have been less dangerous. Had he had an arranged marriage, he might have done his duty and done very well. But in rejecting the nineteenth century's self-deceiving idea of dreamy all-fulfilling love, he also rejects a young woman whose only guilt may be that she too is influenced by this idea. But now she is to become the occasion of self-growth for him (just as the young girl of *Repetition* played a parallel role in that work). We never come to know either young girl, and Quidam did not know her well either. For he declares that he will not stoop to know her by testing and investigating her nature (*SKS*, 6:194; *SLW*, 207)—although we are eventually told that her lack of religious presuppositions removes any basis for the relationship (January 25; *SKS*, 6:211; *SLW*, 226). He is *Tungsind*, and she is the symbol of joy (*Glæden*) (*SKS*, 6:185; *SLW*, 197).

The doomed engagement takes place on January 12 and immediately begins to unravel. He remarks paradoxically that their union is so new that they are separated by the nothing that they have in common, "Lovers ought to have no differences [*Mellemværende*] between them. Alas, alas, we have been united too briefly to have any differences. We have nothing between us, and yet we have a world between us, exactly a world" (*SKS*, 6:202; *SLW*, 216). By January 17, he has a presentiment that it will not work, that it is already over, and that it was over before it began: "It is not with her, it is not with Eros that I must struggle. It is religious crises that are gathering over me. My life view has become ambiguous" (*SKS*, 6:202; *SLW*, 216). By January, he has made his choice: "So I have chosen the religious" (*SKS*, 6:207; *SLW*, 222), and three days later he invokes her lack of religious presuppositions as justifying the break that is coming.

By February 12, he is reading religious books to her, even though he had earlier acknowledged that her lack of religious presuppositions could not be countered by his becoming her religion teacher. He notes that it is not working: she is not attentive. And, meantime, "I myself am growing more and more in the direction of the religious" (*SKS*, 6:224; *SLW*, 240).

When he acknowledges his enclosing reserve (*Indesluttethed*) and its being "an elemental flaw" (*SKS*, 6:225; *SLW*, 241), he comes closer to stating what is, for most, a more comprehensible grounds for his inability to sustain (or even form) a genuine relationship with the unfortunate young girl. Indeed, here he makes a telling self-disclosure about his enclosing reserve, whose very problem, he tells us ironically, is *disclosure* itself. He reveals that enclosing reserve cannot reveal itself and therefore cannot form a union with another.[12] The language of enclosing reserve is, expectably, self-referential. It does not really reach out to another. Hence it is *monologue*, not dialogue.[13] And the reader should not take the diaries for free communication or dialogue. They were never intended for an audience, either by the fictional Quidam or his fictional creator Frater Taciturnus. Hilarius Bookbinder claims to have fished them out of a lake. For all the apparent self-disclosure in recognizing *Indesluttethed* as his problem, there is no hint of real self-transparency on Quidam's part. In the end, his invocation of enclosing reserve is more elemental than he realizes. In it resides the fatal obstacle to love, for, as Haufniensis observed, enclosing reserve is demonic. It is the very opposite of marriage, which Judge William, in *Either/Or*, part 2, called the very symbol of ethical existence. Yes enclosing reserve and all that it represents (unfreedom, being locked up in oneself, unable to open to another) would seem to be Quidam's real problem. However, Quidam has confused his inability to sustain a love relationship with the religious.

By February 20, he is acknowledging the misrelation, sees that she is unhappy, and asks her forgiveness for sweeping her into it. By February 28, he declares, "Courage and perseverance! I shall reach the religious with her" (*SKS*, 6:231; *SLW*, 248), but by which he means "by means of her," not "along with her."

By March 5, he observes that there are "no new symptoms" and repeats this in the next two entries, March 9 and 20. The entry of March 25 has the lovely, melancholy contrast of a young girl sixteen summers old and her young man, who is twenty-five winters old.

By April, the relationship is outwardly coming apart as well, and he reassures himself that the religious is the reason. On April 17 he writes, "The trouble is that she has no religious presuppositions at all" (*SKS*, 6:287; *SLW*, 309), but on April 10, he sums up the solitariness of his religious thinking when he writes, "Spiritually it is with an individuality as it is grammatically with a sentence: a sentence that consists only of a subject and a predicate is easier to construct" (*SKS*, 6:276; *SLW*, 297–98). One senses that his notion of predicates is limited to intransitive verbs, that is, verbs that have no object.

Whatever problems we may have with his solipsistic or narcissistic notion of the religious, he, for his part, sets it emphatically as the obstacle. April 24: "She has no sensitivity whatsoever to the motives I consider to be supreme" (*SKS*, 6:292; *SLW*, 314). April 26: "The deepest breathing of my spirit existence I cannot do without, I cannot sacrifice, because that is a contradiction, since without it I indeed am not. And she feels no need for this breathing" (*SKS*, 6:292; *SLW*, 315).

By May, there is open talk of rupture, and on May 8 he proposes breaking the engagement, a process that will consume the final two months of entries as the diary shifts to a chronicle of dissolution in weekly installments.

On May 30 he explicitly links his enclosing reserve and his melancholia. It is repeated in the final morning entry of July 7: "My life view was that I would hide my [melancholia, *Tungsind*] in my enclosing reserve." (*SKS*, 6:365; *SLW*, 394), that is, attempt never to share with anyone his darkening personal crisis pressing him toward a religious solution. This is nearer to the mark: enclosing reserve protecting the secret of his religiously directed melancholia.

Because he suffers from a combination of naïveté and the age's idealization of romantic love, it never occurs to him his problem might be that he had courted the wrong person. His romantic notion of only one possible beloved combines with a pride that tells him that he cannot have gotten it wrong. And so, *pace* Frater Taciturnus, the reason he could not marry Quaedam may be nothing more than a simple mismatch of Quidam and his Quaedam. In short, he did not have the good luck of a Papageno with his Papagena in *Either/Or*, part 1. But Quidam would have us believe that the fundamental reason is the religious. Yet everything in his narration would suggest that his emotional isolation, expressed as *Indesluttethed* (enclosing reserve), is more nearly the reason and that the inability to disclose oneself as one needs to do in a love relationship has no necessary connection to the religious at all, even if the deep inwardness of religious life is not readily disclosed to another.

In the end, his enclosing reserve (which Walter Lowrie's earlier English translation frequently rendered as "morbid reserve") probably rules out any relationship at all and would do so even if there were no attendant religious crisis. Quidam makes a believable religious crisis into the unbelievable reason for the breakup.

In sum, enclosing reserve is the root problem in the relationship, not the religious and not even melancholia (*Tungsind*). Who was supposed to be persuaded by these repeated attempts to make the religious the justification for a failed human relationship? Quidam, his reader, or Kierkegaard himself?

Midnight Entries

Five months after the rupture, Quidam struggles with his oversensitive conscience in his midnight thoughts. If the midnight entries are considered as counterpoint to the morning reminiscences, they are for the most part the same repetitious, gloomy melody, broken only by six thematic, titled pieces ("Quiet Despair" [January 5]; "A Leper's Self-

Contemplation" [February 5]; "Solomon's Dream" [March 5]; "A Possibility" [April 5]; "The Reading Lesson: Periander" [May 5]; "Nebuchadnezzar" [June 5]). The pattern of fifth-day midnight entries is one of the most striking structural elements of the diary.

The ghostly diarist worries about the young girl. He tells us that he goes to sleep at nine, to rise at midnight for his nocturnal brooding. "Who would not think me a fool if I told him that now in this current year she preoccupies me more than ever?" (*SKS*, 6:203; *SLW*, 217). According to him, he has her life on his conscience and feels like a murderer.

On February 2 he wonders whether he ever loved her, whether he might be too reflective (reserved) ever to love. But this instant of self-clarity vanishes as he asks himself why then all these sufferings and, as he seems ready to accept his suffering as the (romantic) proof that this must have been love, speculates that his tortured and haunted present must be the aftermath of a tragic love.

His repetition compulsion is clearly stated on March 7: "What is all this for? Why do I do it? Because I cannot do otherwise." But at least to his conscious mind this is not mere Freudian repetition compulsion. He has a higher and conscious reason: "I do it for the sake of the idea, for the sake of meaning, for I cannot live without an idea; I cannot bear that my life should have no meaning at all. The nothing I am doing still does provide a little meaning" (*SKS*, 6:236; *SLW*, 253).

His belief that his religious nature is the root of his inability to have continued or consummated the relationship is repeatedly stated. He dismisses her, this year as last,[14] for having no religious presuppositions (February 7; *SKS*, 6:220; *SLW*, 236). Yet he is ambivalent about this too and perhaps gives away the fact that her "nonreligious" nature is not the problem after all when he comments on April 29, "If she had become a religious individuality in the proper sense, it would have been frightful for me" (*SKS*, 6:296; *SLW*, 318). For then he would not have been able to use her lack of interest in the religious as a reason and he might have had to admit that his enclosing reserve alone was the cause. (The young girl never appears as a character in the novel. We see her only through Quidam's eyes.)

On March 7, he remarks that "only a relationship with God is the true idealizing friendship" (*SKS*, 6:236; *SLW*, 253). But he confesses that, whatever a religious person may be, he himself is not yet one: "I am really no religious individuality; I am just a regular and perfectly constructed possibility of such a person" (March 20; *SKS*, 6:240; *SLW*, 257). He declares his enduring need to work himself free of her even a year later in order to turn to "the religious crises" that will then be his task (*SKS*, 6:243; *SLW*, 261). However incorrectly he may understand himself, he does have a definite interpretation of his problem, and it is that his religious nature and impending religious crisis, compounded by Quaedam's lack of religious interest, make a continuation of the relationship impossible. But this is an interpretation after the fact. We have no record of his thoughts during the actual time of the rupture. (And we should not be fooled by the morning reminiscence diary.) Everything is "clearer" in retrospect, now that he has settled on a line of interpretation. Having done the incomprehensible deed of breaking off the relationship, he comments on May 27, "Only religiously can I now become intelligible to myself before God" (*SKS*, 6:326; *SLW*, 351). The rupture may intensify his emotional state and his separate religious crisis, but the religious is not therefore retroactively the cause. It is simple fallacious reasoning (*Post hoc ergo propter hoc*), and he must anticipate that his educated reader can see this.

He seems to come closest to self-transparency when he confesses, "My idea was to structure my life ethically in my innermost being and to conceal this inwardness in the form of deception. Now I am forced even further back into myself; my life is religiously structured and is so far back in inwardness that I have difficulty in making my way to actuality" (*SKS*, 6:327; *SLW*, 351).

Memories are never entirely to be trusted. Fictional recollections should be no exception. And so we should be wary of Quidam's recollections of the past, upon which he has attempted to impose a narrative structure and teleology: things not only happened, but they happened for a reason and lead on to a conclusion that, in retrospect, is now obvious. Quidam has perhaps convinced himself in his "Diary" and maybe Master Kierkegaard as well. Who is Frater Taciturnus hoping to convince?

The reasons given for why the love story could not endure, however many times Kierkegaard tells it, are ultimately more than unconvincing. The story betrays itself, repeatedly and by its repetitions, as having no rational justification for its outcome. If this has the effect of undercutting the attempt to portray a religiously awakening Quidam as tragically unable to marry a Quaedam and reduces it to the probable mismatch of an undefined young girl who agreed to marry a man she hardly knew but who turns out to be emotionally inaccessible, this does not render it comic either, but only very human, both in its confused, irrational dynamism and in the attempt to elevate it to something higher after the fact.[15]

But does the unpersuasiveness of Kierkegaard's intended interpretation of the love story necessarily undercut the meaning Kierkegaard wants to give it? Not at all. For there is no reason to dispute the religious sensibility and divine eros that drives Quidam, only his contention that his brief but haunting romance was made impossible by the religious rather than by his enclosing reserve. However, Quidam himself seems to sense something of this, or else he would not be struggling with Frater Taciturnus's title, "'Guilty?'/'Not Guilty?'"

Even if we do not accept Quidam's self-serving romantic analysis of his religious nature as precluding marriage, we should not pass over the more important point that he is clearly trying to make: that he is a religious individuality, struggling with his religious nature and its unclearly seen but definitely sensed directedness. In his "Letter to the Reader," Frater Taciturnus will counsel studying him even in his excess: "Yet it may well have its importance to pay attention to him, because one is able to study the normal in the aberration" (*SKS*, 6:369; *SLW*, 398).

The Six "Short Articles"

The themes of the six midnight tales sketch enclosing reserve from various angles (despair, secret disease, secret sin, etc.) constitute a series of maudlin reflections.[16]

January 5 is the "voice of quiet despair," about the son who recovers the lost intimacy he had with his now deceased father by imitating his father's voice and saying to himself, as his father once said to him, "Poor child, you are in a quiet despair." Ironically, listening to his father's words is a source of comfort. But of course the voice is really his own—or perhaps an "impersonal," higher voice that belongs to more than father and son. But it is anything but a message of comfort.

February 5 ("A Leper's Self-Contemplation") is a tale of solitude and self-mastery. The disoriented leper Simon calls to and answers himself, reproaching himself for having concocted a salve by which the mutilation of leprosy could be turned inward. But the leper renounces its use and therefore voluntarily suffers the fate of external mutilation.

March 5 ("Solomon's Dream") is the tale of a son discovering that the father is in despair (thus a kind of mirror image of January 5). A son steals a glimpse of his father's secret despair, normally obscured by worldly success and esteem, and dreams that the worldly achievement is not God's blessing of a chosen one but an ungodly man's punishment sharply intensified—for both father and son—by the world's misconstruing worldly station as indicating God's favor.

April 5 ("A Possibility") takes place in Christianshavn, then isolated from Copenhagen and accessed by a narrow bridge, a place where "one feels abandoned and imprisoned in the stillness that isolates." It is the tale of a possibility that haunts and isolates, that renders mad and wise at the same time. The melancholy entry (*SKS*, 6:257–68; *SLW*, 276–288) describes a strange, shy, rich, and mentally disordered young man who loves children and, in the secrecy of his apartment, collects sketches of children's faces for reasons that will come to light when he recovers a (questionable) repressed memory of having been led to a whorehouse once by friends. Now he fears the possibility of having fathered a child, of having responsibility for the life of another. And so he examines the faces of urchins.

His elder cousin thoughtlessly comments about a man never knowing for sure how many children he has, and the young man shudders in recognition. When he gives alms to street children, he is tormented by the possible and horrifying irony of giving alms to his own unknown child. It is the tale of psychological self-torment, of a sickbed fantasy coming back to haunt someone who is supposed to be in restored health.

May 5 ("The Reading Lesson: Periander") tells of a schizophrenic monster personality, one who has slept with his mother, killed his wife, alienated and bullied his children, and inadvertently brought about the murder of his son. He is a revolting figure, a symbol of alienation and isolation. Only in plotting his own death, as escape from life, does he briefly negate the split in his being as he unites in one act his wise side and his tyrannical side. For concealing his true identity, he has the good sense to have himself assassinated and buried anonymously. But as part of the plot and to seal his anonymous burial, he has the assassins also killed.

June 5 ("Nebuchadnezzar") is the tale of the king of Babylon changed in a dream into an ox for seven years. Defenseless against the power of God, alienated, and his true identity unrecognized by others, he cries out, "My thoughts terrified me, my thoughts in my mind, for my mouth was bound and no one could discern anything but a voice similar to an animal's" (*SKS*, 6:335; *SLW*, 361).

The net effect of these entries is to underline the gloom of Quidam, who is haunted both day and night by memories and dreams, unable to live in the present, holding off a crisis that ultimately cannot be escaped and for which he pays dearly in the meantime in self-inflicted torment.

Frater Taciturnus's "Letter"

The taciturn brother weighs in with a lengthy letter that makes no secret of his willful view of the story that he presents. For his "Letter" brings with it his own insistent interpretation of Quidam's tale, not just about melancholia [*Tungsind*] directed toward the religious but also about the role of enclosing reserve. It was already implicit in "Quidam's Diary"; in the

"Letter," it becomes explicit. Taciturnus's first tack is to portray the story as an unhappy love, doomed by misunderstanding between the two principals because the young man exists in (potential) religious categories, while the young woman lives solely in aesthetic categories (*SKS*, 6:389; *SLW*, 420). "Unhappy love implies that love is assumed and that there is a power that prevents it from expressing itself happily in the lovers' union" (*SKS*, 6:375; *SLW*, 405). But what is this power? Frater Taciturnus will want to insist that it is his religious calling. The more skeptical reader will find that enclosing reserve is sufficient explanation. Taciturnus describes Quidam as "a demoniac character in the direction of the religious—that is, tending toward it" (*SKS*, 6:369; *SLW*, 398). In order to emphasize it, he makes the same point again but negatively when he informs the reader that the book is not about the erotic like Constantin Constantius's tale in *Repetition* (*SKS*, 6:373; *SLW*, 402). For *Repetition* was about a collision within the aesthetic. "'Guilty?'/'Not Guilty?'" according to Taciturnus, depicts a collision between a young girl also within aesthetic categories and a darker young man who is "in the power of spirit in the direction of the religious" (*SKS*, 6:389; *SLW*, 420). There can be no mutual understanding, essential for a love union, since she cannot understand his deeper inner life. So argues Taciturnus.

To the extent that the issue is the religious, perhaps Taciturnus has not just *Repetition* in mind but the more famous book issued the same day, namely, *Fear and Trembling*. There Abraham is justified by virtue of the religious. However, the religious inwardness of Abraham is depicted there as merely incommunicable. (It does not make his marriage to Sarah impossible, although it does of course present difficulties.) Taciturnus replaces the merely incommunicable with the more problematical category of enclosing reserve.

For Taciturnus, Quidam's *Tungsind* is nothing less than "the crisis prior to the religious" (*SKS*, 6:398; *SLW*, 430), as he attempts to suggest a necessary link between enclosing reserve and *Tungsind*.[17] He comments that enclosing reserve is a form of *Tungsind* and that *Tungsind* is "the condensed possibility that must be experienced through a crisis in order that he can become clear to himself in the religious" (*SKS*, 6:396; *SLW*, 427). In sum: a crisis must be experienced in movement toward the religious, *Tungsind* is that crisis, and enclosing reserve is an aspect of *Tungsind*. But is it a necessary and universal quality of *Tungsind*? Otherwise put: must every individual facing his religious potential in a crisis of gloomy melancholia (*Tungsind*) also struggle with enclosing reserve? If one accepts this unqualified linkage, then Quidam's moral quandary and emotional-psychological impediment may be absolved by being linked to the religious. However, while the link of *Tungsind* and the religious holds, the suggestion of a universal link of enclosing reserve and the religious seems unnecessary, even if enclosing reserve seems to be a genuine personal problem of one individual, namely Quidam. Enclosing reserve is simply a separate problem from the religious, even if it should prove to be a possible symptom sometimes accompanying the brooding melancholia of *Tungsind.*

In his commentary, Taciturnus goes on to state that Quidam's reserve is the "condensed anticipation of the religious subjectivity" (*SKS*, 6:396; *SLW*, 428). This might allow for the possibility that, once the religious crisis is over and religious subjectivity achieved (*if* achieved), Quidam might be able to come out of his reserve. But nowhere does Taciturnus suggest anything of the kind. And, in fact, the character of Quidam would not hold out this hope either. Were we to imagine him as having completed and resolved his religious crisis, we cannot imagine him as outwardly changed. We can imagine only that he would remain as reserved as ever and have to find some new reason for his isolating reserve. Taciturnus's psychological experiment never systematically explores enclosing reserve. And while Taciturnus maintains that "there is no real healing for him except religiously within himself" (*SKS*, 6:397; *SLW*, 428), he does not suggest that enclosing reserve is itself ever healed or overcome.

Taciturnus speaks of deception on the part of the young man in trying to exit from the relationship. Yet Taciturnus's "Letter," and the whole of "'Guilty?'/'Not Guilty?'" with it, is a kind of deception too: the claim that the religious can now account for the end of a romantic mismatch in a way that the melancholy aesthetic categories of *Repetition* could not. In the process, the linkage between darker melancholia, expressed in the word *Tungsind,* and a religious crisis is established as an important point in Kierkegaard's developing religious psychology. But the invocation of the religious still leaves the secret of enclosing reserve intact. The interlacing of the religious, enclosing reserve, and unhappy love is a dramatic tangle. But it fails to convince those of subsequent times that things had to end as they did.

Kierkegaard's various meditations on impeded or impossible earthly love suggest numerous questions about the object/Object of human desire. In the human desire for a beloved, is there really also some dawning revelation of a greater dynamic of desire? In the insufficiency of the object/s of human desire, is there also a pointer or a pointing toward a greater Object? If so, does the Object represent a spiritual oasis in the parched desert of desire, or only a spiritual mirage? Kierkegaard surely believes in the spiritual oasis, yet through his pseudonyms he conducts his readers through only a tour of earthly mirages.

Kierkegaard's story of failed personal fulfillment—transformed into literature, told repeatedly in different modes, and claiming to point beyond itself—may be a compulsive attempt to justify himself for his irrational conduct in breaking a rashly conceived engagement. But it is also recollection of an older religious truth, triggered by this personal trauma and approached from different angles ("The Seducer's Diary," *Repetition*, *Fear and Trembling*, "'Guilty?'/'Not Guilty?'") as the trauma is reenacted in literary variations. It is ultimately a revelation about the nature and telos of desire that sees beyond itself and its initial object.

Works of Love, published under his own name in 1847, makes clear that Kierkegaard recognized that love of the other is at the center of the Christian message and of the religious life, Christianly understood. Yet the force of his fixation in the aesthetic writings is to make us wonder whether or not he ever successfully reconciled the two in his own life, or whether the enclosing reserve remained a personal emotional obstacle in moving from the *theory* of religious living to *practice* in Christianity.

8

The Dark Ground of Anxiety: Kierkegaard and Schelling

Kierkegaard's *The Concept of Anxiety* is first and foremost a philosophical excursion through human possibility. Highly abstract and speculative, it is deeply insightful in its psychological exploration of the awed experience of unactualized human possibility. This is the only sense in which Vigilius Haufniensis, his pseudonym for this work, considers anxiety, while anxiety clearly has a broader, if often indefinite, meaning. Kierkegaard's work focuses on an analysis of the individual's discovery of him- or herself in a critical state of anxiety—beginning in the existential sense of diminished possibility and its manifestations as a self-inflicted wound—and then discerns in the anxiety experience an intentionality or directedness toward self-recovery. But the work also considers the abstract "history" of human possibility and the fateful sin of Adam that on the one hand theologically actualized a possibility (namely, sin) and on the other hand existentially narrowed human possibilities down to the twofold option of continuing in the same state or else getting out of it. Quite significantly in a Christian author, however, it rejects any notion that human failing, or sinfulness, is the result of inheritance, of any action by Adam.[1] Rather, in the spirit of Enlightenment rationalism, Kierkegaard's pseudonymous Vigilius Haufniensis shows that sin is and must be each human person's own deed. The fact of sin, existentially understood, and the fact of narrowed human possibility are the actual starting point for his 1844 work. Its speculations are probably unconvincing for a contemporary audience, which may not even accept the category of sin, no less the idea that there was a fateful first sin on the part of the first human. Nonetheless, it is valuable as an attempt to make existential sense out of the troublesome Christian teaching of original sin to show that the underlying tale of an Adam and an original sin can still make sense, but only as a mythological portrayal of a deed that everyone has done him- or herself, not a deed done by a historical Adam alone. Despite all the speculative activity in the book, it should be emphasized that its confessed main interest remains existential: cultivating the consciousness, seriousness, and commitment in individuals needed to recover lost possibility and so to fulfill their highest possibility.

Although Kierkegaard's *The Concept of Anxiety* begins formally and theologically as a reflection upon the first human sin, it quickly directs itself to the more profound question of the origins of *all* sin. It proceeds to analyze the structure of the human spirit that makes both sin and overcoming sin possible. It holds that freedom and possibility are central to the essence of the human spirit and explores them as theoretical categories for the sake of existential understanding and follow-up in action.

Kierkegaard is by no means the first or only modern thinker to be concerned with sin, possibility, and freedom, or the relation among them. Kant's "On the Radical Evil in Human Nature" (part 1 of *Religion within the Limits of Reason Alone*, 1793) had considered these same subjects and had also philosophically reinterpreted the theological notion of inheriting Adam's first sin. Kant, for his part, established through a kind of introspective speculation that one's feeling of fallenness and accountability for fall point to a personal deed of one's own whose elements can be discerned with intellectual certainty, even if the when and why of such a deed can never be made entirely clear.

The theodicy question of the eighteenth century about the question of the origin and responsibility for evil was thereby partially answered: humankind is responsible for moral evils and for its diminished state or fall. Sixteen years later, the young philosopher Schelling published a work whose distinctiveness was only much later appreciated, his *Treatise on the Essence of Human Freedom* (1809; hereafter cited as the *Freiheitsschrift*).[2] In publishing his work on freedom, Schelling was emphatically breaking with the still emerging idealist movement just as it was completing its transition from subjective idealism (in Fichte) to objective idealism (in Hegel). In this early work Schelling too sought to explain moral evil, lay the blame at the human door, and in the process acquit God of any share in it. His approach was unique and suggestive in that it acknowledged evil as real and, more striking still, as part of a total reality whose ultimate source was God. Moreover, it did so in such a way that God was viewed as the ground and source of all possibility, including therefore the possibility of evil. This work eventually influenced Kierkegaard's own consideration.

Kierkegaard took up the themes of freedom and fall in his 1844 *The Concept of Anxiety*, with his own special emphases. He was interested in a better explanation than the "inherited sin" of dogmatic theology, and he was concerned with observing, via speculative reconstruction, the movements into sin but with the added practical interest of pointing toward the overcoming of sin. Kierkegaard's treatment of freedom and fall is part of a continuum in modern philosophy that includes Kant, Fichte, Schelling, and also Hegel.[3] On the subject of freedom, the torch passes from Schelling to Kierkegaard (unbeknownst to both), and the treatment of fall is an outgrowth of their respective conceptions of freedom and of their adherence to orthodox Christian interpretation.

Kierkegaard and Schelling

Kierkegaard attended Schelling's Berlin lectures on the philosophy of revelation from November 1841 until about February 4, 1842, when his *Referat*, or lecture notes, break off.[4] Schelling's lectures in Berlin were something of an intellectual event, for Schelling had been summoned out of retirement in Munich by an invitation of the Prussian king Frederick William IV and famously tasked with nothing less than "driving out the dragon tooth of Hegelian pantheism," ten years after Hegel's death in 1831. Much was expected, and the audience included others besides Kierkegaard who were destined for fame in European thought, including Engels and Jacob Burckhardt. Kierkegaard hoped for great things, was originally thrilled to hear the word "actuality" at last uttered in a contemporary philosophy lecture, but was soon disappointed.

Although Kierkegaard's letter of February 6, 1842, to his friend Emil Boesen says that he will return to Copenhagen when Schelling has finished and that he expects this to be in the spring, his letter of February 27 announces his imminent plans to leave Berlin. An undated letter of the same month to his brother Peter complains that Schelling is taking longer than expected (*LD*, 141), derides the lecturer for talking "the most insufferable nonsense," and declares his intention to leave Berlin for Copenhagen as soon as possible.

The lecture notes kept by Kierkegaard cease at the point where Schelling is reviewing the relation of his philosophy of mythology to his philosophy of revelation. Kierkegaard thus heard Schelling up to lecture 19 in the published version of the philosophy of revelation.[5] Consequently, Kierkegaard did not hear Schelling's formal treatment of Christianity with its curious sections on philosophical theogony (the genesis of God) and "Logogony" (the genesis of the Logos).

Why rehearse such details? The reason is simple: of all the German thinkers whom Kierkegaard learned from and reacted to, Schelling is the only one whom Kierkegaard actually heard and saw. However, the full story of Kierkegaard's encounter with Schelling's philosophy has not received the attention it deserves, in part perhaps because of a preoccupation with Hegel in Kierkegaard studies.[6] Indeed, the themes of *The Concept of Anxiety* suggest careful comparison with Schelling. But there is an additional reason that singles out this particular Kierkegaard work for beginning a Kierkegaard-Schelling comparison: of the eleven references to Schelling in Kierkegaard's published works, nine of them occur in *The Concept of Anxiety*.[7]

Despite the cocky young Kierkegaard's 1842 dismissal of the elderly Schelling, there are resonances and striking similarities with Schelling's ideas in his subsequent works. A draft introduction to *Repetition* in 1843[8] refers several times to Schelling's 1809 essay on human freedom.[9] It is not possible to determine with certainty from these references when precisely Kierkegaard read the essay, whether before or after his encounter with Schelling in Berlin. Based on the 1843 publication date of two works by Rosenkranz on Schelling, works that Kierkegaard read and referred to in writings of this period (*Sendschreiben an P. Leroux über Schelling und Hegel* and *Vorlesungen über Schelling*), I believe that Kierkegaard's emphasis on Schelling in his drafts and publications of 1843–44 suggests a careful reading of the *Freiheitsschrift* in 1843 subsequent to his first Berlin visit, or perhaps a rereading prompted by Rosenkranz's works. In addition, it would be most unlikely that this important Schelling work, which had not received much comment at the time of its publication in 1809, would have come much earlier to the attention of a faraway Dane—hence, an even stronger reason for leaning toward the theory of a later reading.

The most important aspect of the *Freiheitsschrift* for purposes here is the notion of good and evil presented in it in relation to the all-important fact of human freedom. Had Kierkegaard kept reading notes on this work, they would have been enormously valuable in assessing Kierkegaard in his critique of idealism, since the *Freiheitsschrift* was the attempted slaying of idealism by one of its founding figures. In it, as Martin Heidegger has noted, Schelling saw through the problems of idealist metaphysics long before Hegel's *Logic* was set to paper.[10] Yet Kierkegaard does not seem to have perceived Schelling's accomplishment, nor is Schelling invoked in Kierkegaard's criticism of Hegel.[11]

Schelling considered his philosophy of revelation to be a "positive philosophy" and a philosophy of freedom. It was to be "positive" in contrast to the "negative" that, in Schelling's view, had culminated in Hegel. Its very fundament was to be freedom—and this in conscious antithesis to the category of necessity in the Hegelian system. On the basis of this fundament, a fully detailed philosophy of freedom was to be constructed, of which the philosophy of revelation would be the culminating section. The philosophy of revelation is, however, the only section that is complete, and it is not a polished piece. A full positive philosophy or philosophy of freedom would require a philosophy of existence, which Schelling did not supply. (Heidegger comments that this ambition is tantamount to a squared circle,[12] and Kierkegaard, without any reference to Schelling on this point, declares that a system of existence is impossible [*SKS*, 7:104; *CUP*, 107] precisely because of freedom.)

The application of the philosophy of freedom in the philosophy of revelation is indeed curious at times, but it bears reviewing precisely because Kierkegaard listened to it in 1841 and then wrote about some of the same themes in 1843 and 1844. The philosophy of freedom expressed in 1841 develops an earlier effort in Schelling's unpublished Munich lectures of 1831 and is an outgrowth of the more important *Freiheitsschrift*. But the discussion of Schelling's works here will follow the order in which I believe Kierkegaard came to know them. Hence, I proceed from the 1841 lectures on the philosophy of revelation to the *Freiheitsschrift*, and then to Kierkegaard's 1844 *The Concept of Anxiety*.

Freedom and Fall in the Philosophy of Revelation

Schelling's God concept lies at the center of the philosophy of revelation. In a sense, his God concept *is* the philosophy of revelation, for all its major themes in effect are an elaboration of God's life. While sticking close to the outline of Christian Incarnation, Redemption theology, Schelling stresses a God in process as opposed to an unchanging God, a living God who realizes and manifests himself in freely creating and redeeming a world. Moreover, in actualizing himself in creation, God attains personhood. Schelling wished at every point to avoid any suggestion of necessity in creation or in God's life (and specifically anything resembling emanationism). He also wished to ward off any appearance of pantheism in his own God concept while at the same time validating pantheism and polytheism as important phases in the history of religion that were part of the restoration of what he believed to have been an original monotheism. In addition, since creation was held to be free and unnecessary, it was in no way required of God that he become incarnate and a historical human person. Thus, when God does become a person, as Schelling accepted, in Jesus of Nazareth, God does so freely.[13]

The details of God's life are set forth in the darkest teaching of Schelling's philosophy of revelation, namely, his doctrine of potencies. Potency is at the center of all that is living, according to Schelling, including the living God. Schelling's is ultimately neither a satisfying nor persuasive teaching, but it remains a central one and is of special interest for its parallel to that underlying what Kierkegaard-Haufniensis will term “the dizziness of freedom” in *The Concept of Anxiety*. Schelling set forth his obscure theory in lectures ten to fourteen of the philosophy of revelation lectures in Berlin. Kierkegaard bore up under it, although he snapped that the doctrine of potencies betrayed the greatest impotence (*LD*, 141).

The doctrine is tied to the root teaching of God’s freedom and attempts to explain how all freedom—including divine freedom—moves from the nothingness of possibility into actuality. In it, Schelling sought to steer equally clear of notions of creation ex nihilo and emanationism, that is, on the one hand the notion that the world arose from pure nothingness and on the other hand the notion that the world emanates from God by God’s very nature. The latter notion is to be avoided because it would constitute a necessary, unfree development. Schelling avoids the former since he will have God create not out of pure nothingness but rather out of that which is not yet.

Schelling’s distinction revolves around a subtle difference in Greek negatives. In that which is held to be *ouk on* (οὐκ ὄν, “permanently not”) the emphasis is on the negative *ouk* (οὐκ) and the term signifies that which not only is not but also cannot be. In *mé on* (μὴ ὄν) the emphasis for Schelling is on being (*on*, ὄν) and the term thus signifies that which is not presently actual but is possible. *Whatever is* mé on, *while not presently actual, can come to be.* And it is out of this “can be,” or potency—which Schelling conceives of as *part* of God and yet *apart* from God—that creation and all that happens in and to creation are held to arise.[14]

The second part of Schelling’s lectures outlines the place of humankind in creation and the role humankind plays in God’s theogony. Creation has not followed its ideal course—not because of any divine or human necessity but because of human freedom. Humankind wished to be lord of potencies and lord of causes, that is, like God. In attempting this, humankind became instead lord of a fallen world “outside God.” Alienation of the world from God was thus humankind’s free but unfortunate deed.

Schelling thus explains speculatively how humankind became responsible for the entrance of evil into the world. The alienation of the world from God has its source in God’s own dark ground of possibility. In this idealist mythology of origins, humankind’s will to be like God led it demonically to wreak havoc upon the created world. In the process, humankind succeeded in becoming “like God,” but not God-like, for humankind emerged as the perverse lord of being. (A striking variation from other accounts of the fall is Schelling’s having the Son, or Logos, immediately and freely follow creation into alienation, or extradivinity, in order to restore it from within at a later point.)[15]

For Schelling, God’s free creation has now broken with God, and

God maintains the world in existence for the sake of eventual restoration by the Son, Logos. This will in time be a great good for the world, but also for God, who becomes actualized as the Trinity in the process. Both creation and redemption are viewed and emphasized as entirely free, and both are part of God's life or theogony. The theological ideas of freedom and fall are thus accounted for, as well as the outlines of redemption.[16]

There are echoes here of positions Kierkegaard himself was to take in *The Concept of Anxiety*. For in his analysis of anxiety, centering on the dizzying experience of potentiality, he followed a course quite parallel to Schelling's, except that Kierkegaard-Haufniensis's analysis is on the human plane only, rather than the divine, and is concerned with *humankind*'s becoming process, or what we might term anthropogony (on the model of "theogony").

Freedom and Fall in Treatise *Of Human Freedom* (1809)

Schelling's philosophy of revelation emphasized human beings as *free* beings in a *free* universe that has been created by and is ruled over by a *free* God with whom human beings are in relation, not just in thought but in experience (which, for Schelling, included revelation).

But the emphasis on freedom began much earlier. Schelling had come to see that in a profound and generalized way things were not as they ought to be. In short, *the world of actuality was not the world that thought would have had him expect,* and it did not follow along the necessary stages that Hegelian thought posited. As he was driven to ask why actuality does not correspond to thought, he was carried beyond his original philosophy of identity and its point of departure in the identity of thought and being. In this, he radically confronted the issue of human freedom, something that idealism, in his view, had not accounted for but merely subsumed into a doctrine of necessity. The *Freiheitsschrift* set out to account for human freedom in ways that speculative thought would not expect, explained evil and fall as an act of human freedom, then sought to go further in order to explain the metaphysical relationship of human freedom to God and to God's own freedom. Heidegger comments that freedom, for Schelling, was defined as in "the original feeling for the unity of all being in and out of its ground."[17]

Schelling clearly thought that the best evidence for human freedom was to demonstrate conceptually its presence in God and thus pursued freedom back to God himself and, out of the hazy sequence Eternal God-

Creation-Fall, derived a new view of creation according to which creation did not issue from pure nothingness but rather from potency—that which was not (yet) actual. Nonetheless, human freedom is his central thesis, even if a human freedom grounded in divine freedom. The separation between freedom and necessity remained the most fundamental category distinction for him. It was more important even than the separation between essence and existence. It is also more fundamental than the distinction between possibility and actuality. For Schelling, then, only a philosophy that built upon the deepest fundament (namely, freedom arising from possibility) and that recognized the relationship between the fundamental categories (in this instance, a nondialectical relationship) could issue in a correct philosophical system. His point was two-sided: the Hegelian model, which was dialectical, based on the logical relationship between being and nonbeing, was not fundamental enough; the new model, his own, was built instead on a fundamental, nondialectical relationship manifested not in any *idea* but in the *phenomenon* of freedom. The consequence was far-reaching: it would require a revision of the entire enterprise of philosophy in light of freedom. To construct a system of freedom, a mode of knowledge had to be sought that went beyond mere ideas and logical necessity.[18] (Schelling also sought a *historical* philosophy of actualized freedom, and this ultimately went beyond the philosophy of freedom to the philosophy of revelation, in which the revelation of the Christian religion is taken as the record of actualized freedom and the key to interpreting all that had gone before.)[19]

The process-God concept of the *Freiheitsschrift* describes two equally eternal beginnings in God that will find its analogy in human being. God is understood as having two poles: (1) God as conscious subject and (2) the dark ground of God, not conscious, inseparable from God and yet also different. This dark ground is not only the ground for the becoming of all that is not God (in particular, the world) but also for the becoming of God himself. With this notion, Schelling sought to describe a living God who is his own creator and who is ground and creator of both that which will be apart from him and that which he himself will become. But the condition for the possibility of God's own becoming is at the same time the condition for the possibility of good and evil.[20]

The bipolar God concept provided the basis for an explanation of both divine and human freedom, including human fall. All freedom is understood as having its base in the dark ground of God, a darkness that is the source of all potential and hence the source of potential good as well as potential evil. The possibility of good and evil is thus grounded in God himself, even while God remains all good. But within his creation is a creature by nature good but endowed with freedom and hence with the potential to choose to actualize good or evil. Historically, this creature chose to actualize evil and thereby perverted the original order of creation: the aboriginal unity of creation was shattered and evil; that which ought not to be was actualized.[21] Evil is thus explained and human freedom is grounded in the life and becoming of God. All that is and that has come to be proceeds from the dark ground of God, including that which ought not to be. *Why is there not perfection from the beginning?* Simply put: because God is a life and a perfecting God, rather than a completed being à la Aristotle.[22]

Certain emphases immediately emerge. First, humankind is responsible for evil. No external evil spirit tempts humankind in Schelling's account; the blame is neither shifted nor shared. God created a good world that humankind perverted.

Evil is thus a reality, although emphatically not a necessity. It is the product of the freedom that is able to act on the potential for good and evil. God acts and creates the good. But one good has its own potential and in the exercise of its freedom has brought forth evil.

Freedom and Fall in *The Concept of Anxiety*

Kierkegaard brings out the psychological insights that derive from Schelling's existential metaphysics. He does not begin where Schelling ended, nor does he begin where Schelling began. Nor does he retrace Schelling's steps. His enterprise is different. He begins with a different problem and a different method, and yet the ground covered is not so different. Kierkegaard's slim volume begins not in the metaphysical poles and potencies of God but rather with the problem of human fallenness and incompleteness. Formally it is the particular dogmatic issue of hereditary sin. Yet in analyzing it, Kierkegaard covers much the same intellectual terrain as Schelling. Kierkegaard begins with the first sin rather than with what made it possible, acknowledges the first sin as being historically first but still just one form of sin, and then penetrates to the deeper ground of all sin in human freedom.

What most immediately distinguishes Kierkegaard's treatment from Schelling's is that Kierkegaard does not carry the analysis of human freedom back to God and *divine* freedom. But the workings of human freedom are essentially the same for both writers. How human freedom relates structurally and metaphysically to God's being is simply not a theme of Kierkegaard's work.

In the form of a theological treatise, Kierkegaard's work sets out with a classic theological theme, the intellectually interesting doctrine of an original sin. But it views this as only the decisive first actualized possibility of evil and springboards into a discussion of all actualized evil, with the repeatedly declared practical interest of overcoming it. For, once it is established that every person brings sin into the world for him- or herself, the important practical question is how to exercise freedom to recover from this deed. Kierkegaard's work moves on to a discernment of the shattering *experience* of one's own dark ground, with its offer of recovered possibility. (Recovery itself and the overcoming of sin extend beyond the scope of Haufniensis's work but lie within the scope of that of the 1849 pseudonymous Anti-Climacus in *The Sickness unto Death.*)

"No explanation," writes Haufniensis, "that explains Adam but not hereditary sin, or explains hereditary sin but not Adam, is of any help" (*SKS*, 4:334–35; *CA*, 28). Ultimately, Kierkegaard-Haufniensis seeks an explanation that will explain Everyman and every sin. Kierkegaard's interest in the Fall is thus universal, whereas Schelling's is particular. Each is interested in the metaphysics and experience of freedom in all human beings. While Schelling's discussion of the Fall confines itself to Adam's fall, there is no inherent reason why it could not have extended to other humans as well. For Schelling would recognize all human beings as fallen and all as having exercised the same freedom that Adam had.

Kierkegaard makes all this explicit as he portrays the first actualization of evil (sin) emerging for every person from an original innocence, and Haufniensis-Kierkegaard's consideration turns to a psychological (but hardly empirical) investigation of spirit in its original dreaming and innocence.

> In [innocence] . . . there is peace and repose, but there is simultaneously something else that is not contention and strife, for there is indeed nothing against which to strive. What, then, is it? Nothing. But what effect does nothing have? It begets anxiety. (*SKS*, 4:347; *CA*, 41)

"Nothing" acts as "something." Moreover, it is not outside but within oneself as its own dark ground, as it were, but then incorrectly understood as being outside oneself: "Dreamily the spirit projects its own actuality, but this in actuality is nothing, and innocence always sees this nothing outside" (*SKS*, 4:347; *CA*, 41). The experience of this nothing is *the experience of the possibility of possibility*. Kierkegaard terms this "anxiety in innocence" and holds that there *is* such an experience, because *there must be* such an experience, even though one has no memory of it. It is therefore a claim about an initial existential anxiety that must have been because thought requires it. (This will strike the contemporary reader as odd but would not seem like an excessive claim in the philosophy of the nineteenth century.)

The passage goes on to observe that anxiety has the same significance for dreaming spirit that melancholia or "heavy spiritedness" (*Tungsind*) has at a later point (*SKS*, 4:348; *CA*, 42). Not only does Kierkegaard see the connection between anxiety and melancholia but also Schelling saw the very same kind of connection, while never using the term "anxiety." In the *Freiheitsschrift*, he spoke of the dark ground of God as a condition relatively independent of God. This is God's unactualized potential, or one might say that "God's Nothing" is a source of melancholia or "heavy spiritedness" to him, and it extends to the whole creation in which this nothing or dark ground is found.[23] "Thus the veil of sadness [*Schwermuth*] which is spread over all nature; the deep, unappeasable melancholy [*Melancholie*] of all life."

In Kierkegaard-Haufniensis's reading of Genesis, the prohibition not to eat of the fruit of the tree of the knowledge of good and evil mythologically represents the spark to the awakening slumbering spirit (*SKS*, 4:350; *CA*, 44). Spirit discovers its freedom, seeks knowledge, and in the process also discovers its own dark ground, or nothing. And so anxiety arises out of the nothing, or dark ground, of the spirit. To be precise, Kierkegaard does not use the term "dark ground" and he does not make the connection, but his "nothing" and Schelling's "dark ground" are parallel categories and function in the same way. For humankind, they are the first inklings of the unactualized potential that is part of every individual and that rises up to confront him or her.

And so Kierkegaard Haufniensis writes that anxiety is the presupposition of hereditary sin (*SKS*, 4:351; *CA*, 46). But the same conditions are true in the sin of Adam and of every descendant of Adam. Adam's sin is merely first. There was no sin before Adam, but other than that, everything is the same.

Having explained the psychological and metaphysical conditions in which the historically first sin and every first sin have taken place, Kierkegaard turns, in chapter 2, to the consequences of the deed of sin. To use Schelling's terminology, that which was able to be but that ought not to have been has in fact come to be; and this actualized possibility has consequences for future possibilities. Both ignorance and innocence are things of the past, and present possibilities are modified by the actualized possibility of sin.

Anxiety has now come to mean two things:

1. the anxiety experience out of which the first deed arose, namely, anxiety at the possibility of possibility, and
2. the anxiety experience subsequent to the deed of lost innocence: restricted possibility and eventually the experience of the possibility of self-recovery (*SKS*, 4:359; *CA*, 54).[24]

Kierkegaard's chapter on subjective anxiety concerns the experience of possibility on the individual level. The experience of the possibility of possibility is compared to the dizziness one feels in looking down into a yawning abyss. But looking into the abyss is a free act (one might have closed one's eyes, for example) and hence is termed the dizziness of freedom. And in this dizziness freedom succumbs. Kierkegaard-Haufniensis announces that this highly metaphysical line of psychological thought cannot penetrate any further back than this point of dizziness. In the very next instant, everything is changed, and the individual intuitively knows that his use of his freedom has made him guilty. While he could not remain in innocence, guilt was not the sole option, since he also could have made a choice in the direction of God, rather than the opposite. Between these two moments lie the leap and mystery that no science has explained and that no science can explain (*SKS*, 4:366; *CA*, 61). *Why* one would choose evil remains mystery; *that* one has chosen it is an intuitive certainty.

Freedom succumbs in the dizziness: the free subject who discovers himself in guilt also recognizes his own responsibility for the moment of dizziness and fall that has gone before. Such subjective anxiety describes the condition from which every individual arises to discover that she or he has fallen into sin. Freedom has changed, and so has the directionality of anxiety. For now it is about further fall or else recovery. Possibilities remain and above all one especially important one: either remaining in this fallen state or rising from it. This either-or is the problem that so much of Kierkegaard's psychological thought revolves around. Kierkegaard-Haufniensis's special, practical interest in overcoming sin is the concern of chapter 5 ("Anxiety as Saving through Faith") and then continues in Anti-Climacus's companion work, *The Sickness unto Death.*

To Kierkegaard's mind, both sin and the overcoming of sin[25]—in secular language, self-alienation and self-recovery—are possibilities proceeding from the dark ground of one's unactualized being, from one's own nothingness that rises up to the level of experience in anxiety to confront one with one's own freedom to choose to create oneself or not, and ultimately with one's responsibility for what one chooses.[26]

Kierkegaard is using the sin language of Christian theology and the metaphysical language of German philosophy, but what he is straining to describe is the development of the human spirit that discovers itself self-alienated and dissatisfied, and then, in escalating fear and trembling, experiences the shattering challenge of reversing self-alienation.

Theologically expressed, the sleeping human spirit is at first nothing more than a possibility that must be awakened by using its freedom and actualizing its possibility; but its first choice—symbolically expressed in the Genesis myth of the violation of the divine prohibition in the Garden of Eden—is a choice of self *against* God rather than a choice of self in relation *to* God. Adam and Everyman were free to do this, and did so. But the action can be overcome, and the marvel is that a greater good can and will be brought out of this actualized possibility. For theology, it is expressed in the teachings of the Incarnation of God's Son and his Atonement. In the reversal, original innocence itself is not restored, but something higher is held to come about: a higher relationship to Divine Spirit made possible by God's taking on human form and proffering a new relationship to the divine-human God. Clearly this is not psychology, although Kierkegaard would insist that the relationship, if established, is experienced and not a mere matter of words.

Thus freedom and freedom's possibilities can be restored, but not the original possibility of sinlessness. Sin has been actualized and cannot be undone. But there arises now the possibility of restoration.

The nothing of anxiety will appear again, and the dialectic of "something" (the actualized self) and "nothing" (possible self) will continue as long as there is life. For Schelling, the dark ground, too, was there at the beginning—even at the very beginning with God himself—and was there at the moment of the Fall and thereafter. It is the source of the exercise of freedom, for freedom acts upon possibility and makes "something" out of what was "nothing." The ground of freedom is God, and this idea is implicit in Kierkegaard's thought. Hence, Schelling and Kierkegaard share the same metaphysical backdrop of human freedom, namely, divine freedom. And freedom acts upon the potential called by Schelling the dark ground and by Kierkegaard the nothing that is something. Out of potential have come good and evil, as both Schelling and Kierkegaard observe. The actualization of evil should not have come about but did so by the misuse of human freedom. Kierkegaard stresses the experiential quality of this, despite language that sometimes sounds every bit as metaphysical as Schelling's.

What has been actualized cannot be undone, but full, original possibility can be restored and even enhanced by virtue of action from God's side. At this point, Schelling and Kierkegaard diverge, mostly because the very structure of their respective works takes the discussion in different directions. In his philosophy of revelation, Schelling is interested in exploring what this means for *God.* In *The Concept of Anxiety,* Kierkegaard-Haufniensis's interest is what it means for *individual human beings.* Schelling's interest is more metaphysical and theological, whereas Kierkegaard's is psychological and anthropological.

Kierkegaard's work gives a new name to Schelling's dark ground, namely, "nothing," and, more important, names its first product: anxiety. Kierkegaard goes on to describe the dynamic of humankind's dark ground in detail that far surpasses Schelling's work or its ambition. In addition, and as an important distinction between the two, Kierkegaard always confines his analysis of freedom to the human plane. God's own dark ground, God's nothing, is a subject never broached by Kierkegaard.

It has been clear to many that the existentialist writings of Heidegger and Sartre (and others) are indebted to Kierkegaard for the theme of anxiety, and to both Schelling and Kierkegaard for the issue of freedom as the decisive divide from idealism. In the end Schelling and Kierkegaard are not so entirely different as Kierkegaard's rejection of Professor Schelling in 1842 might lead one to believe. Kierkegaard's "nothing" indeed seems to be another name for the dark ground that underlies the freedom concept in Schelling's work. There is thus an element of continuity between Schelling and Kierkegaard that Kierkegaard himself never seems to realize. This is not to suggest that Kierkegaard belongs to a Schelling school. Their differences are striking and fundamental: Schelling is a philosopher trying to harmonize his cultural Christianity with his own intellectual experiments; Kierkegaard is a more orthodox Christian writer interested in highlighting the distinctiveness and practical existential meaning of what he held to be psychological truths so that people might in their own interests act upon them and not merely think about them.

9

The Fear of Nothing: Kierkegaard and Heidegger

The previous chapter made clear that anxiety (*Angst*) as discussed by Kierkegaard-Haufniensis does not correspond entirely to the way the term has been used in the twentieth and now the twenty-first century. Kierkegaard and Heidegger, in two very different philosophical projects, use the term for only a subset of anxiety and not the full range of the term's meaning. But Kierkegaard and Heidegger would hold that it is the most essential form of anxiety and reveals us to ourselves as incomplete beings, troubled by our own incompleteness, aware of responsibility for being less complete, anxious about recovering lost possibility, and face-to-face, as it were, with vague and eerily felt future possibility.

While Kierkegaard's and Heidegger's respective theories of anxiety have had considerable influence in psychological, philosophical, and theological circles, Kierkegaard and Heidegger remain very different thinkers overall, by virtue not only of their respective philosophical projects but also of epistemology and methodology. Heidegger is self-consciously extending phenomenology beyond his teacher, Edmund Husserl. Kierkegaard is making a descriptive analysis well in advance of phenomenology but has more recourse to metaphysics, in addition to the Christian presuppositions and interests that he brings to the task. Heidegger seeks to be secular yet follows a remarkably parallel course.

Kierkegaard and Heidegger each link anxiety with *nothing* and explore the *nothingness* that they claim anxiety is about. They each note empirical manifestations in the subject of the experience and identify that which the experience uncovers about the subject's present existence and then go on to identify that to which the experience points. The intentionality of the experience is the most disputable because it is highly interpretive. The speculative intentionality of Kierkegaard proceeds from seemingly unproven and unknowable presuppositions. These include a Christian worldview with Greek metaphysical underpinnings. With Heidegger they are secular but often seem to be a secularized version of a parallel and very similar horizon. In this respect, both Kierkegaard and Heidegger, despite claims to an experiential grounding to their theories, veer off into a kind of meta-psychology.

Nothing

Many would hold that to say "I fear nothing" is to say "I do not fear." But both Kierkegaard and Heidegger emphatically speak of *nothing* as unactualized *something. Nothing* is in their philosophies also the term for that which is not and yet *might possibly be.* One can treat the well-known phrase from Heidegger "Das Nichts nichtet"[1] (Nothingness nihilates) as paradox, as an expression pointing beyond words, or as words that make no sense and are nonsense.[2]

In exploring this theme, it might be well to take a cue from the nominalists, who sought to be on guard against being taken in by our own words, for people have coined words and think that the words designate a reality in itself (e.g., that there really is such a thing as anxiety in itself, independent of anxious people). Etymology does not tell us much either: "anxiety" derives from the Latin *anxietas,* which comes from the verb *ango* (and noun *angor*), which means "to choke." The other suggestion in the etymology is being in a tight situation, in narrow straits, feeling pressed from all sides. Vivid images, perhaps, but not very telling.

Psychological and psychoanalytical explorations of anxiety range very broadly from speaking of an avoidance mechanism to aversive stimuli, to cognitive dissonance as a reaction to incongruent information, to a reaction to a perceived state that seems impossible to master, to a morbid anxiety that is a paralyzing "fear of anxiety" itself. Kierkegaard and Heidegger are not attempting to set out a description or a theory that takes account of this wide range. They have a very specific kind of experience in mind and in view. For the moment, let us grant the possibility that Heidegger and Kierkegaard strain to give voice to the experience of the essential anxiety of every living human, or at least every member of Western culture.

For both, the hallmark of anxiety is its objectlessness. Unlike fear, anxiety has no clear or discernible or distinguishable object. This is *not* because an object is *not yet* clear. Indeed, no clear object will ever emerge, because the essence of anxiety—what makes it the eerie, uncanny experience that it is—is precisely its objectlessness. It is *not* fear of a vague something that could be clarified. There is *no-thing,* and this very nothingness rises to central significance.[3] Neither Kierkegaard nor Heidegger would claim that his language is adequate, or could be adequate, to what either is trying to explore and understand. In fact, Heidegger would say explicitly that the limits of language are met and exceeded by the phenomenon. But he will emphasize that it is indeed a phenomenon for which the only appeal and justification for proceedings are experience itself. (The ultimate appeal back to experience, on the part of both Kierkegaard and Heidegger, should be borne in mind throughout and as a check on any inclination to confuse experience and speculation and slip into a metapsychology.) The indefiniteness of the object of anxiety is precisely what is particular to the experience that both Kierkegaard and Heidegger wish to describe and analyze. And they pursue the indefiniteness of anxiety's object back to nothingness itself.

For Kierkegaard and Heidegger, anxiety relates not to one definite object but to my existence itself. Fear of something that actually exists could of course also at times be fear related to my continued existence—as, for example, one fears a bear in the woods. But anxiety in the sense that Kierkegaard and Heidegger write of it is fear of nothing specific. The anxiety that they seek to describe is about what might be, but *not* in the sense of presentiment and a possible object (as in "I am anxious that there might be a bear in the woods"). In anxiety there is no object that I can run away from or, alternatively, run toward. There is nothing that one can immediately do about it. Yet it is there with me. It unsettles me in another way too by revealing to me that one's very being is not a settled matter, that who one is is essentially not a finished matter but continues to be defined. This consciousness is famously expressed in the phrase of Jean-Paul Sartre "Existence precedes essence." In this understanding, what I *essentially* am is not already a given or established fact but will be established only in the future through my existence.

The possible result of anxiety, as described by Kierkegaard and Heidegger, is what makes it so potentially important for each of them, namely, that it can save the individual from being lost amid others, from becoming a mere herd being rather than being a developed individual. In short, it calls one (back) to an essential self-identity as individual. Neither considers the Darwinian question that might be posed to anxiety: whether any evolutionary purpose might be served by such a psychological mechanism, or whether the truth about individuality that it uncovers or recovers collides with Darwinian notions of who and what *Homo sapiens* is. Anxiety's gain seems to be individual only. There are surely social repercussions for a society of individuals, defined by the individuality achieved. It has no apparent survival or reproductive advantage (unless it might be the intelligence to reckon with population density and environment).

In a popular book, *A Brief History of Anxiety*, Patricia Pearson describes anxiety as "fear in search of a cause."[4] In it, she praises Kierkegaard above Freud as the true psychological genius on this subject (p. 12). The phrase "fear in search of a cause" nicely pinpoints what Kierkegaard and Heidegger will describe as the starting point in the exploration of the objectless nature of anxiety, the fear of nothing definite, the fear of that which *is not* but *might be,* thus the fear of no-thing yet. Admittedly, here we have the linguistic paradox of "nothing" being talked about as "something." This is much less a problem, or not a problem at all, for Buddhist thinkers, for whom emptiness (*śūnyatā*) is a negative ideogram for what the West thinks of as fullness, and not-self (*an-ātman*) is the negative ideogram for the highest possible (im)personal attainment. Perhaps we should think of the philosophical language about anxiety as a negative ideogram as well: negative language trying to point to and express something highly positive about the human self.

The characteristics of this anxiety are *not* the heart palpitations, the sweats, or intestinal symptoms associated with a medical diagnosis of anxiety. Heidegger in fact says that the anxiety about which he writes is characterized by an eerie calm, in which one senses a disconnectedness with one's fellow beings, an isolation that cannot be breached.[5] It is an isolation that brings one face-to-face with the problematic nature of oneself: I realize in the anxiety experience that I am an open-ended question to myself, that I am so by the very nature of my being, and that others cannot define me for myself, despite their pretensions to the contrary. My existence is a problem to myself: not just its contingent, nonnecessary nature, not just its temporal nature, and not merely because I realize that someday I will die and no longer exist.[6] There is something about my very being that does not make rational sense to me: why I am at all, rather than not being, why my being and identity are fluid rather than fixed and stable, and how I face the awareness of eventual nonexistence. (Heidegger will talk of this under the rubric being-unto-death.)

This anxiety experience thus turns me in on myself, makes me reflective, acutely conscious of my incompleteness and of my transience, makes me aware of my ultimate inability to totally lose myself in the crowd. Anxiety for both Kierkegaard and Heidegger is thus an experience of my self at its limits. But it is an experience both of (current) limits and of possibility. Kierkegaard and Heidegger will diverge in the discussion of the latter, and Heidegger will give emphasis to the experienced consciousness of my not inevitable nonbeing as an important horizon for understanding my own becoming.

For Kierkegaard and Heidegger, *Angst* is a sally into the indeterminate itself, and thus the emphasis for both on the absence of a definite object.[7] It is illusion-shattering and at the same time posits nothing clearly in its stead. And yet it is precisely that "absent object" that anxiety is about: my possible future self.

Angst will be portrayed above all as the discover-recovery experience of possibility. It effects a revelatory consciousness of personal possibility ignored and unfulfilled and simultaneously constitutes a first step in recovery from an everyday condition of lostness.

How each proceeds in plumbing the dark and negative depths of anxiety is to a significant extent shaped by the formal philosophical project of each, and is expressed in the philosophical language adopted by each. Kierkegaard from his vantage point in the mid-nineteenth century would wince along with many in the twentieth century at the odd, strained-and-straining language employed by Heidegger.[8] Heidegger for his part would regard Kierkegaard as part of the Old Metaphysics that was prophetically declared dead by Nietzsche at the end of the nineteenth century. At the same time, Heidegger is nevertheless significantly influenced by Kierkegaard's insights and was among the first to see the psychological originality and genius of Kierkegaard. It is a genius that struggles toward its insight from within its own times, along with their presuppositions, concepts, and terminology—a commonsense observation, certainly, but one easily overlooked.

Both discuss *Angst* within large formal treatises, Kierkegaard proceeding from a formal concern to rethink the ur-Christian teaching of original sin,[9] Heidegger from a concern to describe Being by beginning with the being who asks the question about Being and whose own being is brought into question by himself as the questioner. Whereas Kierkegaard chooses the form of a medieval theology treatise, Heidegger applies phenomenological method developed by Husserl. Kierkegaard is more existential in his formal concern, for his analysis of anxiety in relationship to the problem of sin proceeds with the serious practical interest of finding the way out of sin and into recovery from sin. Heidegger would seem no less interested in the existential application of his discussion but indicates his existential interest only indirectly.

As far as this writer is aware, Kierkegaard is also the first to associate anxiety and "nothing"—"nothing" as that which at the moment is not but in the mode of possibly coming into being. But it is no specific thing, and gradually it is made clear that it is interior to one's own self. However, as we have seen in the previous chapter, it was Schelling's meditation on the relationship between freedom and what is not yet (*mé on*) that conceptually prepared the way. In Kierkegaard-Haufniensis *mé on* crystallized into *nothing*.

Kierkegaard sees its manifestations in children in their seeking after, and their attraction to, the adventurous, the monstrous, and the enigmatic. And this points to the "sympathetic antipathy" and "antipathetic sympathy" that he sees as characterizing anxiety: one is simultaneously attracted and repulsed.[10] But if there is an essential ambivalence here, one is not paralyzed by it.

Kierkegaardian Anxiety

The listing of the characteristics of anxiety below is not systematic but simply follows Kierkegaard's order of presentation:[11]

The dizziness of anxiety. Kierkegaard compares anxiety with the dizziness of looking down into a yawning abyss. He writes, "Hence anxiety is the dizziness of freedom, which emerges when the spirit looks down into its own possibility, laying hold of finiteness to support itself. Freedom succumbs to this dizziness."

Anxiety, he asserts, is selfish: "In anxiety there is the selfish infinity of possibility, which does not tempt like a choice but ensnaringly disquiets [*ængster*] with its sweet anxiousness [*Beængstelse*]" (*SKS*, 4:366; *CA*, 61). Anxiety is mine, and mine alone. And it is ultimately about me.

Anxiety is linked with sensuousness and with nothing. Kierkegaard asserts that sensuousness is an "unexplained riddle that causes anxiety" (*SKS*, 4:369; *CA*, 65). Kierkegaard is not much help to us here in understanding what he means, except to say that he is convinced of a causal connection between sensuousness and anxiety. Indeed, the more sensuousness, the more anxiety.

Because he holds to the past sexist view that woman is more sensuous than man (*SKS*, 4:370; *CA*, 66), he asserts that woman is more anxious than man. We probably need to regard this as a sexist error of his times and take his main point more seriously, namely, that the more sensuous a person is the more that person will feel anxiety. In that respect, sensuousness must be regarded as something positive, and Kierkegaard-Haufniensis goes on to point out the error in Christian theology by which sensuousness and sexuality became equated with sinfulness. To repeat: he affirms the link of sensuousness and anxiety but denies any link between sensuousness and sinfulness.[12]

The nothing of anxiety. Kierkegaard refers to the Pythagorean concept of nonbeing (the empty [*to kénon*], that which is not [*to mé on*], and he associates it with the nothing out of which Plotinian Christian theology asserts creation arose—*creatio ex nihilo* (creation from nothing). This is a fascinating association, since Kierkegaard would thereby be saying that anxiety is an experience of the *nihil* out of which the being of the world arose, was created, and that self-completion is creation from out of the same *nihil* out of which the universe arose (albeit, in his understanding, ultimately in cooperation with the Creator God). This is a rich, fascinating, perhaps even awe-inspiring way to think of what it means to complete oneself as a human being, but Kierkegaard has no empirical basis for such an interpretation.

Anxiety is always about the future, for the possible lies in the future. (Anxiety about the past he reduces to anxiety about repeating the past.)

Anxiety is a breaking out of spiritlessness and the breaking out of the empty talk (*Gerede* in Heidegger) associated with spiritlessness. Kierkegaard describes the spiritless person as a "talking machine."

Anxiety is freedom's disclosure to itself in possibility (*SKS*, 4:413; *CA*, 111). He stresses that the high possibility around which it revolves is the "unwarranted actuality of sin" that one can do something about. But it is ambivalent, and to some extent he writes that one also wants the actuality of sin to continue. This is part of what he calls the sophistry of sin (*SKS*, 4:416; *CA*, 114). The greater crisis lurking ahead, according to Kierkegaard's analysis, is that one can repent but not cancel sin (*SKS*, 4:417; *CA*, 115).

Anxiety is always the sign of a deeper nature (p. 116). But he notes a kind of "demonic anxiety" that seeks to close itself off in "enclosing reserve" [*det indesluttede*], a kind of "escape from freedom," for freedom is naturally communicative (*SKS*, 4:424–25; *CA*, 123–24). Ironically, enclosing reserve becomes involuntary self-disclosure, through a word or glance by which one unwillingly reveals that which one wishes to conceal (*SKS*, 4:430; *CA*, 129).

Flight from the true possibility for oneself that anxiety reveals can lead to hypersensibility, hyperirritability, neurasthenia, hysteria, hypochondria. Here Kierkegaard is suggesting psychosomatic illness as a sometime manifestation of the attempt to refuse to act positively in response to the spiritual awakening of anxiety (*SKS*, 4:437–38; *CA*, 136–37). Self-deception, idleness, stupid busyness are also manifestations. In short, they are attempts to flee from seriousness, from taking oneself and one's own incompleteness seriously and seeking to do something effective about it.

Heideggerian Anxiety in *Being and Time* (1927)

Heidegger is clearly influenced by Kierkegaard on the concept of anxiety, and much more so than he acknowledges. (See the appendix for further discussion of this theme.) Heidegger concedes Kierkegaardian influence in (only) two places in *Being and Time*. While Heidegger had misgivings about the Kierkegaard fad in Germany at the time, he nonetheless learned much from him, and many of the categories that Heidegger uses in connection with his phenomenology of *Angst* have direct parallels in Kierkegaard-Haufniensis's description of the same.[13]

Formally, Heidegger's project in *Being and Time* is to develop a phenomenology of Being, beginning with that locus closest to the reflective observer, namely, one's own being, the place where Being is. Heidegger takes the term *Dasein* (which simply means "existence" in everyday German), partitions it into its linguistic elements, *da-sein*: *da* as the "there" and *sein* as "being," and analyzes the There-Being (*Dasein*) of the human being. Put another way, he analyzes the human person as the place where Being is, in one particular and privileged manifestation of Being.[14]

Heidegger seizes upon anxiety as "one of the *most far-reaching* and *most primordial* possibilities of [the] disclosure" of Being in the human person as There-Being (*Dasein*). (*BT*, 226; *SZ*, 182). Its analysis occurs just after the section in which Heidegger has sketched how the human person has fallen away from Being in a tranquilizing state of being-in-the-world in which one's involvement with Being is lulled to sleep, or nearly forgotten. The situation, before the shudder of awakening in anxiety, is that the human person (There-Being) has drifted into an alienation in which its potentiality for being is hidden from it. Its manifestations are the falling into the impersonal and inauthentic world of the "they" (*das Man*): self-alienation from Being and one's possibilities and mistakenly taking the meaning of one's being from the impersonal masses.[15]

According to Heidegger, the eruption of anxiety shakes this state of affairs and initiates a disclosure about one's authentic possibilities. And so Heidegger sets himself the task of working out what he calls the *Befindlichkeit*—literally, "the way one finds oneself"—and then the task of characterizing ontologically what is disclosed in it.

Fear, for Heidegger, is always about some entity in the world that constitutes a danger. In contrast, the threat in anxiety is completely indefinite; it is no entity ready at hand, nor the sum total of entities ready at hand. "That in the face of which one has anxiety is characterized by the fact that what threatens is *nowhere.* Anxiety 'does not know' what that in the face of which it is anxious is" (*BT*, 231; *SZ*, 186). Simply put, anxiety does not initially know what it is anxious about. But in the raw experience, the nothing and nowhere of anxiety first point up the insignificance of entities in the world, while there is simultaneously a positive disclosure about oneself. He goes on to note that anxiety ultimately discloses There-Being's freedom to choose itself and to take hold of itself, with the possibility of recovering authentic Being. What Heidegger claims is disclosed is that one is anxious not in the face of other entities in the world but rather is anxious in the face of one's own being in the world.

But before the ontological discernment comes the feeling of eeriness or uncanniness (*unheimlich*), a sudden feeling of not being at home in one's world, that is, the experience of a rupture in what up to now has been a tranquilized feeling of being at home amid the "they." A once contented mass identity of being part of the many no longer works in that it is no longer felt to be adequate. And so anxiety has the effect of freeing one from absorption in the everyday, tranquilized inauthentic world in which one has been living with other tranquilized inauthethic beings. "This uncanniness pursues *Dasein* constantly, and is a threat to its everyday lostness in the 'they' " (*BT*, 234; *SZ*, 189).

Heidegger returns to discussing anxiety in the section "*Dasein*'s Possibility of Being-a-Whole, and Being-towards-Death."[16] In his discussion of being-unto-death, Heidegger is really talking about the effects of anxiety upon self-awareness, self-consciousness, and self-creation through the unsettling disclosure of personal transiency.[17]

The awareness of one's being-unto-death—that one is a being that will surely die—discloses that there is a completion of one's being lying ahead in the future, when one will have ceased to exist and when therefore one's being will by definition have been completed. And, while one is also acutely aware of the eventual termination of oneself as a locus where Being is present, one simultaneously experiences a disclosure of potential wholeness and a prompting toward actualizing it. Indeed, the quality of "not yet" is understood as an essential quality of the Being of the human person brought to higher awareness by death consciousness.[18] The section is not so much about death as about one's grasping the inevitable fact that one's being is moving toward death and future nonexistence, and then one's being moved by this consciousness not to depression or despair but to a commitment to actualize one's being in the here and now.

One experiences one's own movement toward death, but not of course one's own being dead. For Heidegger, this aspect of one's being—in conscious movement toward death—is thus a catalyst to a disturbing but creative experience, for it too calls one's being into question, shakes one's everyday being in the world, and forces upon oneself the recognition of everyday absorption or lostness. "Death is a possibility-of-being which *Dasein* has to take over in every case. With death, *Dasein* stands before itself in its ownmost potentiality-for-Being" (*BT*, 294; *SZ*, 250).

Anxiety in the face of death is anxiety in the face of one particular and final potentiality that is one's alone, that is not relational and not to be outstripped (*unüberholbare*).

The most important disclosure here is not only that there is an end point of *Dasein*'s being but also the "not yet" quality of its being. For Heidegger, the common reaction is a fleeing in the face of being-unto-death. One does not want to think about it. The result is not just a fleeing from death consciousness but also and more important a fleeing from one's own "not yets," one's other authentic possibilities. But there can be no authenticity until this is faced up to and accepted, in a return to oneself as the being that one actually is (as opposed to the illusions or blank consciousness that one has in the crowd).

> *But the state-of-mind which can hold open the utter and constant threat to itself arising from* Dasein*'s ownmost individualized Being is anxiety.* In this state-of-mind, *Dasein* finds itself face-to-face with the "nothing" of the possible impossibility of its existence. (*BT,* 310; *SZ,* 265–66)

Anxiety in Heidegger's Lecture "What Is Metaphysics?" (1929)

Two years after the publication of *Being and Time,* Heidegger gave his inaugural lecture as professor in Freiburg. In the published version of this lecture, "What Is Metaphysics?,"[19] he elaborated on the themes of "the nothing" and anxiety. He acknowledged how strange it sounds to inquire into nothing, that both question and answer can seem inherently absurd. But he asserted that humans experience the limits of Being, even as they try to ignore them, and spoke of the "common nothing that glides so inconspicuously through our chatter, blanched with the anemic pallor of the obvious." And he scorned attempts to define it metaphysically and merely as an empty idea (i.e., as the complete negation of the totality of beings) (par. 16). He discussed moods as attunements of beings to Being and isolated anxiety as the fundamental mood that reveals the relationship of human being to Being.

Heidegger held that an attunement, in which human beings are brought before the nothing itself, does occur in human existence. It can and does occur in the lives of individuals, although rarely enough and only for a moment, in the fundamental mood of anxiety (par. 21). In fact, the experience rescues them from mere group existence and individuates them.

Anxiety is thus the mood that reveals the nothing in an ambivalent experience characterized on the one hand by what he calls a peculiar calm and on the other by an uncanniness, an ill-at-ease quality (*unheimlich*) that pervades the anxiety experience. The indeterminateness of that in the face of which one has anxiety is, for Heidegger, once again emphasized as an essential characteristic of anxiety. In an objectless experience that is unsettling both for its emotional quality and its objectlessness, everyday existence is unsettled as beings as a whole recede and slip away and leave one alone with one's own problematic individual being. One experiences a shrinking back and a bewildered calm. The anxiety experience is characterized as being repelling but also indicating that there is nowhere to run. Unlike Kierkegaard's description, Heidegger's does not include what Kierkegaard-Haufniensis termed antipathetic sympathy, an element of grudging or unwilling attraction in the experience.

Heidegger goes on to assert that the encounter with the nothing is indispensable to selfhood and freedom and states that without it no authentic selfhood and freedom are possible (par. 34). He remarks that everyday superficial living is a construct to avoid this uncomfortable encounter. But even if the nothing is obscured or ignored, it is there all the same and can succeed in making its presence felt at any moment.

> The original anxiety in existence is usually repressed. Anxiety is there. It is only sleeping. Its breath quivers perpetually through *Dasein*, only slightly in those who are jittery, imperceptibly in the "Oh, yes" and the "Oh, no" of men of affairs; but most readily in the reserved, and most assuredly in those who are basically daring. (par. 41)

For Heidegger, the blank spaces in the phrases "anxiety in the face of . . . ," "anxiety about . . ." are absolutely key. They speak of an absence that is manifested positively in eerie calm.

The temptation and everyday response is to try to ignore the experience, to reduce it to *nothing*!

> Q: "What happened?"
> A: "Oh, it was nothing."

For Heidegger, of course, indeed it is nothing, but this "nothing" is *everything*. It is the potential passage to an enhanced self, to a recovered sense of the strangeness and mystery of Being. Heidegger takes seriously the Greeks' marveling at Being, and at why there is Being and not just nothing. For Heidegger, there is both the experience of Being and the experience of nothing. Both are covered up in modern society, and daring to be open to the experience of the nothing and what it uncovers is decisive for an enhanced, authentic mode of human being.

If Heidegger's philosophy turns very much on the question How is it with Being?, it also turns on the question How is it with the nothing? Heidegger wishes to emphasize that they are not empty words, and not mere concepts, but that they name genuine objects of experience. Thus Heidegger writes, "With the fundamental mood of anxiety we have arrived at that occurrence in human existence in which the nothing is revealed and from which it must be interrogated. How is it with the nothing?" (par. 26)

In sum, anxiety is a discomforting jolt followed by the apprehension of the self-deceptive nature of everyday life that pretends that there is no death and no end of being, that seeks refuge from, and confirmation of, its self-deception (bad faith) in idle chatter and group identity. Anxiety is about one's own nothingness, which no group participation can experience on one's behalf or deal with for one. Ultimately one dies and ceases to be, and no group can help one. Anxiety severs one from forgetfulness in mere group existence and throws one back upon oneself in one's individuality. It tears one from unsuccessful self-tranquilization in group existence, into which one has been lured by the prevailing group think and group speak. It resulted in one's assigning completeness to that which one intuitively knew—and now experientially knows—is not complete, namely, one's own existence. It forcibly frees one from the group (the "they") that can do nothing for one, that can no longer keep one in forgetfulness about one's being. And it is here that one senses one's individual freedom, that one uncovers one's own sense of possibles, and can act upon them.

So *Angst* is a breaking away from inauthentic group existence by a shattering of the illusion of its satisfactory nature. It frees one from the superficiality of discourse that fills up time with themes of unimportance while banishing ultimate questions to the realm of the morbid, the nonsensical, or the imaginary.

It rends the curtain of everyday inauthentic existence that hides from oneself the way things really are.

Unlike fear, which registers a threat to one's continued existence, anxiety is not about a threat to one's existence per se but rather a threat to what one has come to accept and believe about one's own existence. Anxiety reveals that our stories and myths, our theories and concepts about our own existence are unsatisfactory and untrue and announces this so powerfully that one is no longer able to ignore or deny the fact or return easily to everyday tranquilization about it.

Clearly, the effects of the anxiety experience are viewed by Heidegger (and Kierkegaard) as all important. The experience itself is of short duration and is not a major physiological event. Everything turns on the aftermath, that to which anxiety points and that which can be seen, and now possibly grasped, as a result of the shattering liberation from group- and self-deception. It is also in effect an existential mythic call to the heroic life: to the struggle with Being and Nothingness, not as abstractions but as revealed "givens" in human experience.

What one has heard here is in no substantial way different from Kierkegaard. Much of it, in fact, sounds like a translation out of the metaphysical-theological language employed by Kierkegaard into a secular terminology created by Heidegger. Kierkegaard, for his part, would still insist on the language of "grace" that he believes plays a role in the process of self-recovery and self-actualization, but this is ultimately not a major point of disagreement. Kierkegaard is unable to express himself in any other terminology, while Heidegger regards it as a necessity to do so. Yet Heidegger's increasing use of poetic language gradually begins to suggest a very similar course. Kierkegaard would say that the full process needs to be supplemented by grace. However, this insistence on Kierkegaard's part would seem unnecessary and gratuitous for those outside the Christian belief system who hold that they have experienced the same without following a Christian path.

10

Despair as Divided Will and Inner Life Ignored

Kierkegaard's *The Sickness unto Death* at first glance might seem to suggest that there are multiple forms of despair. The table of contents contributes to this impression as section headings announce discussions of despair as conscious or unconscious or as defined by finitude and infinitude, possibility and necessity, and so forth. But despair is a single sickness. In *The Sickness unto Death*, a symptom-oriented psychologist views the manifestations of serious forms of dis-ease while his *meta*physician alter ego analyzes the roots of the disease and steers the patient toward a religious solution. The actual disease is all one thing—a refusal to be who and what one really is—contracted in a primal act in which the will turned against itself. He analyzes its progressing in a maturing individual toward a kind of fever pitch where the fever can be broken and the patient at last be healed. This is what Kierkegaard is essentially talking about in *The Sickness unto Death* and what he had partially portrayed in the "case history" of Aesthete A in *Either/Or*, where the problem of despair was first vividly portrayed. As we have already seen, there the Aesthete's "Diapsalmata" revealed a despairing individual whose life was a burden to him, who felt empty and trapped, without hope, without a way out. Judge William, in part 2, gave the seemingly hopeless Aesthete A the paradoxical counsel to despair as the act needed to break him out of his apparent dead end.[1] The presentation of despair in *Either/Or* as both sickness and required action suggested an illness that has to run its course. Judge William recognized despair in the young man he was observing, but he did not deal with the range and intensity of the forms of despair. Thus, six years after *Either/Or*, another Kierkegaardian pseudonymous narrator would provide a virtual diagnostic manual of despair and correct Judge William's injunction to despair in order to overcome despair and instead assert very clearly in the introduction to *The Sickness unto Death* that despair is *not* the cure for despair. In addition, Kierkegaard per Anti-Climacus will emphasize the source of the cure for spiritual illness as coming from "outside" or "above," in the experience of a grace that is only posited and whose workings are never described in detail.[2]

Judge William's counsel was tantamount to encouraging Aesthete A to take a positive course about his condition ("Do something!") in place of passivity. Where Aristotle in his own notion of health stressed *outward* activity, Judge William meant *inward* activity and became the first spokesman among Kierkegaard's pseudonymns for the importance of the inner life.[3] Kierkegaard followed Aristotle in asserting that health—in this case, psychological and spiritual health—required activity but stressed that the inner dimension is at least equally important in total human health. In this view, health is not the mere absence of illness but the product of positive action on one's part. An essential aspect of Kierkegaard's psychological thought is that a healthy or "cured" self is not the mere result of getting rid of some kind of illness and neutralizing dis-ease but requires active, engaged attention to the inner life and to the sickness lurking there.

Students of Kierkegaard generally view *The Sickness unto Death* as a continuation and sharpening of insights from *The Concept of Anxiety*, where the analysis of everyone's first act against oneself (sin) led to an analysis of the "nothing" that permitted this condition to come into being. *The Sickness unto Death* thus shares with *The Concept of Anxiety* a declared interest in the psychological and in the "upbuilding," or self-improving. Its subtitle, "A Christian Psychological Exposition for Upbuilding and Awakening," should be taken at its word and as indicating greater interest on the part of the author in driving the reader to action than in an exhaustive, intellectually dazzling systematic analysis. But the latter is perhaps the more striking in the work, and therefore perhaps Kierkegaard's need for issuing a warning. Surely nineteenth-century readers were puzzled by the work. It strikes the twenty-first-century reader as a combination of reflection on experience (its phenomenological aspect) and Christian theology. The two parts cannot be easily disjoined, for they are also conceptually intertwined. (Commentators have noted that the psychology of part 1 already presupposes the theology of part 2, while the theological part 2 rests on the psychological foundations of part 1 and lends it credibility.)[4] Surprisingly, Kierkegaard–Anti-Climacus claims in the introduction that any university student could have written *The Sickness unto Death*, but the contemporary university student often prematurely despairs of understanding the work as a whole because of the first paragraph's arresting but confusing definition of the self:[5]

> *What is the self? The self is a relation that relates itself to itself or it is the relation's relating itself to itself in the relation; the self is not the relation but is the relation's relating itself to itself.*

Despite the appearance of a definition, one would not necessarily be expecting a full definition of the self here but rather indications of Kierkegaard's emphases and program. While he begins by defining the self as relationship, what is most striking, but not always obvious, is that the first relationship mentioned is *relationship to one's own self.* This is not what we normally think of when we first think of relationship, but rather relationship to *others.*[6] However, in proceeding in this manner, Kierkegaard is not proposing solipsism but rather an alternative and ultimately complementary perspective to the outer-oriented culture of his (and our) times. Relationship is not just about the external, not just about the other. *It is emphatically also inner.* There is a way of relating to *oneself,* and it is different from the relating to other selves in one's outer life.

The work thus highlights problems in this inner relationship to oneself.[7] And misrelationship to oneself in one's inner life is fundamentally what constitutes despair. Religiously understood, the misrelationship is reflected in an absent or ruptured relationship to God. And it is manifested psychologically above all in a split will: a will that wills two things and tortures itself in an ongoing battle of these two wills and reveals the possibility, on the part of those who wish to bring it to conclusion, of achieving a purity of heart that wills one thing.[8]

Beneath the symptoms of a life in flight from itself into fantasy, illusions, and external things, a divided will as the root phenomenon of despair is a rupture between an individual's existence and his or her becoming, which Kierkegaard views ultimately as a religious task. Thus it is important to keep in mind that Kierkegaard–Anti-Climacus[9] sees himself in *The Sickness unto Death* here as a "*Christian* psychologist,"[10] rather than a *natural* psychologist. He provocatively announces that he brings certain intellectual terms, categories, and beliefs to the analysis of despair, most notably the Christian category of sin, as well as its theological background. Formally speaking, this is not so very different from what happens in Freudian psychology, Jungian psychology, or the newly emerging field of evolutionary psychology: namely, an intellectual framework and foundational point of view are superimposed upon the project and the data to be analyzed. Most significantly, the question posed to the data is how they make sense in light of the postulated theory. Therefore, one aspect of the project in *The Sickness unto Death* is to articulate how the problem of a fragmented or divided self can be understood in light of the Christian category sin.

The opening definition of the self in *The Sickness unto Death* cited above has baffled many a Kierkegaard reader, including that university student who Kierkegaard thought might easily write his book. And a lot of ink has been spilled in trying to puzzle out what it means for a self to relate to itself and for a relation to relate to itself. Strictly speaking, (actual) self does not relate to (higher) self as one human being relates to another (as in the way that John relates to Peter or to Mary, for example) but relates itself in reflection about the present, regret about the past, and anticipation of a future. Kierkegaard's own formulations may not always be the most fortuitous expression of his insights, especially for those unaccustomed to seeing psychological problems expressed in nineteenth-century metaphysical language. However, unpacking the formulation is less difficult than parsing it. The key to understanding Kierkegaard's opening formulation of despair—and, even more important, understanding what to do about it—rests in understanding *how* a self relates to itself and *how* a relationship relates to itself inwardly.[11]

A mistake in contemplating the opening lines of the work would be to think that Kierkegaard is portraying the self merely as a relationship between antithetical metaphysical elements in the personality: finitude and infinitude, necessity and possibility, and so on.[12] The key line is that *the self is the relating to its own self.*[13] How then does a self relate properly to itself? *By an act of the will*: by willing to be that which in essential structure and existential dynamism one truly is. But the factual problem, in Kierkegaard's understanding, is that one has already willed *not* to be the self that one most truly is and can be[14] and, as reflection and analysis reveal, has instead either willed weakly to avoid this higher calling or else defiantly willed to pseudocreate some fantasy self. In the process, a series of psychological repercussions emerge, the most notable brought to clearest expression in Sartre's famous term "bad faith," namely, the individual's uncanny actualized ability to deceive himself about himself and his true state.[15] (The discovery of a false self is, however, still a distance from a clear sense of the self that one should be willing and actualizing.)

Kierkegaard's insight aims to highlight experiential indications of the nonunity of a deceptively unified self, the fact that a person is always to some extent *not yet* who she or he truly is, that the self is a dynamism that one must direct toward that which is greater than oneself and which grounds the self, namely, the Transcendent. The illusion of already being a unified or completed self, and free of any troubling reflection about this, is what Kierkegaard called unconscious despair and named as despair's most prevalent form. While he terms it unconscious, he nevertheless repeatedly suggests that it is not an undisturbed unconsciousness but one in which there are occasional tremors that one chooses not to notice, until and unless there is, as it were, an earthquake. The situation could be analogous to a person's going to a physician unaware of any problem and insisting on feeling fine, while the physician, in contrast, detects a problem in the patient that as yet has no surface symptom; and upon hearing the diagnosis, the patient privileges the surface feeling of well-being over the physician's detection of an underlying condition.[16]

Kierkegaard thinks here of an unconscious condition that has been self-inflicted. Unlike a physical condition whose origins or infliction may not be essential to the cure, in despair, it is quite otherwise. Insofar as one comes to recognize responsibility for the state of affairs of the self, one is brought back to one of the central questions of *The Concept of Anxiety*: how do we undo a primal deed (a first sin) and its aftereffects—a deed that we ourselves individually, and no one else in our stead, must have done to ourselves? The answer is deceptively easy on the theoretical level, excruciating and complex on the existential level. *Theoretically*, one needs to will to be oneself. *Existentially*, one needs to make an act of will from out of the complex, existential, impaired self that one currently is. An impaired self that has already *not* willed to be itself must attempt either (1) to persevere in the bad faith of attempting to keep the problem from disturbing everyday consciousness or (2) try in vain to do away with itself entirely or (3) attempt to undo what has been done and make a new act of the will.[17] The outstanding question remains, how does one fuse together a will that has been split?

The task of Kierkegaard in *The Sickness unto Death* is not to speculatively re-create the original deed or to meditate on the why of this act, as he did in *The Concept of Anxiety*, but instead to recognize the manifestations of the consequences of the deed and to point toward the cure. Moreover, Kierkegaard warns at the outset that this cannot happen by any attempt at going backward and undoing the deed.[18] Indeed, the only path is to go forward, to experience the ultimately redeeming conscious agony of the divided straining to be healed. *Paradoxically, only by going forward—into deeper, conscious despair—is there hope for overcoming despair.* But such a living out of nonselfhood to its *existential* conclusion is described as an anguished act of consciousness, as one takes the full measure of what one has done to oneself and recognizes how hopeless the situation seems to be. Ironically, in the agony of felt hopelessness lies the possibility of actual hope, as expressed in the Christian promise of grace. For when one has come to full consciousness of one's fallenness and brokenness, therein lies the first real hope.

To understand the varieties of being a nonself versus the simplicity of being an authentic self, Anti-Climacus's treatise presents the reader with an abstract cataloging of the manifold ways of being a not-self.[19] His analysis of the forms of despair seems to be an attempt to consider despair from every possible categorical angle (e.g., the despair of finitude as the lack of infinitude, the despair of infinitude as the lack of finitude, the despair of necessity as the lack of possibility, etc.). The underlying point in this analysis of opposites is that despair is an imbalance caused by a misrelationship to one's Ground and resulting misrelationship to oneself. Despite the abstract language, the work tries to point the reader toward an understanding of what the misrelationship to oneself is all about, while theologically asserting that no final cure can arise without correcting the misrelationship to the Grounding Power, or God as understood in traditional Christian thought. The seriousness of the work, on its own terms, lies not only in its analysis but also in directing the reader to do something about despair, Christianly understood. Thus Kierkegaard's seeming speculative and methodical survey of the categories of despair quickly joins up with the Christian theology of sin, where, in the deepest sense of guilt and responsibility, there emerges the hope of forgiveness and establishment of a self regrounded in God. (Secular interpreters of Kierkegaard, such as Heidegger and Sartre, have been able to mine his insights while bracketing the Christian language.)

While Anti-Climacus posits a *universally* applicable cure, he stresses the *individual* nature and destiny of each self, as well as the individual nature of each person's relationship to the Grounding Power. In his view, it is not at all the case that we all become the same self. Each self is radically individual and, to the extent that there is a felt relationship to God (that which is Absolute), it will also *not* be identical for each. The rich religious implication here is that each individual's relationship to God is indeed individual: it is not identical to Abraham's or to Jesus' or to any Christian saint's. It will be uniquely one's own, even if it shares essential aspects with the experience of others. Kierkegaard thus gives new meaning to the phrase of "being alone with one's God." There is thus an implicit existential richness here in Kierkegaard's analysis that can be overlooked in the emphasis on forgiveness and grace.

Through the detailed analyses of the forms of despair, the reader is led to understand that the exit path out of the cave of despair first involves further descent into despair—to experiencing the hopeless situation of continuing as a nonself and, in pained humility, despairing of the illusion of being able to be the creator of some new kind of self on one's own. Finally, it is breaking with hopelessness itself and regaining hope. To employ a different metaphor of descent, overcoming despair by continuing through despair can be thought of as soaring down the slope of despair only to build up enough momentum to soar up the opposite slope. Kierkegaard, for his part, can imagine this happening only with the grace of God, who graciously restores the relationship broken by sin.

Diagnosing the Conflicted Self

Kierkegaard describes the internally conflicted self as cleft in two, torn between opposite metaphysical poles of the self, and severed from its anchoring or grounding principle. He then proposes a cure that initially involves a worsening of suffering: living through the experience of cleavage intensively and self-consciously, to its bitter end in the desperate cry for a rebirth of the self. If it were only psychological rebirth that was sought, his would be a natural psychology. But Kierkegaard means spiritual rebirth and is aware of addressing his prescription to a culture for which the term "spiritual" means increasingly little because the spirit and the spiritual, inwardness and inner life have been overlooked in experience and banished to poetry and theology books.

Authentic and Inauthentic Despair

These are not the terms of Kierkegaard but rather of the German scholar Michael Theunissen, who, in *Kierkegaard's Concept of Despair*, attempts to get to the heart of what he calls Kierkegaard's anatomy of despair and in some cases to find clearer formulations than Kierkegaard arrived at.[20] For, as has been suggested, Kierkegaard's schematization of despair can sometimes have the effect of obscuring what is essentially going on in despair. Theunissen notes that Kierkegaard's cataloguing of the forms of despair initially makes it seem that the forms of despair sketched by Kierkegaard–Anti-Climacus are quite distinct from one another. Yet on closer examination, each seems to contain elements of its opposite. For Theunissen, it all comes down to *the despair of necessity as the loss of the sense of possibility.* This is the form of despair par excellence: a fractured will that feels it impossibe to will what is required (despite the fact that an act of will remains an open possibility) (p. 97). He distills Kierkegaard's schematization even further when he writes, "The existential-dialectical principle of Kierkegaard's analysis of despair is: *We do not will to be directly what we are*" (p. 5).[21]

One is always factically what one is, but the problem is willing or not willing to be who one is, and thus relating or not relating to oneself thereby (p. 14). The general human condition is that we do not will to be what we are, and we sense it, even if we repress it. Theunissen terms authentic despair the rising to the level of knowing it. Inauthentic despair would be *unconscious despair* (which Kierkegaard holds to be the majority case). But, looked at in another way, there really is no such thing as a pure unconscious despair. There is always an inkling about one's condition, even if one strives to repress or deny it. Theunissen comments that one cannot be in despair without some "self-consciousness in the sense of an accompanying self-presence" (p. 15).

But the disruptive, diremptive *not willing* here is really also a kind of willing, in the mode of negation (p. 15). So there is always an element of willing even in what is termed not willing, and always an element of consciousness even in what is termed unconscious despair. Thus, inauthentic despair is not a true parallel category to conscious despair *in fact* but only *in terminology*. It is a subcategory, a less-conscious despair; a kind of virtual unconscious despair, but one that is not unconscious upon fuller scrutiny. For it takes constant effort to keep the sense that one is in despair from rising to awareness. This is a major insight of Kierkegaard's here, picked up by subsequent existential authors (and by Sartre in particular). Theunissen describes it thus:

> In terms of a structural theory, to be in despair in all of its forms means both that we do not want to be what we are and that we want to be what we are not. We do not want to be what we are as human beings who are defined by both necessity and finitude as well as possibility and infinitude, and we want to be what we are not, that is, a pure possibility and infinitude, which in its purity is inhuman, or a pure necessity and finitude, which alienates us from our human being. (pp. 18–19)

We are alienated from our own human being when we yearn to be absorbed in the collective or want to be submerged in another. In effect we yearn for an inhuman existence. But not willing to be who we are is always *primarily* a rejection of who we are and only *secondarily* a desire to be what we are not (p. 19).[22]

But the fact is that even if we want to be rid of ourselves, we cannot do it through an act of will. Failure to do so leads only to a heightened consciousness about despair. Its opposite finds easy expression but remains a very difficult achievement: "Not to be in despair means to accept oneself, and in the depth dimension of our self, it means to ground oneself in the power that has established the self" (p. 22).

This is the essential message of Anti-Climacus's part 1, freed of the metaphysical language and categories in which it is expressed.

Part 2 of *The Sickness unto Death* introduces the Christian theology of sin in order to understand the disease that is at the root of existential "dis-ease" and then the cure. (Recall that the origin of the disease was analysed in *The Concept of Anxiety*, where the original sin is de facto an act of the will: as mythologically represented, not following the command of

God in the Garden of Paradise.) One does not, however, have to accept the Christian doctrine of sin in order to make sense of what Kierkegaard is saying. In fact, most of his diagnosis can be restated without reference to the Christian doctrine of sin—but not completely, of course.

Excursus: Despair in Neo-Darwinian Thought

Evolutionary biologists speculate that despair and depression reflect the cleavage between ancestral highly social conditions that attended the evolution of *Homo sapiens* and the current social and cultural configuration, in which modern humans often find themselves feeling isolated and frequently living alone.[23]

Interestingly, Kierkegaard's *The Sickness unto Death* contains analogous ideas about contemporary society and above all about the contemporary individual's alienation from an original, superior natural condition. Kierkegaard denounced the disappearance of authentic individuality in what he held to be the bourgeois philistinism of the nineteenth century and the resulting intensification of alienation.[24] Kierkegaard attempted to get at a root sense of alienation from an original condition but interpreted it in terms of the accepted Christian theology of his day. Both Kierkegaard and Heidegger roundly criticized the complacency and self-satisfaction of contemporary society and for bringing everyone down to the same level, for its downgrading of the individual and for its elevation of the masses, for empty speech and hollow relationships—all of which combine and conspire to weigh the individual down in "bad faith" about his or her condition and conspire to distract the person from self-recovery.

Surely Kierkegaard and evolutionary psychologists differ about the origin of the problem of despair. As for the cure, both agree that there is no going back, there is only a going forward. For the evolutionary psychologist, even if return to a more ancestral form of social living were possible, it would not be a realistic recommendation, and a utilitarian calculus would suggest that the increased incidence of despair is the unavoidable price one pays for living conditions that in most other ways are preferable to ancestral society (and more conducive to successful reproduction of the species). The answer to the modern condition is to be found in the laboratory of self-actualization. It should be noted that this is something Kierkegaard would never have permitted to be called self-creation, as that smacks of the mythological Lucifer's desire to replace

God and thus to be his own lord. Nor would Kierkegaard have been open to the new evolutionary theologian's idea of co-creation.[25]

But the view from the perspective of current evolutionary psychology (certain to be refined in the future) would *not* be the solution for Kierkegaard.[26] Evolutionary psychology's take on despair as an experience of the cleft between an ancestral condition and a modern condition leaves out of consideration the possibility of internal evolution anytime soon. In short, it considers the contemporary psyche of *Homo sapiens* as de facto a constant vis-à-vis an ancestral human psyche, or at least as still having the structure and role in the glacial pace of evolution as it had two hundred thousand years ago, when *Homo sapiens* emerged as a distinctive species, or even fifty thousand years ago, when the most recent trace of human evolution is held to have occurred.

For his part, Kierkegaard puts the emphasis on a dynamic psyche, and the entire meaning of cure for him is *not* the reestablishment of an ancestral social model but rather a new, exhilarating, and undefined condition that depends for its success on willing to be the dynamic being that one is and on doing so in a felt interaction with the experienced Transcendent.[27]

The severing from the Grounding Power (God) and the current experience of cleavage within oneself are understood as in a cause-effect relationship. It is because of the severing from the Grounding Power that the personality is unbalanced and veers toward one extreme or the other (possibility and necessity, finitude and infinitude, etc.) without ever fully breaking with its opposite. The same phenomenon of separation and cleavage also points toward the solution or cure, namely restoration of relating and reanchoring of the self in its Ground.[28] Kierkegaard imagines the cleavage as constituting the tendency in the personality to overemphasize one or the other opposite poles in the self: possibility and necessity, the eternal and the temporal, infinitude and finitude. He posits instead a "true self" that would reflect a synthesis and balance of these elements.

Each of the forms of despair that Kierkegaard catalogues represents a variation of not being oneself. However, they are not all equal. Much of what he means by despair and by the self can be restated less obscurely. To become oneself is (a) to will to be the dynamic becoming entity that one truly is and (b) *not* to will to try to be static or to be some imaginary other kind of being than the one that one is. But the reality is not nearly as simple as the formulation: one finds oneself in a world that subtly pushes one toward one of the fantasy alternatives that he sketches, and one wonders what is wrong with oneself when one embraces one of these false options that conflicts with the ongoing dynamism within oneself.

His message, in many senses, amounts to, "Go with the flow," not so very different in form from the Stoics in formulation but surely different in the content of the self-knowledge one has in our times, as well as in the understanding of what is meant by "the flow." Kierkegaard's language of analysis is fairly modern, while the language in which he discusses the solution or cure is often ancient, metaphysical, and theological. These latter are cherished categories of medieval and modern metaphysics but pose serious "translation" problems for many contemporary readers. Both the problem and advantage in reading Kierkegaard after absorbing Nietzsche's announcement of the death of Western metaphysics is that we are now able to see how clearly his work proceeds out of a Christianized Plotinian universe via Augustine of Hippo, an intellectual universe that we now know not to be so. Contemporary physics does not in any way suggest that everything will return to the One. On the contrary, the evidence seems to point to its exact opposite.

Thus no contemporary reader can be expected to accept Kierkegaard's articulation of the problem of a split and self-alienated self in the metaphysical language of finitude and infinitude, the eternal and the temporal, possibility and necessity. He is expressing an existential dilemma in the philosophical language then in use. (Of course, there is also an existential connection here to classic and medieval philosophy.) The understanding of the existential dilemma that he is trying to express is in fact as old as Saint Paul and Saint Augustine: a divided self whose will and willpower have been compromised and are not up to the task of restoring themselves. Quite importantly, Kierkegaard locates the problem of the self in the will rather than in knowledge. For it is not a matter here of merely "*knowing* the self," in Socrates's famous adoption of the motto of Delphi. Kierkegaard, like Freud after him, recognizes that part of the problem is that the self *does not know* itself. And yet the Delphic inscription (γνῶθι σεαυτόν) is also not so far away in formulation either. In a sense, one must have some self-knowledge in order to will the self. Kierkegaard certainly recognizes that, but the kind of knowledge called for here would not be the knowledge of metaphysical categories of finitude and infinitude, eternal and temporal, and so on.

Kierkegaard's *The Sickness unto Death,* the titularly gloomy companion to *The Concept of Anxiety* and more importantly its conceptual completion, is in fact far more positive and hopeful than its sister work. *The Sickness unto Death* does not have the originality and striking genius of *The Concept of Anxiety*—a genius that uncovers more than it is aware of and that leaves for succeeding generations to process its findings, as a Heidegger, for example, would do some 80 years later.[29] It appears to be a kind of 1848 Diagnostic Manual of Despair: a work of diagnosis but also schematization in which all the variants are carefully labeled. But if it proceeds through the various forms of despair, the "data" defy conceptual neatness. He recognizes as much and admits that each paired type contains elements of the other in itself and in some senses may be considered a variant of its own opposite, as in the example of the despair of weakness and the despair of defiance, each of which contains elements of its opposite.

Beyond Sin and Grace?

Sin remained a major interpretative category in Kierkegaard's thinking but is problematic for many modern thinkers. Equally problematic is its theological corollary, grace. Kierkegaard accepts the tenets of traditional Christian theology as facts and interprets the human condition filtered through them. He accepted the biblical story of the fall of Adam and Eve and the theological interpretation of it that crystallized in the theology of Augustine of Hippo, namely as constituting an original and inherited sin, even if he added a modern existential twist. Thus in *The Concept of Anxiety*, Kierkegaard had his pseudonymous narrator give modern psychological depth to this old doctrine. That line of thought continues to underlie *The Sickness unto Death*, as well as the theological corollation of grace together with faith, all the while emphasizing not the theological and the traditional so much as the existential and experiential. Kierkegaard's solution to the "bad faith" of despair remains the *experience* of the ancient faith of Christianity in a God who offers forgiveness, salvation, and grace.

For modern secular readers of Kierkegaard, the notion of grace or supplement to human effort is more problematic than the notion of sin itself. Sin at least had been successfully secularized by Kant in *Religion within the Bounds of Reason Alone* (*Die Religion innerhalb der Grenzen der blossen Vernunft*) with its notion of a fall into radical evil and further secularized by Heidegger in *Being and Time* (*Sein und Zeit*) in his concept of *Dasein*'s *Verfallenheit* (fallenness) as a starting point (rather than a self-inflicted wound) from which the human person must extricate him- or herself. And while Kant does allow for a kind of gracious regard by the Moral Law Giver vis-à-vis one struggling to be perfectly moral, there is no equivalent in Heidegger's work, nor is there any phenomenological need for any superhuman supplement.

Kierkegaard's conceptual embrace of grace is not a description of a phenomenologically grounded need but rather the solution offered to him by Christian theology and to which he subscribes and which, he would no doubt assert, conforms to his own experience. It is a sincerely held belief on Kierkegaard's part, but it is an arbitrarily added element, without demonstration or proof. While the majority of commentators on Kierkegaard have been and continue to be believing Christians, their testimony alone does not establish that Kierkegaard was correct either as a psychologist or phenomenologist (rather than as a theologian) in adding this element as a decisive truth in human existence. This goes as well for his requirement that the self relate to its Constituting Power (or Ground) in order to achieve authentic selfhood.[30]

If one had the opportunity to ask Kierkegaard–Anti-Climacus to describe a concrete historical individual of Christian faith who has overcome despair, he would likely respond that he has no access to the inward life of another. (But Heidegger does no differently in his analysis of fallenness and authenticity in *Being and Time* nearly a hundred years later.) It is of course much easier to think of describing historical *non*selves, and here there is an abundant supply, both non-Christian and Christian. However, for this commentator there is no reason to think that important non-Christian individuals such as Socrates and Siddhārtha Gautama should be regarded as having been in despair at the conclusion of their lives. In fact, based on the sources that we possess, there is no more reason to think that they were in despair, in Kierkegaard's sense, than there is to think that the historical Jesus of Nazareth himself was in despair at the end.

In a certain sense, this observation is unfair to Kierkegaard, who addressed his work only to a contemporary and professing Christian audience so that they should understand and do something about their despair along the lines outlined by their Christian faith. But if it is unfair to Kierkegaard to raise the question of authentic selfhood achieved outside Christianity, it is by no means an unfair question in and of itself, nor an irrelevant one for anyone who is interested in the possible psychological truth about overcoming the split in the self that Kierkegaard otherwise so insightfully sketches.

Is there then a model of authentic selfhood that does not require being articulated in the categories of Christian theology? Can one successfully substitute the language of Being or the Ground of Being (Heidegger and Tillich, respectively) for Kierkegaard's Constituting Power? Can one speak meaningfully and in a promising manner about a model of becoming a self where the self is relating to a felt sense of the Transcendent (that is not necessarily visualized or conceptualized in Christian images)? In thinking about such questions, one is ultimately obliged to pass beyond Kierkegaard. One cannot, after all, expect him to rise above his times and culture. Kierkegaard has also given no indication whatsoever that he would be prepared to consider such an option, and his writings, as this writer knows them, would suggest that he would regard this way of speaking as a return to paganism—perhaps even to the golden Greek paganism of Socrates himself—but still a paganism deprived of a higher truth proclaimed by Christianity.

Still, Kierkegaard's radical insight about the tremors of possibility arising within the shattered self (in the anxiety experience of *The Concept of Anxiety*) and their intensification in the pained consciousness of being a shattered self in need of reconstitution, regrounding, and rebirth have a meaning and a validity for others who do not think of the process in Christian terms, as Heidegger and even Sartre demonstrated in their early twentieth-century non-Christian writings so indebted to Kierkegaard.

The thesis of *The Sickness unto Death* still commands our attention, namely, that to overcome or rectify the condition of being an incomplete self one must intensify and accelerate the process of dissolving the false self.[31] In twentieth-century parlance, this was once colloquially referred to as "bottoming out," hitting bottom.[32] But in the end, Kierkegaard's analysis points affirmatively to a dynamic, self-actualizing self with its own unique history and its own unique resolution, not at all in isolation but rather genuinely united with others in an experienced common Ground. But he does not describe it in its actualization. As such, Kierkegaard concludes at the edges of mysticism, affirms what he holds to lie beyond, but, if he enters, does not take the reader with him. Meantime, what he has left behind remains a very rich deposit that continues to be mined.

Appendix

On the Kierkegaard-Heidegger Relationship

Chapter 9 traced the parallels between Kierkegaard and Heidegger in their respective discussions of *Angst* and Heidegger's more than apparent indebtedness to Kierkegaard on that theme. There can be no question but that Kierkegaard had been a significant influence on Heidegger's thought and development, especially as manifested in *Being and Time.* With so many parallels, so many shared terms, and so many similar categories, there must be something to it, one feels. Yet Heidegger never explicitly acknowledged a direct or significant debt. As John Van Buren remarked in his study of the young Heidegger's development,

> The later Heidegger was, as has been well documented, often puzzlingly reluctant to acknowledge his profound indebtedness to those philosophical traditions that originally helped to put him on the way of the being question in his early Freiburg period, such as the young Luther, Kierkegaard, Jaspers, Aristotle's practical writings, Husserl's Sixth Investigation, and Dilthey.[1]

John Caputo was hard-hitting in his criticism of Heidegger:

> Heidegger not only understates his dependence on Kierkegaard, he misstates it. In borrowing upon Kierkegaard's theory of repetition—without acknowledgement—he invokes Kierkegaard at the most crucial ontological juncture in the published text of *Being and Time.* And when he does mention Kierkegaard, it is always to dress him down as an ontico-existentiell author. Yet three central sections . . .—§64 (the constancy of the self), §65 (temporality), and §74 (repetition)—are directly drawn from Kierkegaard's writings. The treatment of the constancy of the self comes from the discussion of the "continuance of sin" in *The Sickness unto Death.* The analysis of temporality is dependent upon the analysis of existential temporality in the second volume of *Either/Or.* And the all-important discussion of repetition is based quite directly upon Kierkegaard. . . . It is clear that Kierkegaard's contribution to *Being and Time* goes right to the heart of the ontology which is defended there. Heidegger differs from Kierkegaard, not as an ontological thinker from an ontic, as he likes to make out, but principally in

terms of the degree to which Heidegger has formalized and articulated Kierkegaard's ontology in a more systematic, professorial manner.[2]

Not only does Caputo counter Heidegger's depiction of Kierkegaard's role as merely a religious thinker but he has also nicely summed up the difference. In addition to *Being and Time*, however, are Heidegger's lectures in the period both before and after *Being and Time*, where important references to Kierkegaard are found that detail a very substantial role in the development of Heidegger's thought. Here one finds many of Kierkegaard's categories virtually intact. Because these lectures have been published only recently, the previous generation of Heidegger readers—except for those who actually attended the lectures or heard about them—could easily fail to appreciate the extent of Kierkegaard's influence. In fact, Kierkegaard belongs to a Lutheran triad of influence upon Heidegger, along with Augustine and Luther. One can go overboard by stressing everything in Heidegger that has a resonance with Kierkegaard (or other writers whom he read). For Heidegger is influenced not only by Kierkegaard but also by major figures who played a significant role in the development of Kierkegaard's own thought, including Socrates, Aristotle, Paul, and Luther. So it is possible for something to sound as though it echoes Kierkegaard when it might actually be an Augustinian or Lutheran influence.[3]

To further complicate the task at hand, Heidegger wrote numerous (and sometimes contradictory) autobiographical statements about his intellectual development. In 1923 he wrote that "companions in my searching were the young Luther and the paragon Aristotle, whom Luther hated. Kierkegaard gave impulses, and Husserl gave me my eyes."[4] In a revisionist utterance of 1943, however, Heidegger seems to dismiss Kierkegaard and to neutralize for the next few decades any reader's suspicions that Kierkegaard was important to him, since the remark was made before the letters and lectures of the 1920s were available. Indeed, one of Heidegger's biographers bristles in his assessment of this statement as he observes that the very same Heidegger "who once modeled his interpretation of Aristotle on Kierkegaard's own reading, said in 1943 that Kierkegaard remains essentially remote from Aristotle. . . . 'For Kierkegaard is not a thinker but a religious writer.'"[5]

Readers will find a full chronicle of Heidegger's intellectual development detailed by several intellectual biographers.[6] The goal here is, far more modestly and based on those biographies, to sketch chronologically Heidegger's engagement with the writings of Kierkegaard and Kierkegaardian themes, including those mediated by Karl Jaspers, and in the process view the extent of that influence.

Heidegger's *formal* concern is not the analysis of a struggling individual that Kierkegaard presents with existential interest and passion. Nonetheless, Heidegger manifests existential concerns in *Being and Time*, with the result that he had to fend off those who wanted to interpret him as an existentialist. Formally, Heidegger's problem is Being, and his project is a phenomenology of Being that takes its point of departure in a phenomenology of human being (*Dasein*). This is neither Kierkegaard's problematic nor his project, of course, even if he makes some distinctive contributions to a phenomenology of human existence in his own writings. In Heidegger's telling, the seeds of his own project were sown as early as 1907, when the seventeen-year-old gymnasium student Heidegger was presented with a copy of Franz Brentano's 1862 dissertation "On the Manifold Meaning of Being in Aristotle." Heidegger recounts it as being nothing less than decisive in his philosophical orientation toward the problem of Being.

Several years later, in the years 1910 to 1914, Heidegger, along with many others in Germany, was reading the new German-language translations of Kierkegaard. During this period he was also reading Nietzsche's *Will to Power*, Dilthey's collected works, and the German Romantics. (The strongest influence at the time was Nietzsche.) During this period, influences on the young Heidegger also included the kairological thinking of Aristotle, Luther, and Kierkegaard, as well as the writings of Augustine and Pascal.[7]

In the period 1919 onward, inspired by Luther and Kierkegaard, Heidegger sought to destroy the Greek conceptuality underlying traditional theological thought and to penetrate to primal Christianity,[8] in the process breaking out of the neoscholastic worldview that he had had. Confirming the role of Kierkegaard in this period is a comment from 1920 by Jaspers to the effect that both he, Jaspers, and Heidegger shared then the same passion for Kierkegaard.[9]

In the summer semester of 1923, Heidegger prefaced his analysis of *Dasein* and factical being in the world with an acknowledgment that "strong influences on the explication presented here come from Kierkegaard's work."[10] Kierkegaard is also considered to have influenced Heidegger's view of Socrates's understanding of the philosophical quest after being as a way of life.[11]

Kierkegaard also mediated Aristotle to Heidegger during this period. As Van Buren remarks,

> Heidegger was certainly aware of not only Luther's, but also Kierkegaard's positive appropriation of Aristotle. Not only did his first lecture course on Aristotle in [winter semester] 1921–22 open with two mottos

> from Kierkegaard, and not only was his reading here of the Platonic-Socratic quest for being organized around Kierkegaard's concept of "passion" and "subjective truth," but in [spring semester] 1923 he discussed Kierkegaard's appropriation of Aristotle through his "connection with Trendelenberg."[12]

During this same period, Heidegger's exposure to an early draft of Jaspers's Kierkegaard interpretation in the *Psychologie der Weltanschauungen* (*Psychology of Worldviews,* untranslated) played a significant role, and this Kierkegaardian work figured importantly in the friendship that developed between the two men. In that work Jaspers viewed Kierkegaard as stressing factical individual existence over against universal man in general and as criticizing idealism for stressing a fantastic being seemingly indifferent to the existing person. Jaspers also stressed the personal and enactment sense of passionate subjective truth. In subsequent years, according to Van Buren, Heidegger continued to rely on Jaspers's detailed expositions of such Kierkegaardian concepts as "the existent," the individual, subjective truth, passion, anxiety, and death, in which Heidegger followed Kierkegaard point by point, also on dispersion, repetition, curiosity, enclosing reserve, conscience, guilt, indirect communication, time, and the moment. Jaspers's "limit situations" concept was derived from Kierkegaard (as well as from Nietzsche) and has its echo in Heidegger.[13] And the Heideggerian concept of "care" is indebted to Kierkegaard's discussion of that concept in "The Lilies of the Field and the Birds of the Air," which Heidegger read in translation as early as 1924. (Heidegger's Augustine readings in 1925 also figure in this.)[14]

The Three Kierkegaard Footnotes in *Being and Time* (1927)

There are three well-known footnotes that refer to Kierkegaard in Heidegger's major work of 1927. The substance of Heidegger's comments is that he values Kierkegaard's religious discourses more than Kierkegaard's more properly philosophical works. It smacks of dismissing Kierkegaard. To put this treatment of Kierkegaard in a larger context, it should be noted that Heidegger does not give much acknowledgment in that work to other at least equally significant influences on his overall development and philosophical program, such as Aristotle and Duns Scotus and Husserl, but he does not dismiss them as he appears to do to in the case of Kierkegaard. They too receive only a few footnote mentions.[15] One reason for the very un-German scarcity of footnotes may well lie in the fact that, in the period just before *Being and Time* was published, Heidegger was under pressure to publish a book-length manuscript for the sake of his academic career. The completion of *Being and Time* thus took place in some haste. (Heidegger also acknowledged that *Being and Time* was only part 1 of a still incomplete larger project, one that was never completed in the originally envisioned form.)[16]

Two of the three *Being and Time* footnotes are worth citing in full. The first is as follows:

> The man who has gone farthest in analyzing the phenomenon of anxiety—and again in the theological context of a "psychological" exposition of the problem of original sin—is S. Kierkegaard.

(Heidegger references the Diedrichs translation of Kierkegaard into German: *Der Begriff der Angst, Gesammelte Werke*, vol. 5 [1923]. See *Sein und Zeit*, 190, 3rd paragraph of note 1.)

The second footnote reads as follows:

> In the nineteenth century, S. Kierkegaard explicitly seized upon the problem of existence as an existentiell problem, and thought it through in a penetrating fashion. But the existential problem was so alien to him that, as regards his ontology, he remained completely dominated by Hegel and by ancient philosophy as Hegel saw it. Thus, there is more to be learned philosophically from his "edifying" writings than from his theoretical ones—*with the exception of his treatise on the concept of anxiety*. (emphasis added; see *Sein und Zeit*, 235n1)

Heidegger here is clearly identifying Kierkegaard's *The Concept of Anxiety* as the exceptional place where something is indeed to be learned from Kierkegaard philosophically—as manifestly was the case in that work but also in others.[17]

(The third footnote references Jaspers's mention of Kierkegaard and the summary review of Kierkegaard, found in *Psychologie der Weltanschauungen* [on pp. 108–9 and 419–32, respectively].)

This is as much as Heidegger has to say about the Kierkegaard whom one can rightly view as having enormous influence in and upon Heidegger's text and thinking, if not his declared formal project. It is far too ungenerous, and not just in Kierkegaard's case. But it is not altogether unusual academic behavior either, historically speaking. In 2015 an author would be far more severely criticized for obscuring and ignoring important sources. John Caputo once remarked in conversation that there was a time when he introduced students to *Being and Time* with the dramatic caveat that Heidegger's work had "made in Denmark" stamped on every page. While that may have been overcompensation for Heidegger's neglect, it does point to an earlier psychological genius on whose shoulders Heidegger stands.

Notes

Introduction

1. The 1996 U.S. publication of the novel *Primary Colors* by Anonymous was a striking and successful example of the added attention pseudonymity can bring to a work. (Some months after publication, the *New Yorker* writer Joe Klein admitted to being the author of this roman à clef of American politics.)

2. See Rudolf Bultmann, *Kerygma and Myth* (1948; repr., New York: HarperCollins, 2000), and *Jesus Christ and Mythology* (1926; repr., Prentice Hall, 1997).

3. See Friedrich Schleiermacher, *On Religion: Speeches to Its Cultured Despisers* (1799).

Chapter 1

1. On the Copenhagen philosopher Sibbern, see Kirmmse, *Encounters with Kierkegaard*, 241

2. Ibid., 242.

3. Cited in Nordentoft, *Kierkegaard's Psychology*, 352. (Original Danish edition published 1972.)

4. Ibid., 245.

5. *Papirer* VII 1 A 126. (Also cited in Nordentoft, *Kierkegaard's Psychology*, 311.) In the same entry from 1846, Kierkegaard mentions his formally consulting a physician, despite his disinclination to speak with anyone about his innermost being and his not being in favor of confidants. He seems to have done so out of a sense of duty to authority. Whether or not his physician would have been able to rise to the challenge of such an unusual patient, Kierkegaard so controls the conversation that the answer is merely the formal answer that Kierkegaard sought and is of no personal help. See Nordentoft, *Kierkegaard's Psychology*, 313. Kierkegaard testifies to the power, attractiveness, and strong hold of melancholia and has Aesthete A speak of loving his melancholy and being loved in return.

6. Among other places, in "'Guilty?'/'Not Guilty?'" in *Stages on Life's Way*, as "An Imaginary Psychological Construction"; in *The Concept of Anxiety*, the subtitle is "A Simple Psychologically Oriented Reflection on the Dogmatic Problem of Hereditary Sin." Kierkegaard also used it as a subtitle for "Silhouettes" in *Either/Or*, part 1: "Psychological Diversion," which represents a change from the

proposed first subtitle, "A Venture in the Black Arts"! (See *E/O* 1, supplement, p. 544, quoting *Papirer* II B 173:1).

7. See Nordentoft, *Kierkegaard's Psychology*. While Kierkegaard read and quoted Rosenkranz, on the whole it cannot be said that he is influenced by Rosenkranz and Rosenkranz's working out of psychology of subjective spirit in Hegel.

8. And which the Hong translations frequently mistranslate as "depression," which is a twentieth-century term.

9. Rosenkranz, *Psychologie*, 389n9.

10. The first university institute for psychology opened in Germany in 1879. Source: *Historisches Wörterbuch der Philosophie* (hereafter *HWdP*), 1599.

11. In Fregius's *Ciceronianus*. Source: *HWdP*, 1599.

12. See *HWdP*, 1602.

13. See Kresten Nordentoft's remark, "At any rate, it is scarcely in technical psychology that one must look for the important and profound literary inspirations behind Kierkegaard's psychology, but in his extensive, not especially systematic reading of fiction, drama, poetry, and aesthetic writings, which, together with theology, constitute the tonal background from which he takes now an example, now an impulse, or an idea. Shakespeare's importance is inestimable . . . but in addition to this must be reckoned German and Danish romantic literature and various folk tales and legendary literature" (*Kierkegaard's Psychology*, 389n9).

14. See chapter 3 for a more detailed discussion of sexuality, narcissism, and anxiety.

15. I have tried several terms, including "religious melancholy," for this represents the directionality of the mood in Kierkegaard's presentations. No term fits precisely.

16. Tammy Clewell writes, "By the time he wrote *The Ego and the Id* Freud understood that explaining the dynamics of mourning demanded a more nuanced view of ego formation, one that no longer reduced object-love to a species of self-love" ("Mourning beyond Melancholia," 47).

17. Although Freud later speaks of melancholia as finally passing; see *SE*, XIV:252.

18. However, Freud later in the essay notes that melancholia is sometimes twinned with mania, something that does not happen in mourning. See ibid., 243–55.

19. *New Introductory Lectures on Psycho-Analysis*, *SE*, XXII:86, quoted in Nordentoft, *Kierkegaard's Psychology*, 145.

20. *SKS*, 9:111; my translation, emphasis in original. See *WL*, 107.

Chapter 2

1. The fact that Kierkegaard engages the music of Mozart (1756–1791) might even be viewed as conservative. After all, Mozart had been dead fifty years when Kierkegaard wrote his Mozart essay. Notable by absence are any references to contemporary musicians such as Beethoven (1770–1827, overlapping the life of Hegel, 1770–1831) or Liszt (1811–1883). Kierkegaard was, however, involved

in a group in Copenhagen that discussed the musical ideas of Robert Schumann (1810–1856). In July of 1841 Liszt performed at the court and in the city of Copenhagen. (Kierkegaard was going through the last phases of his dissertation acceptance at this time and was still in Copenhagen. He did not depart for Berlin until November 1841.) See Elisabete de Sousa, "Kierkegaard's Musical Recollections," in *Kierkegaard Studies Yearbook,* 85–108 (Berlin: de Gruyter, 2008).

2. Strictly speaking, Socrates was repeating a story told to him by Diotima, but it is generally held to be Socrates's own view. See Plato's *Symposium,* 210a–212b.

3. Garff, *Søren Kierkegaard,* 106–8 (*SAK: En Biografi* [Copenhagen: Gads, 2000]). On page 106, Garff sums up the matter nicely: "The naked truth seems to be that even though in *The Concept of Anxiety* Kierkegaard has Vigilius Haufniensis provide us with a detailed examination of the relationship between sexuality and history, Kierkegaard himself remained silent about the role sexuality played in his *own* history. Occasionally, however, goaded by the exhibitionism that often conceals itself deep within modesty, Kierkegaard did yield to the temptation to insert little keyholes in his texts, both published and unpublished, through which the reader can peek and draw his or her own conclusions."

4. See *JP,* entry 6472; *Papirer* X5 149 (1849).

5. Fenger, *Kierkegaard,* 210.

6. *JP,* 5664; *Papirer* IV A 107 (1843).

7. *JP,* 5431; *Papirer* II A 806.

8. *JP,* 5403; *Papirer* II A 520 (July 28, 1839); see also Green, *Kierkegaard and Kant,* 200, 282n37.

9. *SKS,* 6:XX; *SLW,* 283–84.

10. *JP,* 5622; *Papirer* IV A 65 (1843).

11. *JP,* 5664; *Papirer* IV A 107 (1843).

12. *SKS,* 3:117; *E/O,* 2:117.

13. *JP,* 5517; *Papirer* III A 161 (1841).

14. *JP,* 5664; *Papirer* IV A 107 (1843).

15. See Lore Hühn, ed., *Schopenhauer und Kierkegaard: Von der Metaphysik des Willens zur Philosophie der Existenz* (Berlin: de Gruyter, 2011).

16. Nordentoft believes that Kierkegaard's discussion of this theme in *The Concept of Anxiety* has been frequently misinterpreted. For Nordentoft, Kierkegaard is critical of the separation of flesh and spirit that Christianity introduced into the world. In his view, Kierkegaard does not see it as normative. See Nordentoft, *Kierkegaard's Psychology,* 58.

17. In *Either/Or,* part 1.

18. For Kierkegaard and traditional Christians, while the Greeks may have had genuine insight about the sensual in relation to the spiritual, it is only Christianity that is able to actualize it in individual lives.

19. *SKS,* 4:371; *CA,* 67. "With Adam's sin came sin into the world, and sexuality, and for him that came to signify sinfulness" (my translation). Both sin and sexuality enter the world in Adam's sin. The Hong translation misses this.

20. *SKS,* 4:372, 382–83; *CA,* 68, 79–80. But this line of thought is blurred, since *Anxiety*'s pseudonymous Haufniensis holds that Adam's sin, while not a

sexual sin, is nonetheless the cause of sexual desire (pp. 49, 79). This reflects traditional Christian theology, but Kierkegaard's view is free of the negative sexual theology of early and formative Christian writers such as Paul of Tarsus and Clement of Alexandria. He never advocates celibacy or repression of the sexual, rather its enhancement by being incorporated into a fuller human existence that is characterized by a spiritual striving.

21. *SKS*, 3:117; *E/O*, 2:116.

22. *SKS*, 3:39; *E/O*, 2:31.

23. *SKS*, 6:46; *SLW*, 42–43.

24. *Papirer* XI2 A 152; *The Last Years: The Kierkegaard Journals 1853–1855*, edited by Ronald G. Smith (New York: Harper and Row, 1965), 265.

Chapter 3

1. In an undated entry of 1844, Kierkegaard wrote in his *Journals*: "Danish philosophy—if there ever comes to be such a thing—will be different from German philosophy in that it definitely will not begin with nothing or without any presuppositions whatsoever or explain everything by mediating, because, on the contrary, it begins with the proposition that there are many things between heaven and earth which no philosophy has explained" (*JP*, 3299).

2. The first Kierkegaard biographies, such as Walter Lowrie's, tended to be hagiographies of a newly discovered intellectual hero. Josiah Thompson, in *Kierkegaard*, was perhaps the first to debunk that approach. Most recently, the Joakim Garff biography has rendered Kierkegaard as the more complex human being that he was.

3. In his own terminology, his procedure is "dialectical" and "pathetic."

4. There is an implicit sense here of one being one's cocreator as one actualizes possibilities grounded in a divine source recognized as the ultimate source of creation.

5. *Confessions*, I, ii.

6. See Poole, *Kierkegaard*, which offers a very different interpretation. Poole criticizes and rejects the traditional theological interpretations from Lowrie to Thulstrup, with which I agree, but then seems to view Kierkegaard as a very deliberate, if unconscious, proto-postmodernist of the school of Jacques Derrida. This is a challenging theory but one that I find finally unpersuasive. Approaches similar to those of the deconstructionists and postmodernists do emerge, but I believe that Kierkegaard's program emerged and was not fully under way in his first publications. See above all the introduction in Poole's study.

7. By "transparent pseudonym," I mean authorship that is formally and technically pseudonymous but that can be construed as representing the personal thought of Søren Kierkegaard. This interpretation is supported by the fact that, for example, up until shortly before publication he had planned to issue *The Concept of Anxiety* under his own name.

8. In the "Occasional Discourse," previously known in English as "Purity of Heart," Kierkegaard, in his own name, writes, "Alas, it is terrible to see a person

rushing headlong to his own downfall; it is terrible to see him dancing on the edge of the abyss without suspecting it; but this clarity about himself and his own downfall is even more terrible. It is terrible to see a person seek solace by plunging into the vortex of despair, but even more terrible is the composure that in the anguish of death a person does not call out in a scream for help . . . but calmly wants to be a witness to his own perdition" (*SKS*, 8:146–47; *SUD*, 33–34).

9. Kierkegaard has, however, *four* cardinal moods rather than the expectable Hegelian triad. There are many additional departures from and twists on Hegelian structure, of course.

10. "The immediate Don Juan must seduce 1,003; the reflective needs to seduce only one, and how he does it is what occupies us" (*SKS*, 2:111; *E/O*, 1:108).

11. In the nineteenth century, irony is repeatedly referred to as a mood, and Kierkegaard cites Solger's attempt at a philosophical grasp of irony and his definition of irony as "that very mood in which contradictions annihilate themselves" (*SKS*, 1:351; *CI*, 322).

12. *SKS*, 1:355; *CI*, 328. This is also thesis XV of the dissertation itself.

13. *SKS*, 1:320; *CI*, 285. Kierkegaard continues this theme pseudonymously in his witty, ironic analysis of boredom in the "Rotation Method" in *Either/Or*, part 1.

14. It is another paradox of his terminology that the cure for anxiety, that is, actualizing possibility, is termed despair. Here it is conceived in the same sense as in *Either/Or*: choice of the self.

15. Equally, Judge William remarks that there will always be a little melancholia even after the crisis is resolved. One is never complete as a human being so long as one lives and breathes.

16. Of the moods that Kierkegaard explores in detail, one notes that melancholy (as well as boredom) does not have a treatise explicitly devoted to it. There are *The Concept of Irony*, *The Concept of Anxiety* [*Dread*], and *The Sickness unto Death* to deal with irony (as a mood, among other dimensions), anxiety, and despair, respectively. But there exists no formal treatise on melancholy. However, melancholy is a major theme and category throughout most of what may be termed Kierkegaard's earlier authorship, in which he engages aesthetic categories. The pseudonymous Johannes Climacus remarks that the first part of *Either/Or* has melancholia as its essential character (although *Melancholi* is the major terminus employed) (*SKS*, 7:229; *CUP*, 253, mistranslated as "depression").

17. For a history of melancholy, see Radden, *The Nature of Melancholy*.

18. A simple rule of thumb is that when there are in Danish both a Danish root word and a foreign loanword for the same general concept, in Kierkegaard's usage the Danish root word often acquires a special meaning. Not every Kierkegaard scholar agrees with me about this distinction. I concede that one cannot construe it as a precise distinction, but it is a distinct usage nonetheless, in arguably changed context. At minimum, it is clear from a careful reading of the text that Kierkegaard does not merely equate them.

19. Literally, "shut-up-ness" (*Indesluttethed*).

20. The passage continues, "Therein lies the limitlessness of [*Tungsind*]. This answer is altogether correct, because as soon as he knows what it is, it is

eliminated, whereas sorrow in the sorrowing one is not eliminated by his knowing why he sorrows."

21. *Repetition* and "'Guilty?'/'Not Guilty?'" are highly autobiographical, but Kierkegaard's point is not indulgence of his own undeniable susceptibility to melancholy but rather an analysis of the mood.

22. The formalistic presentation of four elements that need to be balanced—possibility, necessity, finitude, and infinitude—is reminiscent of the medieval notion of needed balance of the four humors.

Chapter 4

1. Meantime, Burton's famous *Anatomy of Melancholy* (1621) has a cultural standing that has nothing to do with the believability of its seventeenth-century analyses.

2. See Garff, *Søren Kierkegaard.*

3. For she, as Joakim Garff stresses in his biography, is also a rich source of case material for anxiety (*Søren Kierkegaard,* 270–79).

4. Or equally an Oxbridge graduate, a *normalien* in France, or a classic Tübingen-Marburg-Heidelberg graduate.

5. And, for that matter, while Aesthete A is the recipient of B's letters in part 2, he never formally replies to William, as William himself observes. None of A's papers addresses B's letters and therefore would give the reader the appearance of having been composed before receipt of B's letters.

6. "A Venture in Experimenting Psychology" is the subtitle of *Repetition.*

7. William, who evidences no formal acquaintance with the papers that are part 1, does not employ, or comment upon, the *Melancholi* that at times is at the center of Aesthete A's self-observations in part 1. (The Danish wordplay that runs throughout the section is impossible to reproduce in English, and I note again that the choice of the Hongs to translate *Tungsind* with the contemporary term "depression" is misleading.)

8. I propose to consider Aesthete A and Johannes separately, and, while following Victor Eremita's ascription of "The Diary" to Aesthete A, I propose to follow the fiction of the fiction in treating "The Seducer's Diary" as a literary production of Aesthete A, a work in the subjunctive. However, I do propose to attend to the character of Johannes without conflating the subjunctive mood of Johannes with the indicative mood of Aesthete A, as I did in my 1978 study *The Phenomenology of Moods in Kierkegaard.*

9. See Mandel, *The Theatre of Don Juan.*

10. Demipho in Terence's play *Phormio,* II, 265: "Unum quom noris omnis noris."

11. The remarks that follow, both in reference to *The Concept of Anxiety* and *The Sickness unto Death,* in no way pretend to be a full account of either work but rather only a consideration of what each work contributes toward understanding the psychology of Aesthete A in *Either/Or.* See McCarthy, *The Phenomenology of Moods in Kierkegaard.*

12. A glance at the table of contents of *The Concept of Anxiety* and an observation of page distribution will tell a reader what is at the heart of *The Concept of Anxiety*. For while the work is divided logically, one might even say systematically, it is by no means divided evenly: "Objective Anxiety" has four pages, "Subjective Anxiety" thirty; "Anxiety about the Evil" has five pages, "Anxiety about the Good" has forty-five, and, in the subdivision of "Anxiety about the Good," the discussion of "Freedom Lost Somatically-Psychically" is one page, whereas "Freedom Lost Pneumatically" is twenty-five.

13. The German that Vigilius cites is theologically more pregnant than the original English of Shakespeare, which reads, "O, ruin'd piece of nature! This great world shall so wear out to naught" (*King Lear*, IV, 5). The German of Tieck-Schlegel lends itself more not only to theological reflection but also to nihilism.

14. Implicitly Kierkegaard is following here a Platonic distinction that Schelling had emphasized between οὐκ ὄν and μὴ ὄν in Greek, between that which is not in the definitive sense (is and *cannot not be*) versus that which *is not* in a contingent sense (*is not* but *might possibly be*). Anxiety is freedom's actuality as the possibility of possibility (*SKS*, 4:348; *CA*, 42).

15. What Vigilius terms the despair of possibility.

16. His is not what Vigilius calls anxiety for the evil, for that is the anxiety of one who makes some movement but not the whole movement into self-consciousness as sinner.

17. Even Augustine of Hippo, the chief opponent of Pelagianism, has himself sometimes been accused of semi-Pelagianism by the "grace extremists" in faith versus works controversies.

18. More famously expressed in the ironic anecdote about Voltaire, who, supposedly surrounded by a mob in England shouting "Hang the Frenchman," won them over with the lament of lost possibility (= impossibility): "Am I not punished enough in not having been born an Englishman?" According to the story, they then cheered him and let him go.

19. According to the best genetic evidence currently available, all humans are the descendants of one original woman (presumably from an early group of human females whose descendants died out). Only the descendants of this one woman, sometimes described as the Mitochondrial Eve, have survived and evolved. Estimates vary from 105 to 120 billion humans born since the (estimated) time two hundred thousand years ago when *Homo sapiens* attained its current form.

Chapter 5

1. Sigmund Freud, "Mourning and Melancholia," in *SE*, XIV:246.

2. This thesis is developed in Cole, *The Problematic Self in Kierkegaard and Freud*. On Kierkegaard and Freudianism, see also Nordentoft, *Kierkegaard's Psychology*.

3. Naecke's use of the term is far more specific than Freud's or the psychoanalytic movement's. For Naecke, according to Freud, "narcissism" is a term

to denote the attitude of a person who treats his own body in the same way in which the body of a sexual object is ordinarily treated—who looks at it, that is to say, strokes, and fondles it till he obtains complete satisfaction through these activities (*SE*, XIV:73). Taken in this narrow usage, the term could not justifiably be attributed to Aesthete A on the basis of the text. Later Freud attributed it to Havelock Ellis.

4. And also twentieth-century culture. In this connection, see Lasch, *The Culture of Narcissism*, which suggests that narcissism, with its attendant "diffuse dissatisfactions," is to late twentieth-century culture what hysteria was to turn-of-the-century Vienna.

5. The context refers specifically to "perverts" and "homosexuals."

6. "Energy postulated by Freud as underlying the transformations of the sexual instinct with respect to its object (displacement of cathexes), with respect to its aim (e.g. sublimation), and with respect to the source of sexual excitation" (Laplanche and Pontalis, *The Language of Psycho-Analysis*, 239). *Libido* is of course the Latin for "desire" or "wish."

7. Alford, *Narcissism*, 3 and 98, respectively.

8. Kohut, *Analysis of the Self*, and Kernberg, *Borderline Conditions*, are considered the best contemporary psychoanalytic discussions of the subject. Alford, *Narcissism*, contains a contemporary overview of the discussion informed by philosophical interests.

9. Kernberg, *Borderline Conditions*, 264.

10. Ibid., 227–28.

11. Kernberg, *Borderline Conditions*, adds that such persons also demonstrate an incapacity for experiencing depressive reactions (228–29). This last-named quality, the absence of depression, is particularly problematic in probing *Either/Or*. Freud, himself not always consistent or clear, connects melancholia and narcissism. Yet psychoanalysis generally removes depression from narcissism. For English-language usage of the word prior to Freud and psychoanalytic culture, the *Oxford English Dictionary* cites Burton's *Anatomy of Melancholy* (1621) with reference to those "afflicted . . . [and] depressed." George Eliot's *Middlemarch* (1872) has one of the first uses of "depressed" in a contemporary sense: "I thought he looked rather battered and depressed." The term begins as denoting a reaction to external influences or events.

12. *SKS*, 2:27; *EO*, 1:19. Actually, the Danish Qoheleth Aesthete A begins with a quote in French from Paul Pellisson that is evocative of Ecclesiastes:

> Greatness, knowledge, renown,
> Friendship, pleasure, and possessions,
> All is only wind, only smoke:
> To say it better, all is nothing.

Qoheleth would have called it *hevel*, which is usually translated as "vanity" or "emptiness" but which may also be translated as "irony." "Irony of irony, all is irony" is an interesting possible alternative translation for the opening of Ecclesiastes.

13. *SE*, XIV:244.

14. The relationship of boredom, ennui, melancholia, and narcissism is explored in Kuhn, *The Demon of Noontide.* Of particular interest is the chapter on Goethe's Werther and Chateaubriand's René (of the novella of the same name contained in *The Genius of Christianity*). Werther's *Langeweile* is complemented by René's ennui, and Kierkegaard knew both characters. For Goethe himself, boredom was the mother of all invention. For Chateaubriand, by the way, Christianity brought melancholia into the world, in the same way that Christianity posits sensuousness, in the language of Aesthete A. (See Kuhn, *The Demon of Noontide,* 201.)

René's ennui is summed up in the following entry, which has its echoes in the "Diapsalmata":

> I am bored with life; ennui has always consumed me. What interests other men does not concern me in the slightest. Shepherd or king, what would I have done with my crook or crown? I would have tired as quickly of glory as of genius, of work as of leisure, of prosperity as of adversity. In Europe and in America society and nature fatigued me. I am virtuous without pleasure; if I were a criminal, I would be one without remorse. What I would like is never to have been born or ever to be forgotten. (François-René Chateaubriand, *Oeuvres romanesques et voyages* [Paris: Gallimard, 1957], 502)

Chateaubriand thinks of René as embodying the malady of the century, and it is not surprising to hear Judge William, whose volume opens with a quote from Chateaubriand's Atala, speak of Aesthete A's melancholy [*Tungsind*] and term it the defect of the age (*SKS,* 3:32; *E/O,* 2:23). Kierkegaard never uses Chateaubriand's term "diffuseness of passions" (*le vague des passions*), but he does have William speak about melancholia as the refusal to will and thus as self-dispersal.

The posthumously published autobiographical fragments of Chateaubriand (1768–1848), unknown to Kierkegaard and too late for *Either/Or,* give us a possible glimpse of what an unreformed Aesthete A grown old in ennui might be like:

> . . . grown old on this earth without having lost anything of his dreams, of his follies, of his diffuse sorrows, ever searching for what he cannot find and adding to his former ills the disillusionment of experience, the solitude of desires, the ennui of the heart, and the affliction of the years. (François-René Chateaubriand, *Memoires d'outre-tombe* [Paris: Gallimard, 1959], 2)

15. The earlier Walter Lowrie English translation has "Echo" capitalized. The Narcissus myth figures in the background of *Either/Or,* to be sure. In "The Seducer's Diary," Johannes feigns the role of Echo, wasting away to nothing out of love for Cordelia, when he writes, "My love consumes me; only my voice remains" (*SKS,* 2:395; *E/O,* 1:407).

16. The quotations here are, admittedly, out of context. Both are from posturing letters by Johannes. The second goes on to say that "what is an expression of the utmost egotism in the world's profane eyes is in your initiated eyes an expression of the purest sympathy" (ibid.). It might be added here that Freud offers an observation on the attractiveness of narcissists that may explain

Cordelia's falling for Johannes in "The Seducer's Diary," beyond Johannes's own theory: "For it seems very evident that another person's narcissism has a great attraction for those who have renounced part of their own narcissism and are in search of object-love" (*SE*, XIV:89). To be sure, we know little about Cordelia Wahl as a personality.

17. *Metamorphoses* 3.464–68; emphasis added.

18. Benedict de Spinoza, *The Ethics*, trans. R. H. M. Elwes (New York: Dover, 1955), 173 ("Definitions of the Emotions," in part 3). The linkage to Spinoza is confirmed by Hegel's remark, in *The History of Philosophy*, that "to be a follower of Spinoza is the essential commencement of all philosophy." See *Hegel's Lectures on the History of Philosophy*, trans. E. S. Haldane and Frances H. Simson (New York: Humanities Press, 1974), 3:257, quoted in Butler, *Subjects of Desire*, 12. The latter is a valuable history of desire in Hegelian and post-Hegelian thought.

19. Among others, Taylor, *Journey to Selfhood*, 77, cites both works in this way.

20. Butler, *Subjects of Desire*, 23, writing of her Nietzschean reading of Hegel's *Phenomenology*.

21. In conversation, Edna Hong, prompted by my questions about the various translations for *Attraa* and *Lyst* in *Either/Or* in the early 1990s, conceded the inadequacy and the inaccuracy of the translation in places, particularly where many "desire" words are used together.

22. This is a subject that might well profit from thorough study using the computer programs that Alastair McKinnon has developed. His *Index Verborum* lists the full range of the forms of each word as used in the writings.

23. *SKS*, 5:31; *EUD*, 22. See also the earlier English translation in *Edifying Discourses: A Selection*, trans. David F. and Lillian M. Swenson (New York: Harper Torchbooks, 1958), 20, where the terms are translated as "wishes," "craving," "yearnings," and "desires," respectively.

24. See *SKS*, 1:106; *CI*, 45. While *Attraa* is usually associated with *Elskov*, the Danish term used there for "love" is *Kjaerlighed*. See *The Symposium*, 200a, for Socrates's speech.

25. One must wonder how much this section is also a Hegelian spoof. For, while the requisite triadic divisions are present, Aesthete A argues that music is higher than thought and that we should not attend to the characters or the dialogue but rather to the music that expresses them in their mythological essentiality. For the Hegelian, thought is the highest form of abstract expression, not music, which is a much lower form of representation.

26. Which, uncannily, turn out to be the Mozart operas that the relatively unmusical Freud found of interest.

27. Indifference is noted very perceptively in Dunning, *Kierkegaard's Dialectic of Inwardness*, 38.

28. Jean-Paul Sartre, *The Transcendence of the Ego* (New York: Noonday Press, 1957), 56; quoted in Butler, *Subjects of Desire*, 104. This seems to be a sharpening of Hegel's assertion that desire is conditioned by its object.

29. The Augustinian viewpoint, which Kierkegaard shares, would use the language of rupture, loss, and fall to characterize every person's relationship to God, until there is repentance and restoration. The school of the French neo-

Freudian Lacan speaks of the lost object for which the pre-Oedipal relationship of child to mother is symbol.

30. Certainly the sinfulness and God estrangement of aesthetic existence, combined with the need for a religious solution, is already more than dawning in the closing piece of *Either/Or*, part 2. There the Jutland priest meditates on the meaning, and origin, of the fact "that in relation to God we are always in the wrong" (*SKS*, 3:320; *E/O*, 2:346).

31. Severed in the loss of the imaginary phallus. This is the meaning of castration in Lacan's thought.

32. ". . . that for both partners in the relation, both the subject and the Other, it is not enough to be the subjects of need, or objects of love, but they must stand [*tenir lieu*] as the cause of desire" ("The Signification of the Phallus," in Lacan, *Écrits*, 187).

Chapter 6

The chapter epigraph is from Lacan, *The Four Fundamental Concepts of Psychoanalysis*, 61.

1. See *SKS*, 8:93; *TA*, 98.

2. "Reconstruction" is the term that Alastair McKinnon used for his computer-based study of Kierkegaard texts. Some critics would dismiss McKinnon as a mere word counter. His ambitious method aimed to penetrate to and reconstruct the very mind of Kierkegaard from a study of his vocabulary. In his late work, McKinnon finally returned to a revaluation of context as well. McKinnon's work has met with very mixed reactions, but it does have some value in highlighting terms and vocabulary that then need to be considered by other methods as well. It may finally be more useful in raising text questions than in providing persuasive answers.

3. Equally notable is the fact that Constantin is apparently untroubled by publishing his young friend's confidential letters.

4. It should be noted that my own division of the work into eleven units is in no way formally reflected in the text. They also do not represent sections of equal length: the shortest is a two-page prologue, the longest the nearly forty-page section of letters.

5. Constantin comes close to this formulation in his oft-cited assessment of the young man's predicament: "Now I grasped the whole situation. The young girl was not his beloved: she was the occasion that awakened the poetic in him and made him a poet" (*SKS*, 4:15; *R*, 138).

6. Constantin is never named as the addressee of the letters. Instead, "My Silent Confidant" is the form of address. Except that both Constantin and the young man appear two years later as independent personae at the banquet in *Stages on Life's Way*, one might well accept Constantin's suggestion that the young man is a fiction on the part of Constantin. In that case, it would be tempting to view the young man as Constantin at an earlier life phase, the letters as diary pieces, and Constantin as the commentator of later years reflecting back upon

an earlier episode in his life. Of course, if one were to follow this line, one would have to account for the tale of the meetings of Constantin and the young man at a café, etc. The reader of *Repetition* alone might then be misled by Constantin. The truth of the separate existence of the young man warns us retrospectively not to trust Constantin, despite the promise of his name (constancy).

7. Intriguingly, Freud comments in his exploration of repetition in *Beyond the Pleasure Principle* (*SE*, XVIII:9) that the principle of constancy is a necessary inference from the pleasure principle. Freud defines the principle of constancy as the mental apparatus functioning to keep the quantity of excitation as low as possible or else to keep it constant. Constantin represents constancy and achieved *ataraxia*, in contrast to the storm-tossed young man. Freud's French "heir," Jacques Lacan, would, by the way, probably suggest that Constantin's name is a determining influence on his personality.

8. To be precise, 643 times for lowercase *jeg* and 88 times for capitalized *Jeg* as the first word of a sentence.

9. Also near the center of a vocabulary graph of aberrant frequency words stands *Pige* (the girl), who, though absent, is very much at the center of the work.

10. Needless to say, one can do something for the first time only *once*. To do it again may repeat the externals of the act, but its newness cannot be repeated. Doing the same thing for the second time is, paradoxically, its own first time and so on, ad infinitum. In this sense there is no repetition. Ultimately this line of thought—akin to the early Greek observation about the problem of stepping into the same river twice—would suggest the illusory nature of everything, including of course the possibility of external repetition.

11. *SKS*, 4:66 and 72; *R*, 197 and 204, respectively.

12. *SKS*, 4:69; *R*, 201. The explicit appeal on this point is to the principle of *cui bono* in Cicero. Since he feels he has not benefited by making himself and the girl unhappy, he argues that the absence of any benefit is warrant for his being held not guilty. Interestingly, this letter anticipates *Stages on Life's Way* in its consideration of being guilty or not guilty.

13. Given the Hegelian backdrop (including of course the anti-Hegelian polemical interest) to Kierkegaard's writings, one ought not pass over the fact that the closing pages of Hegel's *Phenomenology of Spirit* discuss recollection (*Erinnerung*) as the inwardizing (*Er-Innerung*) of experience. See the translation by A. V. Miller (Oxford: Oxford University Press, 1977), 492.

14. If any wonder at the introduction of Freudian thought here, one can probably do no better in reply than to cite Freud himself at the end of *Beyond the Pleasure Principle*: "It may be asked why I have embarked upon such a line of thought as the present one, and in particular why I have decided to make it public. Well—I cannot deny that some of the analogies, correlations and connections which it contains seemed to me to deserve consideration" (*SE*, XVIII: 60).

15. *SE*, XII:150.

16. Freud goes on to comment that the subject is always some portion of infantile sex life (*SE*, XVIII:18).

17. The young man's conflicting desire for restoration to the young woman and for freedom is a clear indication of his desire to rise above instinctual gratifi-

cation. It is hardly a death wish. On the other hand, it appears that Kierkegaard originally planned a suicide ending for the young man.

18. Kierkegaard's awareness of this theme is reflected in his allusions to Aristophanes's myth of the double beings split by the gods, described in Plato's *Symposium* (and paralleled by "The Banquet" in *Stages on Life's Way*). Most analyses focus on Aristophanes's apparent intention in his *Symposium* speech to describe the origins of sexual orientation. A deeper point that emerges from the speech and that may or may not have been Aristophanes's is frequently missed, namely, that the gods, by creating the desire for one's missing earthly "half" effectively succeeded in distracting humankind from the desire for the heavens themselves, to which they were originally aspiring.

19. Howard Hong, in the historical introduction to the English-language edition, noted that there are marginal remains of a final five pages that Kierkegaard deleted after the news of Regine Olsen's engagement to Schlegel. The ending was then revised with fifteen new pages replacing those deleted. Naturally, the same event affects *Fear and Trembling*, which, behind the equally silent pseudonym Johannes de Silentio, had begun with an Abraham-like Kierkegaard wondering if the love object he was willing to sacrifice, namely, Regine/Isaac, might be restored to him in the end, and he went on to assert his belief that Regine would be his in eternity. At least in the sense of a literary eternity, he proved to be correct.

20. *Papirer* IV A 156 (1843); *JP*, III 3793, cited in Hong in *Supplement*, 326.

21. *Papirer* IV B 120 (1843).

22. Constantin proudly contrasts the existential significance of "motion" (*Bevaegelse*) to the abstract "commotion" (*Ophaevelse*) of Hegelian philosophy. English allows a nice pun here. Kierkegaard's pun had to do with *Ophaevelse* as the Danish translation term for Hegelian *Aufhebung*. See note to the Hong translated text, 370n18.

Chapter 7

After the quote in the first epigraph from "Quidam's Diary," the section continues, "If my repetition [*min Repetition*] is perhaps not always imploring, ah, it nevertheless preferably ends in this final solace" (*SKS*, 6:346; *SLW*, 372). This is one of the few uses of the Danish-English cognate *Repetition*, and where we might expect Kierkegaard's usual term, namely, *Gjentagelse*.

1. Specifically in the first series of discourses drawn from the verse "You shall love thy neighbor" (Matt. 22:39).

2. One can be faulted for taking something like this too far, but Quidam (Someone) is not just Anyone (Quisquis). He is indefinite, but the definite indefinite, a certain someone.

3. Frater Taciturnus offers to return the document to the author, who will be recognized by the handwriting. Meantime, he has no hesitation about its publication. Frater Taciturnus also estimates that the year of the events related is 1751. Is this further distancing?

4. Sales records indicate that fewer than half the original copies were sold (245 copies sold, 280 remaindered). The work was well reviewed by P. L. Møller, and Hong quotes Emmanuel Hirsch (writing in 1930) as saying of *Stages on Life's Way* that, despite the earlier lack of attention, it "has become, in Denmark, as well as in Germany, Kierkegaard's most famous and influential work" (*SLW*, xviii). The high estimation was no doubt due largely to "In Vino Veritas."

5. 64 percent, to be exact.

6. The morning and evening entries give the impression of having been separate compositions subsequently interlaced. Both draw material from Kierkegaard's personal diaries. The longer midnight pieces (Solomon's Dream et al.) are taken directly from Kierkegaard's notebooks and sketchbooks.

7. But Taciturnus anticipates his critics by announcing his expectation that "two-thirds of the book's few readers will quit before they are halfway through . . . out of boredom they will stop reading and throw the book away" (*SKS*, 6:369; *SLW*, 398) and does not overestimate his own writing as he speculates, in the conclusion, "My dear reader—but to whom am I speaking? Perhaps no one at all is left" (*SKS*, 6:446; *SLW*, 485).

8. Hong translated *Psychologisk Experiment* as "An Imaginary Psychological Construction," thereby losing the parallel Danish terminology between the two works.

9. The following outlines the use of the first person pronoun in *Stages on Life's Way*, a work of approximately five hundred pages, of which nearly three hundred compose "'Guilty?'/'Not Guilty?'": (a) morning entries: 789; (b) midnight entries: 1,630; (c) "Quidam's Diary" (a + b): 2,419; (d) "'Guilty?'/'Not Guilty?'": 2,726; (e) *Stages on Life's Way*: 3,630. Most of the occurrences of the pronoun within "'Guilty?'/'Not Guilty?'" are in the diary entries. One can expect a diarist to use the pronoun "I," but the count here is striking all the same. The rest of *Stages on Life's Way* is slightly less "I" centered. The next most "I"-centered work in the aesthetic writings is the hundred-page novella *Repetition*, in which the pronoun occurs 731 times.

10. Except that the young man of *Repetition* makes a reappearance in his surprise May 31 announcement of the young girl's marriage and his (partial) repetition.

11. In her indefiniteness given the parallel indefinite Latin pronoun Quaedam in Taciturnus's "Letter."

12. The pseudonymous Vigilius Haufniensis considered enclosing reserve in detail in 1844 in *The Concept of Anxiety* (*SKS*, 4:424–30; *CA*, 123–29). There enclosing reserve is described as unfreedom and silence, periodically bursting into unfree disclosure.

13. "For monologue is precisely its speech, and therefore we characterize an inclosed person by saying that he talks to himself" (*SKS*, 4:429; *CA*, 128). Or, in this case, as one who writes to himself, night and day.

14. But, of course, it was not really last year at all but merely last year as recollected and reported *this* year.

15. Taciturnus argues, in his "Letter," that "the girl is entirely suitable to him, as is meet and proper for the imaginary construction" (*SKS*, 6:436; *SLW*,

473), but the suitability that he has in mind concerns her dialectical role, not her suitability as love object.

16. The six fifth-of-the-month entries were originally planned as seven, drawn from Kierkegaard's journals (the "A" *Papirer*, *JP*, V B 124). At some point, Kierkegaard dropped a planned Abelard article (*JP*, IV A 177, 31), and so July 5 has no article.

17. Taciturnus allows that "there is a difference between [melancholia] and [melancholia]," which is to say a difference between the melancholia of artists, poets, and thinkers and the melancholia that is prior to the religious, and which is the form of Quidam's melancholia (*SKS*, 6:398; *SLW*, 430), *pace* those Kierkegaard scholars who disregard this difference. Abrahim H. Khan wrote in 1985 that I had once made too much of this, and perhaps he was right. (See "Melancholy, Irony and Kierkegaard" in *International Journal for Philosophy of Religion* 17 [1/2]:67–85 [1985].) I still insist that there is a significant difference, a view with which, in conversation, he agreed. Very few have written on this subject, and Karl Verstrynge in his 2003 article "Hysteria of the Spirit" cited me as the first to develop the distinction and would seem to be in general agreement with me. See also "Hysteria of the Spirit: On Melancholy and Kierkegaard" in *Immediacy and Reflection in Kierkegaard's Thought*, edited by Paul Cruysberghs, Johan Taels, and Karl Verstrynge (Leuven: Leuven University Press, 2003), 143–58.

Chapter 8

1. Danish, like German, expresses the Latin term *peccatum originarium* (English "original sin") as "inherited sin" (*Arvesynd* and *Erbsünde*, respectively).

2. Schelling, *Philosophische Untersuchungen*.

3. Some detect the influence of Schleiermacher as well. See the translator's notes to *The Concept of Anxiety*, 228–29nn47, 49. A much longer list could be compiled, beginning with Socrates and Aristotle.

4. Kierkegaard's first journal entry about Schelling's lectures (*Papirer* 111 A 179; *JP*, 5355) refers to the second lecture, November 11, 1841.

5. *Philosophie der Offenbarung*; Schelling, *Philosophische Untersuchungen*, 13–14.

6. Thus even Kant has been neglected in Kierkegaard studies, although in recent years some fine work by Ronald Green has appeared. (See Green, *Kierkegaard and Kant*.) One frequently feels that Kierkegaard is reacting to Kantian material, particularly to *Religion within the Limits of Reason Alone*, and this would have been expected in religious philosophy of the German-speaking world even into the middle of the nineteenth century. The sense of unannounced dialogue with Kant is especially strong in *Fear and Trembling*. See Robert L. Perkins, "For Sanity's Sake: Kant, Kierkegaard, and Father Abraham," in his *Kierkegaard's "Fear and Trembling": Critical Appraisals*, 43–61 (Tuscaloosa: University of Alabama Press, 1981).

7. There is a single reference to "Schelling" in the *Concluding Unscientific Postscript to Philosophical Fragments* and another to the Danish possessive form

"Schellings" in *Either/Or.* In addition, there is a single mention of "Schellings" in *The Concept of Irony.* There are also four adjectival references (*schellingske*), but *The Concept of Anxiety*'s being the preeminent locus of Schelling discussion is not undercut thereby.

8. *Papirer* IV B 117, 118.

9. Schelling, *Of Human Freedom.*

10. Heidegger, *Schellings Abhandlung,* 117. Heidegger provides a rich commentary on Schelling's work.

11. All of which may serve only to underline the view that Kierkegaard's polemic was more essentially and substantially directed against Copenhagen Hegelians than against Hegel himself.

12. *Schellings Abhandlung,* 26.

13. Schelling's heavy emphasis on freedom is not without its price. For, since the incarnation of God is not necessary, it is in a sense unessential, and with this arises connotations of ultimately being not just "accidental" but "incidental" as well.

14. The first potency, which is able to be (A1), has been actualized but also actualized in sin: that which was able to be and ought not to be has come to be. Having done so, it must go further, on to resolution, by moving *ab actu ad potentiam*: by progressing from actualization to restoration as pure potency. This resolution is caused by the movement of the second potency that, in fulfilling itself, restores the original potency of A1. Schelling's obscure mathematical notations A1, A2, and A3 take on new meaning when one learns that A1 refers to the Fall, A2 to God's Logos who restores, and A3 to the Spirit. The full actualization of the potencies thus represents fall and restoration but also—and synonymously—the actualized life of an actual God, or theogony. Ultimately, the three potencies come to stand for the trinitarian life of God and the three personalities of God's life that result from the process.

All three potencies are potencies of God's being. God is thus the source both of all being and of all potency. God is the lord of possibilities, actualized and unactualized. Moreover, God would be fully and really God even as lord of mere potencies had he never actualized a world. This point contrasts with Hegel's philosophy. For Hegel's philosophy suggested that God would not be God without a world. Creation is there reduced to a divine necessity and as such must be viewed as unfree.

As the Logos, or second potency (A2), actualizes itself, creation is held to be restored. And he, along with the actualized Spirit, comes then to constitute God as a trinity of actualized persons. This constitutes theogony, or God's becoming, for Schelling.

All three members of the potentially actual Trinity were active in creation. All three in fact acted as creator: the creator as Father is he who goes out in exclusive being, the creator as Son is he who overcomes this exclusive being, and the creator as Spirit is he who completes or perfects arisen being. In this, the Father provides the "stuff" of creation and is its material cause; the Son gives creaturely form and is thus its formal cause; while the Spirit as the common will of both brings creation to what it should be, perfects it, and is thus its final cause.

Schelling finds this reading of Aristotle into the Trinity supported by Saint Paul himself in the Epistle to the Romans (11:36), where he wrote of all that is created as "from him, through him, and in him." The principal novelty of this reading consists in the view of the Son as formal cause or demiurge.

15. This might sound Manichaean, except that in the Manichaean teaching primal man is taken prisoner in the creation and is thus under a kind of necessity.

16. Kierkegaard heard this much and heard also the details of the Son of Man lecture. Schelling describes the Son of Man as the hidden principle of paganism present while paganism struggled under necessity toward restored monotheism, when the Son freely revealed himself in Christianity. Kierkegaard's *Referat* breaks off during the survey of the pagan mysteries, just after the discussion of Demeter and Persephone, still well before the large-scale Christology and philosophical interpretation of the Christian religion. Kierkegaard had obviously heard enough, realized his hopes for a significant new philosophy from Schelling were to be disappointed, and left Berlin on March 6, 1842, approximately one month after his *Referat* breaks off. Whether he attended additional lectures without note taking is unclear, but it would seem unlikely.

While Schelling's God is free, he could seem to be the unfortunate victim of caprice in his own creation. He allows free actions that affect not only creation but also his own being. And he might even appear foolish to some for having allowed himself to be determined by others' use and misuse of God-given freedom, even if the eventual outcome seems to have justified the risks.

17. Heidegger, *Schellings Abhandlung*, 82–83.

18. But if Schelling was freed from certain idealist presuppositions, he was still not freed from the idealist ambition of system construction. He still held to a "system of freedom" as his goal.

19. Even if it is a key that only Schelling's own philosophy can turn.

20. See Heidegger, *Schellings Abhandlung*, 143.

21. Despite his new theodicy, Schelling would not really escape his French Enlightenment predecessors' rebukes regarding philosophical attempts to justify God. One might well imagine a Voltaire's reaction to the account of a God who does not need a world but then creates one anyway, and such a troublesome and manifestly mixed world at that. A French *philosophe* might well have quipped that, if God had needed the world, he might have taken the trouble to create a better one!

22. Schelling, *Philosophische Untersuchungen*, 403; Schelling, *Of Human Freedom*, 84.

23. Schelling, *Philosophische Untersuchungen*; Schelling, *Of Human Freedom*, 79.

24. The discussion then turns formally and briefly to the strange and unconvincing category of "Objective Anxiety"—the abstract, metaphysical, and cumulative effect of deeds of sin on the part of human beings—before rejoining Kierkegaard's preeminent interest: subjective anxiety.

25. The latter being the only subject of practical interest since all have already fallen, individually.

26. Kierkegaard is describing here the ontological structure of the human

person as made up of being and nonbeing. The suggested dialectic of being and nonbeing evokes Hegel's *Logic.* The difference here is between a free and existential dialectic rather than a necessary and logical one.

Chapter 9

1. "What Is Metaphysics?" (1029), par. 31.

2. Jean-Paul Sartre, for his part, has the French equivalent in *le néant* and the verb *anéantir* in *L'être et le néant* (*Being and Nothingness*).

3. The separation of "nothing" into "no-thing" is not possible in Danish or German but is useful wordplay in English.

4. Pearson, *A Brief History of Anxiety,* 3.

5. This parallels the importance that Kierkegaard assigns to enclosing reserve (*Indesluttethed*) in his discussion of anxiety.

6. Of course there is also the fact that there was a time when I was not, but anxiety does not look to the past. One of its hallmarks is that it is oriented toward the future, but with a sense of my present being intimately connected with my future and its possibilities.

7. However, both would hold that to be an important aspect of self-awareness as well. The consciousness of this is discussed by Kierkegaard as consciousness of the familiar philosophical categories finitude and necessity, and by Heidegger, straining to stay clear of the old metaphysics, in the language of "facticity" and "thrownness."

8. Not that his own vocabulary is without its problems.

9. Given its classic formulation by Augustine of Hippo in the fifth century.

10. *SKS,* 4:348; *CA,* 42. For Heidegger, the anxiety experience manifests repulsion, but not attraction.

11. The structure of Kierkegaard's work first takes him into a discussion of the relationship of anxiety and original sin going forward, including a very odd-sounding consideration of "objective anxiety" that is required for conceptual symmetry. In keeping with his emphasis on the subjective over the objective (a swipe at the Hegelians, quite likely), objective anxiety receives four pages, while subjective anxiety receives twenty-one. Kierkegaard makes the claim that there is such a thing as objective anxiety—the sum total of human possibilities—and that this increases as the population of the race increases, and that objective anxiety represents the sum total of unactualized human possibilities. The thought of there actually being such a thing, beyond being an idea, is itself frightening. What, after all, could any person do, as a single individual, about the collective unactualized possibilities of the entire human race up to this moment, except to feel overwhelmed, perhaps saddened, by this very melancholy thought?

12. This may seem a fine point to some, since Kierkegaard-Haufniensis does hold that sinfulness arises out of an initial condition of anxiety (which, admittedly, is linked to sensuousness). But it is not the sensuous itself that leads to sinfulness.

13. See Kisiel, *Heidegger's Way of Thought,* 26. While Heidegger had already

read some Kierkegaard in the 1910–14 period, it seems that the strongest Kierkegaardian influence upon him was mediated by Jaspers through his 1919 work *Psychologie der Weltanschauungen* (*The Psychology of Worldviews,* untranslated into English). Although Heidegger's review of the work as a whole was not positive, the large summary section on Kierkegaard proved to be very influential. See Jaspers, *Psychologie der Weltanschauungen,* 419–32.

14. Apparently, Heidegger considered *Zu-Sein* as an alternative term, which some think would have been a better choice since it stresses the directionality or intentionality of Being.

15. This corresponds step for step to the Kierkegaard-Haufniensis analysis; see the appendix.

16. Division 2, title of section 1; see *BT,* 279; *SZ,* 236.

17. Kierkegaard does *not* associate it with death or being-unto-death. It would seem that both Kierkegaard and Heidegger name in a different way the "ownmost possibility" around which *Angst* revolves: Kierkegaard views it as the sin consciousness of not being whole, whereas Heidegger sees it as being-unto-death and the consciousness of the possibility of one's no longer being (the nonbeing that one is no longer there to experience).

18. Heidegger compares this with the "not yet" quality of a quarter moon, or of an unripened fruit, to argue that the kind of "not yet" quality that humans have is essentially different. He, no more than Kierkegaard, makes no reference to Schelling's notion of *mé on,* from which both Kierkegaard's and Heidegger's views seem derived. What is missing here is a comparison with the being of other mammals that are also beings-unto-death, even if they do not seem to manifest any consciousness of being troubled by the prospect. We do know, whereas Heidegger most probably did not, that there are higher mammals that are aware of the death of their pack members and, at least in the case of elephants, have something resembling a mourning ritual, even a commemoration.

19. "What Is Metaphysics?," trans. David Farrell Krell, in *Pathmarks,* ed. William McNeill (Cambridge: Cambridge University Press, 1998), 82–96. German original: "Was heißt Metaphysik?" in *Wegmarken,* 2nd ed. (Frankfurt a. M.: Klostermann, 1976), 103–22.

Chapter 10

1. He also anticipates the definition of a self in *The Sickness unto Death* when he writes,

> The self the individual knows is simultaneously the actual self and the ideal self, which the individual has outside himself as the image in whose likeness he is to form himself, and which on the other hand he has within himself, since it is he himself. Only within himself does the individual have the objective toward which he is to strive, and yet he has this objective outside himself as he strives towards it. . . . Only within himself can the individual become enlightened about himself. . . . When the individual has known himself and

> has chosen himself, he is in the process of actualizing himself, but since he is supposed to do that freely, he must know what it is he wants to actualize. What he wants to actualize is certainly himself, but it is his ideal self, which he cannot acquire anywhere but within himself. If he does not hold firmly to the truth that the individual has the ideal self within himself, all of his aspiring and striving becomes abstract. (*SKS*, 3:246–47; *E/O*, 2:259)

The Sickness unto Death will make clear that the ideal self does not yet exist, that it is something that one is moving toward. See also Watkin, "Søren Kierkegaard's Psychology of the Self."

2. This view of Kierkegaard admittedly rings very Augustinian, although Kierkegaard himself does not cite Augustine. However, Augustine has so influenced the history of theology that his influence would have been mediated by theology studies and the Lutheran theological tradition of which he is part, and which is so heavily indebted, via Luther, to Augustine. See Pattison, *Kierkegaard and the Theology*, 124, for a discussion of sin and the Augsburg Confession and the "extreme Augustinian-Protestant understanding of the Fall and its consequences" present in *Philosophical Fragments.*

3. See Westphal, "Kierkegaard's Psychology," 40, 44. Augustine, following in the Aristotelian line, declares happiness to be active willing (*De libero arbitrio*, Liber I).

4. Westphal, ibid.

5. The actual opening paragraph of *The Sickness unto Death* does not begin immediately with the infamous sentence but rather the declaration that a human being is spirit, that spirit is the self, and that the self is the relating to, or willing to be, the self that one knows oneself to be, which includes a relationship to the Transcendent. Willing to be itself in fact seems to be a synonym for relating to the Transcendent ("in relating itself to itself and in willing to be itself, the self rests transparently in the power that establishes it" (*SKS*, 11:129; *SUD*, 15).

6. See also Paul Ricouer, *Oneself as Another* (Chicago: University of Chicago Press, 1995). Interestingly, the classic Confucian value of fulfilled humanity is expressed in the *Analects* by the Chinese ideogram for *rén*, which includes two elements, person and relationship to other.

7. The fact that Kierkegaard in this work does not discuss these outer relationships does not imply that he is not aware of them or that he is not concerned with them. It is simply that they are not the theme of his book.

8. See Kierkegaard's religious discourse *Purity of Heart Is to Will One Thing*, trans. Douglas Steere (New York: Harper, 1956).

9. Technically speaking, Anti-Climacus is the volume's pseudonymous author. However, there is seemingly universal agreement that pseudonymity in this work is a technicality and that the views are those of Kierkegaard himself and not of a fictional character or of a Kierkegaard at a different stage in his own development (as is the case in the "Diapsalmata" of *Either/Or*, which are taken largely from Kierkegaard's youthful journals). Thus I make no distinction here between Kierkegaard and Anti-Climacus.

10. See also Tietjen and Evans, "Kierkegaard as a Christian Psychologist."

11. To repeat, Kierkegaard does not think out the nature of a self systematically. And so he does not discuss the relation of the self to other selves and its role in constituting the self, or the relation of the self to nature, and to the totality of being, of which it is a part, etc.

12. See Nordentoft, *Kierkegaard's Psychology*, 187.

13. It is the *relating* that is the self, not the relation. See Hannay, "Spirit and the Idea of the Self," 31.

14. This willing *not* to be that self occurred in the first, or original, sin of each individual.

15. See Sartre's 1943 play *The Flies*, act 1.

16. See Westphal, "Kierkegaard's Psychology," 51, where he considers this phenomenon as Kierkegaard's depth psychology revealing itself to be a Heideggerian hermeneutical phenomenology "which refuses to take what is self-evident to everyday consciousness as the last word on anything."

17. As such, it parallels Kant's famous essay "On the Radical Evil in Human Nature" by suggesting a different original choice from that posited by Kant: thus not à la Kant myself as having taken priority over the moral law, but a self that seeks an imaginary self in the place of a self progressing according to the laws of becoming.

18. This Freudian type of analysis is ruled out in advance as nothing but idle naval gazing. This is not a neurosis and the analysis in this case is not the solution.

19. *SKS*, 11:145–64; *SUD*, 27–49.

20. Theunissen, *Kierkegaard's Concept of Despair* (German original: *Der Begriff Verzweiflung: Korrekturen an Kierkegaard* [Frankfurt: Suhrkamp, 1993]). Page references hereafter are to the English-language edition. The English edition unfortunately deletes Theunissen's telling subtitle, *Corrections to Kierkegaard*. Theunissen translates Kierkegaard into Heideggerian language at times, as when he writes, "Authentic despair is not to will to be what we are in our pre-given *Dasein*" (10). Theunissen's *Kierkegaard's Concept of Despair* is a powerful example of moving beyond Kierkegaard exposition to evaluation and critique, including pointing out errors of logic and analysis on Kierkegaard's part.

21. Emphasis in original. Theunissen ultimately views all the various angles on despair sketched by Kierkegaard as weakness of the will, connected to the refusal to recognize the data of one's own experience that is telling one that one is not what the spiritual dynamism of one's being is pressing one toward becoming. He also criticizes Kierkegaard's concept of, and privileging of, despair of defiance as problematic (ibid., 13).

22. Perhaps a metaphor from the animal kingdom will illustrate the problem and not confuse it: If there were such a creature as a cheetah that wanted to be a tiger, rather than a cheetah, Kierkegaard's analysis would hold that the primary fact here is that the cheetah does not want to be what it is: i.e., it does not want to be a cheetah. Its wanting to be a tiger is secondary to the primary psychological phenomenon of not wanting to be what it truly is, namely a cheetah. The wish to be a tiger can be a distraction from this primary phenomenon. *Thus all despair is the absence of will to be who it is that one truly is*, even if accompanied by a stated desire to be something else. It all boils down to this: *we do not accept our-*

selves, we do not will to be who we are, we want to be rid of ourselves, we want to be rid of the challenging dynamism that is the self.

Another version of this phenomenon is reflected perhaps in the Simon and Garfunkel song *El Condor Pasa (If I Could)* (1970): "I'd rather be a sparrow than a snail. . . ."

23. See Robert Wright, "The Evolution of Despair," *Time,* August 18, 1995. Wright, however, is a journalist, writing extensively and provocatively about evolutionary themes. But, interestingly, he begins his article with a rather insightful and sane-sounding quote from the otherwise insane Unabomber, Ted Kaczynski, an American serial bomber of universities and airlines (thus the *Una-* of the FBI code name Unabomber) between 1978 and 1995: "I attribute the social and psychological problems of modern society to the fact that society requires people to live under conditions radically different from those under which the human race evolved."

24. See Kirmmse, "Psychology and Society."

25. According to which God and humankind now together shape a living universe, including shaping *Homo sapiens.* See Philip Hefner, *The Human Factor: Evolution, Culture, and Religion* (Minneapolis: Fortress Press, 1993), 27.

26. In fairness to Kierkegaard, one should recall that Kierkegaard was addressing a specific audience, namely, contemporary early nineteenth-century Danes who were culturally Christian, and was intending to criticize the complacent bourgeois Christianity of his day, as well as to provoke individual readers so that they might go on to the "upbuilding" that his treatise intended. *The Sickness unto Death* was as much an "in your face" kind of treatise as *Fear and Trembling,* which challenged the complacent notion of Danish Christian faith as something conferred in a birth certificate by contrasting it with the kind of troubling, dynamic existential faith manifested in the biblical Abraham, who was supposedly the model of faith.

27. Clearly, in his times, Kierkegaard would have defined that Transcendent in the language of the Christian God and in fact did precisely that.

28. "Separation" and "cleavage" are reflected in the terms used, *Tvivl* and *Fortvivlse.* The archaic English term *twayning* corresponds to the meaning of the Danish *Tvivl:* a split, a twoness.

29. Nordentoft, *Kierkegaard's Psychology,* 181: "Where *The Concept of Anxiety* is a detailed, partially unclear upwelling of ideas, *The Sickness unto Death* is a compressed and explanatory book." Bruce Kirmmse, on the other hand, sees it as Kierkegaard's most perfect book ("Psychology and Society," 167).

30. Haim Gordon takes on this theme in a refreshing and liberating way in his essay "A Rejection of Kierkegaard's Monism of Despair," in *The Sickness unto Death,* ed. Robert L. Perkins, International Kierkegaard Commentary, vol. 19, 239–57 (Macon, Ga.: Mercer University Press, 1987). Alastair Hannay touches upon the same problem in his essay in the same collection, "Spirit and the Idea of the Self as a Reflexive Relation," 23–38.

31. This much is a thesis shared by the *Diamond Sutra* of Mahayana Buddhism, which goes even further in emphasizing the misleading nature of all words and concepts.

32. As in the theory of R. D. Laing that in the case of mental problems one must complete the breakdown in order to be reconstituted in a healthy way; see *The Divided Self: An Existential Study in Sanity and Madness* (Harmondsworth, U.K.: Penguin, 1960) and *The Self and Others* (London: Tavistock, 1961).

Appendix

1. Van Buren, *The Young Heidegger,* 12. See also Caputo, *Radical Hermeneutics,* chapters 1 and 3. The immediately following pages are highly indebted to Van Buren's work.

2. Caputo, *Radical Hermeneutics,* 82–83.

3. Or, for that matter, a Socratic or Aristotelian influence—although Heidegger was influenced in important ways precisely by Kierkegaard's own understanding of Socrates and Aristotle.

4. Quoted in Van Buren, *The Young Heidegger,* 222.

5. *GWH* 5, 249; *QCT,* 94. Quoted by Van Buren, *The Young Heidegger,* 390. With Caputo (*Radical Hermeneutics,* 16), "One wonders how Heidegger can possibly have taken Kierkegaard to be only a 'religious writer' with no ontological concerns. One wonders how he could have written the ontology of 'temporality,' which constitutes the meaning of the Being of *Dasein* in *Being and Time,* without so much as acknowledging Kierkegaard, when the whole analysis, in my view, derives in its main lines from Kierkegaard!"

6. See John Van Buren, *The Young Heidegger;* Theodore Kisiel, *Heidegger's Way of Thought;* John D. Caputo, *Radical Hermeneutics;* and Otto Pöggeler, *Martin Heidegger's Path of Thinking.*

7. Van Buren, *The Young Heidegger,* 25, 63–64.

8. Ibid., 147.

9. Ibid., 150.

10. *G* 63, 108, 29–30, quoted in Van Buren, *The Young Heidegger,* 169.

11. Van Buren, *The Young Heidegger,* 169.

12. Ibid., 223.

13. Heidegger published a lengthy review of Jaspers' *Psychologie der Weltanschauungen,* in addition to engaging in polite surface correspondence with Jaspers about the work. In Heidegger's review itself, he scarcely mentions Kierkegaard and scarcely comments directly on the *Referat* section (although he does cite it in one of the three Kierkegaard footnotes in *Being and Time*). Moreover, the *Referat* itself revolves chiefly around Kierkegaard's *Sickness unto Death,* many of whose categories find parallels in Heidegger's work but overall are not as central to Heidegger's phenomenology of *Dasein* as are those in *The Concept of Anxiety.* Heidegger's emphasis on being-unto-death (in *Being and Time*) has nothing to do with the sense of "sickness unto death" in Kierkegaard's work of the same name.

14. Van Buren, *The Young Heidegger,* 170–75. The very title of chapter 6 in *Being and Time* is "Care as the Being of *Dasein,*" the section in which Heidegger's concept of anxiety is laid out.

15. All of Heidegger's footnotes are obscurely placed as endnotes in the Macquarrie-Robinson English translation of *Being and Time.*

16. Strictly speaking, the published version of *Being and Time* contains only part 1, divisions 1 and 2 of the larger project. Even division 3 of part 1 (promised in *SZ,* 160; *BT,* 202) never appeared.

17. Magurshak, "The Concept of Anxiety."

Bibliography

Agacinski, Sylviane. *Aparté: Conceptions and Deaths of Søren Kierkegaard.* Translated by Kevin Newmark. Tallahassee: Florida State University Press, 1988.

Alford, C. Fred. *Narcissism: Socrates, the Frankfurt School, and Psychoanalytic Theory.* New Haven: Yale University Press, 1988.

Brandes, Georg. *En kritisk Fremstilling in Grundrids.* Copenhagen: Byldendal, 1877.

Burton, Robert. *The Anatomy of Melancholy.* 1621.

Butler, Judith. *Subjects of Desire: Hegelian Reflections in Twentieth-Century France.* New York: Columbia University Press, 1987.

Caputo, John D. *Radical Hermeneutics: Repetition, Deconstruction, and the Hermeneutic Project.* Bloomington: Indiana University Press, 1987.

Carlisle, Clare. *Kierkegaard: A Guide for the Perplexed.* London: Continuum, 2006.

Clewell, Tammy. "Mourning beyond Melancholia." *Journal of the American Psychoanalytic Association* 52, no. 1 (2004): 43–67.

Cole, J. Preston. *The Problematic Self in Kierkegaard and Freud.* New Haven: Yale University Press, 1971.

Collins, James Daniel. *The Mind of Kierkegaard.* Princeton: Princeton University Press, 1953.

Diem, Hermann. *Kierkegaard's Dialectic of Existence.* Edinburgh: Oliver and Boyd, 1959.

Dunning, S. N. *Kierkegaard's Dialectic of Inwardness: A Structural Analysis of the Theory of Stages.* Princeton: Princeton University Press, 1985.

Elrod, John W. *Being and Existence in Kierkegaard's Pseudonymous Works.* Princeton: Princeton University Press, 1975.

Evans, C. Stephen. *Kierkegaard's "Fragments" and "Postscript": The Religious Philosophy of Johannes Climacus.* New York: Humanity Books, 1983.

Fenger, Henning. *Kierkegaard: The Myths and Their Origins.* New Haven: Yale University Press, 1980.

Ferguson, Harvie. *Melancholy and the Critique of Modernity: Søren Kierkegaard's Religious Psychology.* New York: Routledge, 1995.

Ferreira, M. Jamie. *Transforming Vision: Imagination and Will in Kierkegaardian Faith.* Oxford: Clarendon Press, 1991.

Freud, Sigmund. *The Standard Edition of the Complete Psychological Works of Sigmund Freud.* Edited by James Strachey. London: Hogarth Press, 1953–74.

Fuhrmans, Horst. *Schellings letzte Philosophie: Die negative und positive Philosophie im Einsatz des Spätidealismus.* Berlin: Junker and Dünnhaupt, 1940.

Garff, Joakim. *Søren Kierkegaard: A Biography.* Translated by Bruce H. Kirmmse. Princeton: Princeton University Press, 2005.

Gouwens, David J. *Kierkegaard as Religious Thinker: Passions, Virtues and Praxis.* Cambridge: Cambridge University Press, 1996.

Grøn, Arne. *The Concept of Anxiety in Søren Kierkegaard.* Translated by Sinead Ladegaard Knox. Macon, Ga.: Mercer University Press, 2008.

Green, Ronald M. *Kierkegaard and Kant: The Hidden Debt.* Albany: SUNY Press, 1992.

Hannay, Alastair, ed. *The Cambridge Companion to Kierkegaard.* Cambridge: Cambridge University Press, 1997.

———. *Kierkegaard.* London: Routledge and Kegan Paul, 1982.

———. *Kierkegaard: A Biography.* Cambridge: Cambridge University Press, 2003.

———. "Spirit and the Idea of the Self as a Reflexive Relation." In *The Sickness unto Death,* edited by Robert L. Perkins, International Kierkegaard Commentary, vol. 19, 23–38. Macon, Ga.: Mercer University Press, 1987.

Heidegger, Martin. *Being and Time.* Translated by John Macquarrie and Edward Robinson. New York: Harper and Row, 1962.

———. *The Fundamental Concepts of Metaphysics: World, Finitude, and Solitude.* Translated by William McNeill and Nicholas Walker. Bloomington: Indiana University Press, 1995.

———. *Gesamtausgabe.* Frankfurt a. M.: Klostermann, 1975 ff.

———. *Schellings Abhandlung über das Wesen der menschlichen Freiheit.* Tübingen: Niemeyer, 1971.

———. "What Is Metaphysics?" Translated by David Farrell Krell. In *Pathmarks,* edited by William McNeill. Cambridge: Cambridge University Press, 1998, pp. 82–96. German original: "Was heißt Metaphysik?", in *Wegmarken,* 103–22. 2nd ed. Frankfurt a. M.: Klostermann, 1976.

Hennigfeld, Jochem, and Jon Stewart. *Kierkegaard und Schelling: Freiheit, Angst und Wirklichkeit.* Kierkegaard Studies 8. Berlin: de Gruyter, 2002.

Jaspers, Karl. *Psychologie der Weltanschauungen.* 5th ed. Berlin: Springer, 1960.

Jegstrup, Elsebet, ed. *The New Kierkegaard.* Bloomington: Indiana University Press, 2004.

Kernberg, Otto. *Borderline Conditions and Pathological Narcissism.* New York: Aronson, 1971.

Khan, Abrahim. "Melancholy: An Elusive Dimension of Depression?" *Journal of Medical Humanities* 15, no. 2 (1994): 113–22.

———. "Melancholy, Irony, and Kierkegaard." *International Journal for Philosophy of Religion* 17 (1985): 67–85.

Kierkegaard, Søren. *Ausgewählte christliche reden: Mit einem Anhang; Kierkegaards Familie und Privatleben nach den persönlichen Erinnerungen seiner Nichte, Fräulein Lund.* Trans. Julie von Reincke. Gießen: Ricker, 1901.

———. *The Concept of Anxiety: A Simple Psychologically Orienting Deliberation on the Dogmatic Issue of Hereditary Sin (Kierkegaard's Writings VIII).* Ed. and trans. Reidar Thomte with Albert B. Anderson. Princeton, N.J.: Princeton University Press, 1980.

———. *The Concept of Irony, with Continual Reference to Socrates. Together with Notes of Schelling's Berlin Lectures (Kierkegaard's Writings II).* Ed. and trans. Howard V. Hong and Edna H. Hong. Princeton, N.J.: Princeton University Press, 1992.

———. *Concluding Unscientific Postscript to Philosophical Fragments (Kierkegaard's Writings XII.1 and 2).* Ed. and trans. Howard V. Hong and Edna H. Hong. Princeton, N.J.: Princeton University Press, 1992.

———. *Eighteen Upbuilding Discourses (Kierkegaard's Writings V).* Ed. and trans. with introduction and notes by Howard V. Hong and Edna H. Hong. Princeton, N.J.: Princeton University Press, 1992.

———. *Either/Or (Kierkegaard's Writings III and IV).* Ed. and trans. with introduction and notes by Howard V. Hong and Edna H. Hong. Princeton, N.J.: Princeton University Press, 1987.

———. *Fear and Trembling and Repetition (Kierkegaard's Writings VI).* Ed. and trans. with introduction and notes by Howard V. Hong and Edna H. Hong. Princeton, N.J.: Princeton University Press, 1995.

———. *Letters and Documents.* Ed. and trans. Hendrik Rosenmeier. Princeton, N.J.: Princeton University Press, 1978.

———. *Philosophical Fragments, Johannes Climacus (Kierkegaard's Writings VII).* Ed. and trans. with introduction and notes by Howard V. Hong and Edna H. Hong. Princeton, N.J.: Princeton University Press, 1985.

———. *The Point of View (Kierkegaard's Writings XXII).* Ed. and trans. with introduction and notes by Howard V. Hong and Edna H. Hong. Princeton, N.J.: Princeton University Press, 1998.

———. *Practice in Christianity (Kierkegaard's Writings XX).* Ed. and trans. with introduction and notes by Howard V. Hong and Edna H. Hong. Princeton, N.J.: Princeton University Press, 1991.

———. *The Sickness unto Death: A Christian Psychological Exposition for Upbuilding and Awakening (Kierkegaard's Writings XIX).* Ed. and trans. with introduction and notes by Howard V. Hong and Edna H. Hong. Princeton, N.J.: Princeton University Press, 1980.

———. *Søren Kierkegaard's Journals and Papers.* Edited and translated by Howard V. Hong and Edna H. Hong. Bloomington: Indiana University Press, 1976–78.

———. *Søren Kierkegaards Papirer.* Edited by P. Heiberg, V. Kuhr, E. Torsting, N. Thulstrup, and N. J. Cappelørn. Copenhagen: Gyldendal, 1909–48; 1968–70; 1975–78.

———. *Søren Kierkegaards Skrifter.* Edited by Niels Jørgen Cappelørn, Joakim Garff, Jette Knudsen, Johnny Kondrup, and Alastair McKinnon. Copenhagen: Gads, 1997–2013.

———. *Stages on Life's Way: Studies by Various Persons (Kierkegaard's Writings XI).* Ed. and trans. with introduction and notes by Howard V. Hong and Edna H. Hong. Princeton, N.J.: Princeton University Press, 1988.

———. *Two Ages: The Age of Revolution and the Present Age, A Literary Review (Kierkegaard's Writings XIV).* Ed. and trans. with introduction and notes by Howard V. Hong and Edna H. Hong. Princeton, N.J.: Princeton University Press, 1978.

———. *Upbuilding Discourses in Various Spirits (Kierkegaard's Writings XV).* Ed. and trans. with introduction and notes by Howard V. Hong and Edna H. Hong. Princeton, N.J.: Princeton University Press, 2009.

———. *Works of Love (Kierkegaard's Writings XVI).* Ed. and trans. with introduction and notes by Howard V. Hong and Edna H. Hong. Princeton, N.J.: Princeton University Press, 1998.

Kisiel, Theodore. *The Genesis of Heidegger's "Being and Time."* Berkeley: University of California Press, 1993.

———. *Heidegger's Way of Thought: Critical and Interpretive Signposts.* New York: Continuum, 2002.

Kirmmse, Bruce H., ed. *Encounters with Kierkegaard: A Life as Seen by His Contemporaries.* 3rd ed. Princeton: Princeton University Press, 1998.

———. *Kierkegaard in Golden Age Denmark.* Indianapolis: Indiana University Press, 1990.

———. "Psychology and Society: The Social Falsification of the Self in *Sickness unto Death.*" In *Kierkegaard's Truth: Disclosure of the Self,* edited by Joseph H. Smith, Psychiatry and the Humanities, vol. 5, 167–92. New Haven: Yale University Press, 1981.

Kohut, Heinz. *The Analysis of the Self: A Systematic Approach to the Psychoanalytic Treatment of Narcissistic Personality Disorders.* New York: International Universities Press, 1971.

Kosch, Michelle. *Freedom and Reason in Kant, Schelling, and Kierkegaard.* New York: Oxford University Press, 2010.

Kuhn, Reinhard. *The Demon of Noontide: Ennui in Western Literature.* Princeton, N.J.: Princeton University Press, 1976.

Lacan, Jacques. *Écrits: A Selection.* Edited by Alan Sheridan. New York: Norton, 1977.

———. *The Four Fundamental Concepts of Psychoanalysis.* Translated by Alan Sheridan. New York: Norton, 1981.

Laing, R. D. *The Divided Self: An Existential Study in Sanity and Madness.* London: Tavistock, 1960.

Laplanche, Jean. *Life and Death in Psychoanalysis.* Translated by Jeffrey Mehlman. Baltimore: Johns Hopkins University Press, 1976.

Laplanche, J., and J.-B. Pontalis. *The Language of Psycho-Analysis.* Translated by Donald Nicholson-Smith. New York: Norton, 1973.

Lasch, Christopher. *The Culture of Narcissism: American Life in an Age of Diminishing Expectations.* New York: Norton, 1978.

Law, David R. *Kierkegaard as Negative Theologian.* Oxford: Oxford University Press, 1993.

———. *Kierkegaard's Kenotic Christology.* Oxford: Oxford University Press, 2013.

Léon, Céline, and Sylvia Walsh, eds. *Feminist Interpretations of Søren Kierkegaard.* University Park: Penn State University Press, 1997.

Magurshak, Dan. "The Concept of Anxiety: The Keystone of the Kierkegaard-Heidegger Relationship." In *"The Concept of Anxiety": A Simple Psychologi-*

cally Orienting Deliberation on the Dogmatic Issue of Hereditary Sin, edited by Robert L. Perkins, International Kierkegaard Commentary, vol. 8, 167–95. Macon, Ga.: Mercer University Press, 1985.

Mandel, Oscar, ed. *The Theatre of Don Juan: A Collection of Plays and Views, 1630–1963.* Lincoln: University of Nebraska Press, 1986.

Marino, Gordon. *Kierkegaard's Anthropology*. Milwaukee: Marquette University Press, 2001.

Matuštik, Martin J., and Merold Westphal, eds. *Kierkegaard in Post/Modernity*. Bloomington: Indiana University Press, 1995.

McCarthy, Vincent A. *The Phenomenology of Moods in Kierkegaard*. The Hague: Martinus Nijhoff, 1978.

Mooney, Edward. *Selves in Discord and Resolve: Kierkegaard's Moral-Religious Psychology from "Either/Or" to "Sickness unto Death."* London: Routledge, 1996.

Nordentoft, Kresten. *Kierkegaard's Psychology*. Translated by Bruce H. Kirmmse. Pittsburgh: Duquesne University Press, 1972.

Pattison, George. *Kierkegaard and the Theology of the Nineteenth Century: The Paradox and the "Point of Contact."* Cambridge: Cambridge University Press, 2013.

———. *Kierkegaard: The Aesthetic and the Religious*. London: Macmillan, 1992.

Pearson, Patricia. *A Brief History of Anxiety: Yours and Mine*. New York: Bloomsbury, 2008.

Perkins, Robert L., ed. *International Kierkegaard Commentary*. 24 vols. Macon, Ga.: Mercer University Press, 1984–2008.

Pöggeler, Otto. *Martin Heidegger's Path of Thinking*. Translated by Daniel Magurshak and Sigmund Barber. Atlantic Highlands, N.J.: Humanities Press, 1987.

———. *The Paths of Heidegger's Life and Thought*. Translated by John Bailiff. Amherst, N.Y.: Humanity Books, 1998.

Poole, Roger. *Kierkegaard: The Indirect Communication*. Charlottesville: University of Virginia Press, 1993.

Radden, Jennifer, ed. *The Nature of Melancholy: From Aristotle to Kristeva*. New York: Oxford University Press, 2002.

Rosenkranz, Karl. *Psychologie, oder die Wissenschaft vom subjectivem Geist*. 1837.

Schelling, F. W. J. *Of Human Freedom*. Translated by James Gutmann. Chicago: Open Court, 1936.

———. 1809. *Philosophische Untersuchungen über das Wesen der menschlichen Freiheit und die damit zusammenhängenden Gegenstände*. Vol. 7 of *Sämtliche Werke*, edited by K. F. A. Schelling. Stuttgart: Cotta'scher Verlag, 1860.

Schrag, Calvin. *Existence and Freedom: Towards an Ontology of Human Finitude*. Athens: Ohio University Press, 1960.

Taylor, Mark C. *Journeys to Selfhood: Hegel and Kierkegaard*. Berkeley: University of California Press, 1980.

———. *Kierkegaard's Pseudonymous Authorship: A Study of Time and the Self*. Princeton, N.J.: Princeton University Press, 1975.

Theunissen, Michael. *Kierkegaard's Concept of Despair*. Translated by Barbara Harshav and Helmut Illbruck. Princeton, N.J.: Princeton University Press, 2005.

Thompson, Josiah. *Kierkegaard*. New York: Knopf, 1973.

Tietjen, Mark A., and C. Stephen Evans. "Kierkegaard as a Christian Psychologist." *Journal of Psychology and Christianity* 30, no. 4 (December 1, 1998): 274–83.

Van Buren, John. *The Young Heidegger: Rumor of the Hidden King.* Bloomington: Indiana University Press, 1994.

Wahl, Jean. *Études Kierkegaardiennes.* Paris: Aubier, 1938.

———. "Heidegger et Kierkegaard." *Recherches philosophiques* 2 (1932–33): 349–70.

Walsh, Sylvia. "On 'Feminine' and 'Masculine' Forms of Despair." In *The Sickness unto Death,* edited by Robert L. Perkins, International Kierkegaard Commentary, vol. 19, 121–34. Macon, Ga.: Mercer University Press, 1987.

Watkin, Julia. "Søren Kierkegaard's Psychology of the Self." *Journal of Psychology and Christianity* 17, no. 4 (December 1, 1998): 362–73.

Westphal, Merold. *Becoming a Self.* West Lafayette, Ind.: Purdue University Press, 1996.

———. "Kierkegaard's Psychology and Unconscious Despair." In *The Sickness unto Death,* edited by Robert L. Perkins, International Kierkegaard Commentary, vol. 19, 39–66. Macon, Ga.: Mercer University Press, 1987.

Wyschogrod, Michael. *Kierkegaard and Heidegger: The Ontology of Existence.* New York: Humanities Press, 1954.

Zimmerman, Michael E. *Eclipse of the Self: The Development of Heidegger's Concept of Authenticity.* Athens: Ohio University Press, 1981.

Index